The Basic Arts of
MARKETING

Econometrics:
model which can
take account of changes
in the variables +
re-project.

Better Business Guides

Getting to YES
Roger Fisher and William Ury

Effective Delegation
Clive T. Goodworth

Janner's Complete Letterwriter
Greville Janner QC, MP

The Telephone Marketing Book
Pauline Marks

The Basic Arts of Financial Management
Third edition
Leon Simons

RAY L. WILLSMER

The Basic Arts of
MARKETING

Second Edition

Business Books
London   Melbourne   Sydney
Auckland   Johannesburg

Business Books Ltd
An imprint of Century Hutchinson Limited
62–65 Chandos Place, London WC2N 4NW

Hutchinson Publishing Group (Australia) Pty Ltd
16–22 Church Street, Hawthorn, Melbourne,
Victoria 3122

Hutchinson Group (NZ) Ltd
32–34 View Road, PO Box 40–086, Glenfield, Auckland 10

Hutchinson Group (SA) Pty Ltd
PO Box 337, Bergvlei 2012, South Africa

First published 1976
Second edition 1984
Reprinted 1986
© Ray L. Willsmer 1976, 1984

Set in 10 on 12 Times
Phototypeset by AKM Associates (UK) Ltd, Southall, Greater London
Printed and bound in Great Britain by
The Guernsey Press Co. Ltd., Guernsey, Channel Islands

British Library Cataloguing in Publication Data

Willsmer, Ray L.
   The basic arts of marketing – 2nd ed
   1. Marketing
   I. Title
   658.8   HF5415
  ISBN 0 09 164061 X

To Jean

Contents

Preface to the Second Edition

The bulk of the content from the first edition remains in this second one. On the one hand, that may seem disappointing: has there been so little development in marketing theory and practice? On the other hand, it is reassuring to think that perhaps the reason for so little change is that we got it right fairly early on. It is certainly untrue to say that there has been little new in marketing theory. Unfortunately, little of it is of practical benefit in anything other than a descriptive sense. Indeed, a generation of marketing students is now growing up having returned from their placement periods in industry convinced of the irrelevance of all marketing theory to practical business matters.

It is partly to redress a little of that balance that this new edition has been written. The book was always primarily addressed at business men and women who wanted to know something about marketing. Hence the avoidance of jargon, theory and techniques. With the introduction of marketing studies into so many business courses and degrees, students at the Foundation level, especially those preparing for placements, have turned to the first edition and found some omissions. This second edition is an attempt to widen the scope slightly to take in those students doing Foundation courses in marketing and, at the same time, to extend the scope relevantly to those to whom the book was originally addressed. It makes no attempt to be a comprehensive textbook. Its aim is still to describe the essential arts of marketing. However, a significant bridge has been formed toward marketing theory and marketing techniques. On the theory side, some of the best-known theories of buyer behaviour are now briefly described and more space has been given to portfolio analysis, an important practical tool for all businesses. Two chapters have been added. The first concerns the marketing mix: an important concept that describes so many of the differences to be found in marketing and prepared the ground for those who wish to

1

know more about the techniques of marketing. The other is a separate chapter on pricing. Price has always been one of the most important areas of marketing technique and theory and a place where the two sit happily together. Recent recession, following upon rampant inflation, has put an emphasis on price which many of us believe has gone too far.

Marketing remains, and always will be, a dynamic subject, and that makes it difficult for theories to have universal applications or predictive powers. It has often been said that, in business, it doesn't matter what you do as long as you know why you are doing it. This new edition retains the original aim of helping existing and would-be managers make better decisions about what to do in the marketing of their goods and services.

Ray Willsmer

Preface to the First Edition

One of the biggest problems associated with teaching and writing about marketing is that one is always talking about basically the same topics but with increasing degrees of sophistication. This can be frustrating in several ways. On the one hand, there is the danger of learning to run before one has mastered walking, whilst, on the other, there is always the possibility of opting for too low a level of accuracy and sophistication simply because nothing better was available at the time.

This book sets out to provide a universal basis on to which the available techniques can be grafted. In that sense, it is a book concerned with the practical direction of any business which really concerns itself with customer-satisfaction, knowing where it is going and having definite aims about where it wants to go in the future. It sets the ground for the use of the individual techniques.

It is the argument of this work that the basic principles of marketing are appropriate at all levels of a business and thus to all kinds of management. Nevertheless, time constraints – if nothing else – may well justify a separate marketing department. Thus, this book has been aimed at providing a framework of basic matters that will be of value to the specialist marketing executive, those who plan their careers in that direction, senior and general management whose understanding is fundamental to the marketing process and managers with other specializations who want to know what this thing called 'marketing' is all about. For them, in particular, I have tried to avoid the mumbo-jumbo so often used in an attempt to give the subject something approaching scientific status.

Wherever possible, anecdotes have been used to illustrate and amplify. Many of these have been related to me over the years by students and participants in the many seminars and courses I have lectured to. It is mainly from those students that the whole approach to this book has been developed and the practice proved.

Ray Willsmer

3

1
A Rose by Any Other Name

I do not believe in a fate that falls on men however they
act; but I do believe in a fate that falls on them unless
they act.

G. K. Chesterton

Among the many who fear that marketing is just another of those
transitory management vogues, a good deal of unjust criticism is
ironically prefaced by 'Isn't it just'. Isn't it just another name for:

Common sense?
Selling?
Advertising?
What business is all about?
The managing director's job?

It's all of those and that alone shows how different it is from any of
them. It helps to illustrate how difficult marketing is to explain. For
marketing is used both to describe an essential philosophy of business
and a relatively specialized management function. Much of the
problem of definition and the lack of understanding derives from this
confusion between the attitude of mind and the function; the
philosophy and the techniques.

The marketing man, like Chesterton, believes in a fate that
overtakes businesses unless they act. He wants to know all the time
why things happen, what the implications of his actions will be and
how they interrelate with other events. Given that continuing
information, he believes that the inevitable can often be avoided, that
disasters can frequently be predicted and anticipated. Those are big
claims and they need explanation and qualification. Some of that
must be deferred until the appropriate chapter. However, two
underlying aspects of what marketing is all about will begin to
illustrate the force and validity of the marketing man's claims.

4

1.1 Understanding and action

The first precept is that any business will be all the better for fully understanding what it is they are all about. A company celebrating its diamond anniversary invited me to take part in a special seminar for retailers. During the course of my talk, I gave an example (similar to one which will come later in this book) about a company that had discovered that its real opportunities lay in promoting its existing product into another, much larger, sector of the market. This impressed them and brought to the surface a number of thoughts that had been in several managers' minds. The company was celebrating 60 years of success in the hand-cream market. It knew that the market for body lotion was bigger and that their product could effectively compete with the lotions. They had not seriously considered it because of the fear of damaging their prime market. Similarly, they knew that their product had significant properties as a sun-barrier cream. Again, they had not promoted it that way for fear of confusing their market. Prompted by the seminar, the company undertook extensive studies into the usage of their product. After 60 years in the business they discovered that the prime use of their product was as a body cream; second place was taken by the use of the cream for avoiding sun burn and the smallest usage was as a hand-cream. Sixty years of not fully understanding what the business was about!

The second of the two underlying aspects is that appropriate management action will be taken as a result of understanding what the business is about. There is not much point knowing that what you thought you were selling accounts for the smallest part of your business unless you do something with the fact. A few years back, one of Britain's largest publishing groups launched a new magazine aimed at women. The concept behind the magazine was not researched: it was generally believed that 'publishing flair' would be sufficient. Practically everything else was and it revealed a very high probability that the magazine would fail. It even threw serious doubts on the whole concept. The magazine was launched and the initial sale appeared to confound the researchers. However, follow-up studies had been planned and these revealed an alarming number of women who said they would not buy again. They didn't and the magazine was withdrawn from the market, an expensive failure only partly redeemed by swift management action to restrict losses. There had been another course of action open to that management; they need not have launched.

It is in that sense that marketing is a chief executive's responsibility.

Unless that basic way of thinking and caring about the business is practised at a level where effective action can be guaranteed, the best marketing people in the world, the most refined techniques, the best salesmen and the most effective promotion will not succeed. Although arguments about the role of marketing have become a hardy annual, marketing is in fact a still fragile bloom that requires careful and sometimes delicate handling. It thrives in the right conditions. It cannot grow on barren ground, neither does it respond well to hot-housing. Marketing provides policies for profitable action. Someone has to ensure that action. If the marketing attitude permeates the whole business, that action will be swifter and more certain.

1.2 Philosophy and techniques

Am I saying that everyone can be a marketing man or woman? In one very real sense, I am. For marketing is not a precise art with easily defined skills that can be taught, examined and licensed. It is not a business confined to certified practitioners, although that may well come. After all, some 300 years ago, no-one could see why accountants should be any different from any other businessman: every business had to keep accounts and wasn't accountancy just another name for business? Accountants are licensed to practise, yet that has not in any way stopped efficient businessmen from realizing that a basic knowledge of the principles of accounting is essential. Can a basic knowledge of the principles of satisfying your customers be any less so? That fundamental part of marketing that is an attitude of mind is for everybody. That part which seeks to break out of the conventional rut of business thinking, which is prepared to seek to understand what you are doing and appreciate the implications of every activity; that is something every manager should strive to possess.

However, just as the manager with a sound background awareness of the principles of accountancy still requires a qualified accountant to attend to both the highly skilled aspects and the detail, so experienced specialist marketing executives may be required in the business. Yet again, just as some businesses are too small or too specialized to require the full-time services of an accountant, many businesses will not employ marketing specialists. A marketing organization is not a business necessity: acceptance of the marketing approach is.

Within marketing as a management function, there are two distinct streams. The first is that of the marketing generalists. That is where the function began and it grew up with people who tended to be Jacks-of-all-trades . . . and masters of some. Their mastery tended to be sales and advertising and that, in turn, created some of the misconceptions. However, as the study of consumer behaviour became more serious, the need for specialists grew and so did the need for people within the business who could understand and communicate the new specializations. Thus we now have the generalists – with titles like Marketing Manager, Brand Manager, Product Manager – and the specialists. The latter themselves split into the generalist-specialist and the real narrow expert. The former may be, for example, a Market Research Manager conversant with the many techniques available to him, whilst the latter may be especially skilled in psychological research, industrial or medical market research.

In other words, there is a clear distinction between the philosophy and the techniques of marketing. You can have the philosophy without the techniques; you can have the techniques without the philosophy. Under many circumstances, the first can make a lot of sense: under no circumstances does the second alternative. The ideal is to have the two together. Unfortunately, as we shall see later, it is not often that one can afford to completely ignore the use of some of the techniques. The key is always profitability. In commercial businesses, the marketing approach seeks to maximize profits over chosen periods of time. We must never lose sight of that, for even when our definitions and statements do not actually say it, the reason is always profit. We adopt the philosophy for profit: we should adopt the techniques for the same reason – and that may lead us to reject them when they do not contribute to our objective.

Philosophy and techniques – the need to encompass both causes the complications of definition. Virtually every writer and lecturer on marketing has felt the need to phrase his own definition of marketing: the result is a confusion of definitions. What usually confuses them even more is the attempt to cover every possibility of action, rather as though one were framing a law. The almost inevitable result, as with a law, is to draw attention to what has been left out rather than what has been included. Any definition can be argued with. Here are three statements about marketing which, if you insist, can be regarded as definitions: The first relates to the philosophy.

Marketing is selling goods that don't come back to customers who do

That simple cliché type of statement encompasses all the thoughts about consumers' rights: the right product at the right time at the

7

right price affording the right degree of satisfaction – so that they will come back to you for more. But it's more than just a once-only activity. It implies continual quality control, awareness of market attitudes and requirements, fighting off the blandishments of competitive claims, and so on. It can be read also as the art of providing services so acceptable that the recipient wants to go on dealing with your enterprise. It also implies that, in order to market effectively, you may need recourse to some of the specialized techniques of marketing. Hence our second statement.

Marketing takes the guesswork out of hunch

Any new business starts with an idea. Any change of business direction has the same beginning: an idea. An untested idea can be very expensive. If an advertising agency creates a purely speculative campaign for one of its clients, the cost is mainly time, a few materials and some share of total overheads. Not a vast sum and rather akin to a small gamble. A speculative nuclear reactor is unthinkable. In between is a whole host of risk decisions of different kinds. Many hunches about market behaviour can be tested. Some of the specialist areas of marketing are themselves susceptible to testing before any major commitment is undertaken. Marketing techniques do not eliminate risk completely; they can reduce it substantially. They can help to quantify risk so that management does truly know what it is about and what the consequences of its actions could be.

This second statement is of vital importance because of what can be called the 'marketing match'. Every enterprise should seek to match its products or services to what the customer requires. In the vast majority of cases, customers are notoriously bad at articulating what they want. You normally have to give them something to try. In this way you reconcile what you would like to be able to provide with what the consumer is willing to accept. If the customer doesn't like the result, he will go elsewhere – or nowhere as the case may be. If the business doesn't like the result, it can change the product or it can give up. Either way, it has taken away the guesswork and significantly reduced the risk attached to the original idea.

Before looking at an all-embracing definition for marketing, we really should stop and examine an important implication of the last paragraph. It is that activity starts with the manufacturer. Among the more popular alternative definitions are variants of 'Marketing starts and ends with consumer satisfactions'. These derive from Adam Smith and the concept of consumer sovereignty. When Adam Smith wrote, in *The Wealth of Nations* (1776):

8

'Consumption is the sole end purpose of all production; and the interest of the producer ought to be attended to only in so far it may be necessary for promoting that of the consumer'

he was describing what he meant by 'the sovereignty of the consumer'. He was also pointing the way for marketing. Unfortunately, both economists and marketing men lost their way for a long, long time. Whilst economists moved further away from business practicality, marketing men went overboard on consumer sovereignty.

It is certainly not to be dismissed. It has to be put into perspective. By and large, customers are less articulate, less inventive and less inclined to take risks than those who supply them. You cannot sit back and wait for feedback. Moreover, actually asking potential customers what they want is seldom rewarding and the odds are heavily stacked towards failure. Ask one thousand people what their ideal car will be. Put all the answers together and design a car round it. Perhaps you will end up with a car with a long boot, a long bonnet and plenty of room inside the car. However, there would also be a strong possibility that those who wanted the long boot didn't want a long car: in other words, they required a short bonnet. You have the design of a car that you think is what everyone wants but which no-one will buy. (The Edsel car experience in the USA is a prime example and one British car manufacturer has a piece of research which 'proves' that the ideal car has a roomy, separate boot – with estate car doors!) In short, research tends to deal in average consumers. Average consumers seldom lead to products: products lead to average consumers. The message is to assess consumer needs and satisfactions, check your ideas against them, and keep on checking. That way, your business is in harmony with customer needs, guesswork is reduced, risk minimized and repeat business enhanced.

Having travelled so far along the line towards a unified definition of marketing, here is the most widely accepted one, that of the Institute of Marketing.

Marketing is the management process of identifying, anticipating and satisfying customer requirements profitably.

Marketing is a management skill. Not a science; not a technique that can be taught to operatives in the way that, say, woodturning on a lathe can be. A skill of identifying opportunities; of deciding what risk to take when anticipating how customers might act or be persuaded to act. The appropriate techniques will be used but, in the

9

end, the management skill of judgement must be applied. Consumers' requirements are satisfied to make a profit, not just today but well into the future and against reasonable yardsticks that ensure the viability of the company.

A criticism of the Institute of Marketing definition is that it does not adequately allow for social marketing (the adoption of the marketing philosophy and many of its techniques to non-commercial activities). If the concept of 'social profit' or 'welfare benefit' is included under the heading of 'satisfying customer requirements profitably' then it may be claimed that the definition is, indeed, all-embracing. However, this book is devoted to the marketing of commercial activities and for our purpose the Institute of Marketing definition is appropriate, whilst the two earlier statements emphasize the division between marketing philosophy and marketing techniques.

1.3 Types of company

Broadly speaking, there are three types of company and most pass through the first two stages before reaching the third. They are:

1 Production orientated.
2 Sales orientated.
3 Marketing orientated.

A company starts with an idea for goods or services. They then go out and sell it. As sales progress, pressure for more items to sell comes from the sales force (unless surplus capacity exists, in which case the production domination may remain). It is often when the company begins to run into sales difficulties that it looks to marketing as a sort of instant Guru to get the factory back into full production, cover the overheads of the business and produce profits for the shareholders – in that order. The case for the marketing outlook being in at the very beginning is made stronger by dwelling for a moment on the worst excesses of the other two stages of the business.

The production-orientated company literally 'hands over' its production to the sales force to sell. It knows its product is the best in the world therefore, if it doesn't sell as well as the owners think it should, there can only be two reasons:

1 The sales force is no good.
2 The customer is ignorant.

Not so very long ago, a company had designed a completely new form of roof insulation material offering, it was claimed, significant

10

consumer advantages. Firstly, it was made of recycled wastepaper; secondly, it was in flat panels made up as squares to fit the space between roof rafters; thirdly, it was far more efficient in retaining heat in the house, provided at least three layers of panel were used. Unfortunately, said the manufacturer, the trade were stupid and just would not realize what advantages the product offered the householder; why, they could even buy these panels one at a time and carry them home in the shopping bag instead of the inconvenience of carting a great reel of insulation wadding. The company had ignored two things. The cost of the new panels was markedly higher than existing products and they took at least three times as long to lay. The dealers were not so stupid and the householders most certainly were not.

That anecdote, and there are hundreds more where that came from, is a crushing example of two important things for any manufacturer or provider of services to appreciate:

1 The customer is the only arbiter of quality.
2 An 'improvement' the customer cannot understand or doesn't want is no kind of improvement at all.

A good example of the first point exists in the UK tea market. The producing countries and the packers use the term 'quality teas' to describe teas of above a certain retail price. (Since price is a fair reflection of ingredient cost, the choice of price as a quality indicator is not unreasonable.) However, consumer research shows that housewives have another name for them – 'funny teas'. They taste 'funny', that is different from what they usually buy. What they usually buy reflects their opinion of quality and that is the only definition that is meaningful. (In the same way, I recall a high level of complaints from an Officers' Mess near Grimsby. Officers tasting truly fresh fish for the first time in their lives thought it was 'off'.)

The story of the roof insulation panels was an example of an improvement the customer didn't understand. A prime example of one the customer didn't want happened with the *Daily Mirror*. That newspaper thought it could gently move its readers a little more upmarket: gradually wean them away from the more sensational presentation of news, towards the more serious and away from what some might think the trivial; away from a surfeit of flesh and femininity towards a more broadly based newspaper. All was to be very gentle and very gradual. Whilst they were doing this, they sold an ailing newspaper to Rupert Murdoch who promptly relaunched it – right to the slot vacated by the *Daily Mirror*, and with enormous success. Over a long period, *The Sun* was the only daily newspaper to continually increase its circulation. I can speak from personal experience of the enormous difficulty of getting people to change their newspaper, yet *The Sun* now vies with the *Daily Mirror* for the position of most widely read daily newspaper. Whatever personal opinions one may have about the newspaper, it has to be admitted that it does show what a very large number of people want from their daily paper.

It isn't always comfortable sitting on such knowledge. Most people feel a sort of moral obligation to upgrade other people to something approaching their own standards. In this respect, many of the statements made by prominent consumerists are just as production orientated. Marketing teaches us that 'quality' is relative, not absolute: thus it means very different things to different people. The moral obligation to keep large numbers of workers in employment meeting the consumers' definition of quality is far more important than changing those standards.

The difference between the production approach and the marketing outlook is summed up in this example. A British company which had achieved spectacular growth in the do-it-yourself market had been well aware of the growth in polystyrene tiles. After a while, it decided to enter the market directly and build a plant. It wasn't long before the venture began to look very sick indeed. Capacity was being badly under-utilized. The company began offering sales discounts, running promotions and, when those did not produce the desired results, began to search for new markets. Their attitude was one of 'We've got a damned good product; there must be someone, somewhere we can sell to'.

In fact, they had got it all wrong. Firstly, their market analysis was faulty. Certainly, the market for ceiling tiles had exhibited an exponential growth rate. However, they had forgotten to temper their efforts at sophistication with practicality. Had they even asked themselves how often they expected to replace the ceiling tiles in their own homes, they would quickly have realized that there would be a significant difference between initial demand and annual repeat buying. They had been so excited by projecting the market growth rate and expanding it to allow for the effect of their superb new products that they had quite overlooked a basic fact of market behaviour.

At that point, the question they should have asked was: 'We have the technical skill to manufacture and mould polystyrene: how can we match those skills to existing profitable markets – preferably without any change in our facilities and capacity or, alternatively, with only minor modifications'.

12

In the same situation, Polycell turned to the manufacture of polystyrene boats!

Sales orientation can lead to a number of excesses, several of which will appear in later chapters. The cardinal sin, however, is the pursuit of volume.

The marketing approach is synonymous with profit motivation. Profit and volume are hardly ever maximized at the same point. A professional consultant with more demands on his time than he can meet might equate demand and supply by raising his fees until all his hours are filled at the maximum price and all the work done in his own office or consulting room. He would maximize profit and volume at the same time. Most businesses find that the very things which allowed the consultant to maximize both are the very problems which prevent it happening to them. They usually have distribution costs which vary with load and distance and they seldom have the opportunity to use differential pricing to cover the variance in costs. The pursuit of volume fails to realize the application of Pareto's Law – often called the 80:20 rule. Simply stated, the law as applied to marketing says that a few important customers will account for the bulk of profits whilst a large number of small customers will yield only a low proportion of profits. One of the problems which leads to the arrival of marketing as the third stage in a company's development is the way production and sales tend to develop in ways which are contrary to each other. Increasing the scale of production usually leads to economies and greater efficiency. Diminishing returns for sales cost and efficiency tend to arrive much earlier. Thus, whilst the factory is pushing for more sales to improve factory costings, the sales force is increasing costs by spending more time gaining conversions, taking more time in travelling, making several visits to obtain an order and making special runs to deliver. Thus, economies of scale in manufacturing can easily lead to diseconomies of scale in selling.

There are two major methods by which the marketing approach would attack this problem. Firstly, it would seek to improve profitability by concentrating efforts on influencing the major customers and find more cost-effective ways of servicing the rest. For example, both Lyons-Tetley and Brooke Bond Oxo previously sold tea from vans which called on virtually every retailer who might have sold tea. Both now concentrate their own efforts on the top end of the grocery trade leaving the wholesalers and the cash-and-carry outlets to cater for the rest of the trade. Tea is still in virtually 100 per cent distribution but the sales costs of those two companies have been successfully contained. Secondly, a marketing approach would have

13

been more aware of interrelationships and the implications of apparently separate decisions. Starting with 'what is our market' and progressing through 'how many do we want to serve direct' to 'how do we maximize profit' might have led to decisions about production capacity at an early stage. It is a difficult emotional decision for a sales-trained manager to take, but at some time most businesses have to face the decision 'what risk are we prepared to take of not supplying a proportion of our possible customers?'

1.4 What marketing does

We have come back to the point of considering the implications of everything we do. Implicit in our three statements about marketing is an awareness of what you are doing, why you are doing it and what the implications are – now and in the future. It is very difficult to be certain about anything in business. Given the same facts, one company will make one decision and another will take an entirely different direction. One will probably be wrong. However, if it knows why it is doing what it is, the chances of remedying an unfavourable situation and avoiding a similar error in the future must be far greater.

Hopefully, by now you will agree that marketing isn't just common sense, is more than selling alone and certainly isn't only advertising. It isn't entirely what business is all about but if business isn't concerned with the most profitable directions, it isn't concerned with much of value. And the managing director obviously has a great deal more to do than conduct the marketing function, and far too much to be able to exercise any of the specialist roles. On the other hand, if he doesn't set the example, a marketing department cannot achieve very much. Nevertheless, the impression is invariably given that marketing does tread on an awful lot of toes. Just how many can be seen from simply listing the major activities in a co-ordinated marketing company. They would be:

1 *Assessing markets* Measuring existing and potential markets, defining market segments, recommending which to attack, monitoring progress, etc.
2 *Specifying products and services* From market assessment and product potential, ensure that the end user's views and opinions are adequately represented in the goods and/or services offered; that is, offer customer benefits rather than production features.
3 *Pricing policy* Based on the preceding sectors, recommend that

14

policy which will afford maximum profits at least risk. Consider possible competitive reactions and devise competitive ploys.

4 *Channel policy* How goods should reach the end user. The levels through which they will pass. Are sales to be entirely direct; only indirect; or some combination of the two? How will intermediaries be selected, remunerated, trained, motivated, retained?

5 *Sales and physical distribution policy* The functional consequences of channel decisions. Size and duties of the sales force. Number and location of warehouses and depots. Calling and delivery rates and frequency. Profit *versus* volume.

6 *Advertising and promotion* How much (if any), when, to whom? Packaging, service manuals, training as part of product promotion, etc.

7 *Co-ordination*

The last is vital. If there is any single role that transcends all others in distinguishing a marketing man from other managers it is that of co-ordinator. Marketing can be seen as a sort of federated union. The component states include selling, market research, advertising, public relations, promotion, merchandising and so on. Integrating and co-ordinating not only those individual parts but also the efforts of those components with production, accounting, buying, and so on is the way that the full ramifications of all actions will be best understood. To understand is the prerequisite of effective management action. If you don't know what is going on in your market you will be borne along like a leaf on a stream: know what you are about and you can influence your fate.

It isn't easy. In subsequent chapters, some of the pitfalls will be pointed out and some of the more useful marketing practices considered. It is only fair to issue a warning at the outset that cultivating the marketing philosophy is to adopt a way of looking at things that is not always comfortable. It frequently involves the individual in quasi-moral dilemmas with himself until he learns to accept that it is the ultimate arrogance to impose his standards on others. The day he learns that lesson, he understands that he has no personal right to speak on behalf of his customers; for example, he cannot be a fair judge of promotion aimed at them, simply because it is not aimed at him. Only by studying his market continuously will he be able to speak for his customers – using their words. We are all human and we all have lives to live outside our work, and this duality does lead to dissatisfaction, discomfort and anxiety. That is the marketeer's lot. He knows there is a fate that will befall him unless he acts: he often wants to act altogether too quickly.

1.5 Summary

Marketing is not just another word for common sense or some particular discipline. It is a way of thinking that links a host of separate activities and unifies them in the search for profit. Because the marketing man is always asking questions about his market, a number of techniques have grown up. In the ideal situation, the techniques go hand in hand with the philosophy. Often the techniques cannot be afforded or are not appropriate to a particular industry or situation. That is no barrier to adopting the marketing way of thinking, of continually wanting to understand what the company is doing, why and what the consequences might be now and in the future.

The underlying concept behind all marketing thinking is that profit arises from satisfying customers.

1.6 Checklist

1   Who is the ultimate marketing authority in your company?

2   Is this delegated? Wholly or partially? How?

3   How is the company organized to:
    a   Identify customer requirements?
    b   Anticipate them?
    c   Satisfy those needs?

4   Does a mechanism exist to check continuing levels of satisfaction; monitor quality complaints; deal with service complaints?

5   How widely disseminated is the essential marketing philosophy of profit through meeting customer needs (that is, producing what the customer wants rather than what it suits you to make)?

6   At what state is your company?
    a   Production orientated?
    b   Sales orientated?
    c   Marketing orientated?

7   Key areas for marketing attention:
    a   Assessing markets.
    b   Specifying products and services to meet market needs.

16

c   Pricing policy.
d   Channel policy.
e   Sales and physical distribution policy.
f   Advertising and promotion.
g   Co-ordination of the separate activities of company depart-
     ments to achieve corporate marketing goals.

2

A Rose is a Rose is a Rose

Vive la difference

The management consultant learns to spot it a mile off: that moment when his client draws himself up to his full height and from that lofty pinnacle declaims 'But my business is different'.

Of course it is. No two businesses are precisely the same. However, experience shows that not only do businesses that appear to be very different from each other behave in remarkably similar ways, but some businesses that appear to compete in the same market are, in fact, operating in quite different ones. In this chapter, some of the more common business groupings will be examined to see what they have in common and what characteristics separate them. The choice is somewhat arbitrary for, as we shall see, strict definitions of the type usually employed seem to leave a large number of companies hanging in limbo. There are, for example, a number of consumer durable products that are almost industrial in their complexity but, nevertheless, sell to private individuals for domestic use (like an electric drill), and there are many products that appear to be obviously industrial but are sold through shops to both individuals and companies who are the final users (like certain kinds of stationery and office equipment). Somehow they have to be fitted in.

We could divide businesses by their size, but that has always caused considerable problems. Most of the standard definitions of a small business, for example, allow some with very considerable turnover and profit to creep in. Even the nature of the final product is not a watertight method of differentiation, for service industries could be divided between consumer and industrial services whilst each could be divided even further. For simplicity, the headings under which we will examine some of the particular characteristics and problems of individual sectors will be:

Consumer markets
Industrial goods
Service industries
International marketing
Small businesses

2.1 Consumer markets

Probably the two major reasons for the slow acceptance of the marketing philosophy in the United Kingdom has been the belief on the one side that marketing only applies to consumer products (especially soap powders) and the conviction on the other that techniques are readily transferable from consumer marketing to quite different markets. Both are false. The wise businessman knows that techniques and tactics are not always transferable between different parts of the consumer market. Newspapers are obviously consumer products but they don't have '3p off' promotions. Although the worst excesses of both types seem to be in the past, there is still a widespread belief that marketing is really only effective when you spend millions of pounds on television advertising, have hordes of product managers, spend a fortune on market research and do all your sales analysis on a computer. With all that, goes the argument, consumer marketing is dead easy!

On the contrary, it is the hardest of the lot. That is why all those techniques are used and why so much money has to be spent making potential consumers aware of your products and motivated to buy them. At its crudest, it is the difference between trying to address your message once a week to 16 million housewives and contacting 300 buyers four times a year. It is the difference between a sane, rational discussion with a buyer about the objective factors of price, performance, delivery and service, and dealing with emotive and unpredictable purchasing behaviour by someone confused with a shelf full of competing hair shampoos all at round about the same price. It is the difference between trying to convince the housewife that her family will love this new flavour that you have just invented, without asking her whether she thinks she would like it, and responding to the demands for new processes, new ingredients, or new performance standards from a long-standing customer.

Both positions are obviously extremes but they do help us to both kill the myth that consumer marketing is easy and to explain part of the confusion that exists between different types of marketing. On the first, consumer businesses use the advanced techniques and spend large sums on promotion because they have to – not because they enjoy doing it. On the second, it becomes clear that the key ingredients in the confusion are what might be termed 'distance' and frequency.

When most people talk of consumer marketing they are, in fact, thinking of fast-moving goods – groceries, confectionery, cigarettes – goods which have those two characteristics of distance and high frequency. The problems of communication and understanding are the greater the more is the effective distance between the manufacturer and the final user and the more there are of the latter. Only in direct-mail selling is there a one-to-one relationship. Frequently, there are wholesalers, buying groups, store managers and shelves between the two ends of continuum. The efforts devoted to persuading those links in the chain to stock your goods, promote them and generally be enthused by them are often greater than those aimed direct at the final consumer. Many food products, for example, are only promoted to the grocery trade, relying on the retailer to pass on part of the deals he receives in the form of price promotions that make the product attractive to the housewife at the very moment of purchase.

Frequency can compound those problems. The more often the product is purchased, the greater the store that has to be set upon regularity of repeat purchasing and holding customer loyalty. Not only is the great bulk of consumer promotion aimed at first creating and then maintaining loyalty but also the necessity for considerable quantities and sophistication of market research is determined by the need to be aware of buying rates ahead of that awful day when orders on the factory simply dry up. There are, of course, other characteristics of this sort of market. The average volume purchased tends to be low. Most of the products in these markets are characterized by relatively high turnovers and relatively low profit margins. Goods are bought for personal use and satisfaction (including the whole family in that statement) and the buying decision-making group is more often than not the user. On the whole, this type of business is very widely dispersed.

There are, however, many consumer products and services that have quite different characteristics. Many of them are far less frequently purchased, more expensive, are subject to careful consideration and have technical features and attributes. Washing machines, refrigerators, cars and television sets fall into this category of product, whilst many financial services (from banks and insurance companies, for example) and overseas holidays have the same sort of characteristic. Not only will the buyer look around, compare performance, check prices and possibly try out the product, but, in many cases, the purchaser will carry working skills and disciplines into the purchasing situation. The man who works all day in a scientific atmosphere will not completely switch his mind over into some new gear simply because he is making a personal purchase. Indeed, a great deal of fairly skilled consideration has to be given to many consumer purchases if satisfaction is to be assured. A packaged holiday, for example, involves not only consideration of destination but also hotel within the resort, length of holiday, type of room, price, and some thought to other activities that might be pursued when actually there. Quite apart from the complex interrelationships between all those decisions, there is the all-important consideration that the holiday involves a heavy capital sum yet it cannot be seen, touched or experienced at the time of deciding.

We have moved into the field of consumer services, although many would argue that a packaged holiday is a product that involves putting together a number of services rather than a service in its own right. The special position of services will be examined later in this chapter. At the moment it is sufficient to point out that consumer services can be sub-divided into three categories:

Domestic services
Direct personal
Public personal

Examples of the first might be window cleaning, plumbing and milk delivery. Direct personal services are those which are rendered to one person at a time such as haircutting, bank accounts and life assurance. The opposite is the service which a person receives as an individual although it is actually performed simultaneously to many others (or is intended to be). A train journey is an example of this kind, as are all other services performed by public utilities. Thus, pure commercial marketing merges gradually into the spheres of social services and what is beginning to be recognized as 'social marketing' – the application of the principles of consumer satisfaction and the awareness of the effects of interrelated yet separate activities upon both the user as an individual and as a member of a larger society.

2.2 Industrial goods

Although it is comparatively easy to produce a definition of industrial marketing, almost any attempt does have the effect of leaving a large number of businesses hanging in the air. However, the mere fact that so many businesses regard themselves as 'industrial' simply because of the technology involved in the manufacturing process indicates how far we still have to go in recognizing the importance of the customer. The customer we are concerned with, in any attempt to categorize industrial markets, is the end user, the person who finally 'consumes' the product. If a thoroughly pedantic view is taken, no kind of clear definition is possible. Many of the industrial products that are involved in the production of other goods are completely consumed; many food products that are clearly consumer items (such as cooking fat) are only used as an aid to the production of an end product. Obviously, products and services fall into a lengthy spectrum on which the two ends are light years apart, yet near neighbours shade and overlap.

The classic, and most useful, description of industrial marketing is that it is concerned with derived demand, that is it is linked to a demand for goods and services at a consumer level. At times, the distance between first producer and final end user may be enormous. A raw material is an ingredient in a process which transforms it into a form suitable for manufacture as part of a plant which produces packaging which protects a product an operative will use as a service to a householder in his own home. Not only are these industrial services performed for other companies in the manufacturing field but also for institutions, local and central government and for farmers. Even where the product is identical, the selling method will have to vary with the type of buyer and the use he has for the product.

The definition is useful but not entirely satisfactory. Just as we could distinguish sub-divisions of the consumer markets, so we can provide other categories of industrial market which help to scoop up those businesses left floundering without a parent. We can look at businesses by the length of benefit they provide and by the degree of interdependence.

Firstly, benefit. What most people in consumer industries think of as industrial products are really capital items whose benefit lasts over a very lengthy period which covers a considerable number of production cycles (often millions). Although they may be regarded as epitomizing the industrial market, in fact demand is seldom very closely derived, especially when a plant has several alternative uses. That, of course, assumes that the products are tangible. Where they are, they are capitalized in the balance sheet and depreciated over relatively long periods of time. Intangible items cannot be dealt with in the same way but are written off very shortly after purchase. Goods and services that fall into this category are what might be termed one-to-one transaction items. The market for products which cannot be related closely to the process for another is virtually an end-user market and in that respect exhibits many of the tendencies to be found in consumer markets.

Other kinds of product provide their benefits over a much shorter time-span; typically, one production cycle. Thus, they are charges against revenue and, in so far as demand is usually closely derived, are regarded as variable costs in the purchaser's accounts. Examples would include raw materials converted into an end-user product and the fertilizers used to promote crop growth. (In many cases, agricultural products fall rather between two stools, in that demand is not closely derived from a single product and does not vary directly with output in all cases. The farmer will regard the expenditure as a fixed cost but the benefit will be effectively confined to one growing season.)

It is usually reckoned that closely derived demand is relatively satisfying in the respect that one only has to be concerned with the customer's output. Recent events have underlined the effect that changes in stock levels can have on the prime producer. Many companies have found their sales falling even though the final end product to which they contribute is selling as well as ever. The search for increased efficiency as well as cash shortages has caused many companies to learn how to live with lower stocks.

The other alternative form of classification is by the interdependence between products. We can separate out three types of product which are technically linked in some way and one which is not. Stationery, for example, is not usually technically linked with an end product or process: the letters and forms a company employs are an essential part of being in business but have no direct connection with an end product (unless it is for a printer). In cases like this, other considerations determine the buying cycle. Services, such as contract plant maintenance, would also come into this category.

The sub-divisions of the technically linked products and services are based on the ability of the end user to recognize and be concerned about the supplier of an intermediate process or product. Where the demand is very closely derived but the product is not identifiable to the user (for example, a chemical), the possibility of substitution is generally higher. Products in this category live and die by their appeal to their direct customer on the conventional industrial grounds of cost, efficiency, reliability and service. Where the ingredient or component is identifiable by a company or brand name, the owner of that name can take positive steps to not only defend his position as supplier but also to develop an end-user market, safe in the knowledge that he will benefit from the derived demand. This is known as 'back-selling' and classic examples in this country are the synthetic fibres, on the one hand (Terylene and Crimplene, as examples), and the efforts of the International Wool Secretariat, on the other, to promote products made of pure wool.

In between, there are other technically linked products for which the demand is closely derived and where the end user is very well aware of the generic product but not aware of the company who supplied it. A good deal of switching gear comes into this category. Back-selling would be obviously wasteful here and substitution is again much more possible than would be the case if the supplier's name were important to the customer. Control over one's destiny is obviously more difficult and it is clear that the fundamental problems of industrial marketing are precisely connected with the amount of influence a company can have over its own market.

Many of the characteristics of buyer behaviour in industrial markets will be the mirror opposites of those we saw for final consumers. Such is the diversity of businesses that come under this generic heading, however, that it becomes near impossible to tabulate meaningful distinctions without constant qualification.

The term 'business to business' is now being increasingly adopted to cover a far wider area of activities than the traditional description of 'derived demand' items can. For the moment, it is enough to say that the principal considerations of industrial marketing concern the question of control over one's own destiny, the greater concern with selling into, rather than through, one's customers and the more complex nature of the decision-making process before placing an order.

2.3 Service industries

Businesses whose function it is to provide services to others may do so to private individuals, to companies and to local and central government. They cover all those occasions when a benefit is provided without being accompanied by a tangible product. Frequently, a tangible product is the direct result, as when a decorator papers your walls. Often, the tangible aspect is several stages removed (as is the case with most services provided by banks and insurance companies), and in very many instances the service is performed in order to prevent something tangible happening; a chimney sweep may prevent a fire. In many of the cases, such as the chimney sweep, there is no visible evidence of any kind and this can often give rise to considerable criticism of the service. This is especially true of preventive servicing of all kinds. In a well-maintained car, as with a regularly serviced piece of machinery, there is nothing to show. Criticism will be prompt if a mishap occurs soon after servicing but few bouquets are offered when nothing untoward happens between services.

A characteristic of a service is that it is intangible. Most are very difficult to describe and to measure. Payment often has to be made well before the benefit is obtained; holidays and life assurance are good examples. In many cases, the benefit will be received by someone else and frequently, as with most kinds of insurance, there is always the hope that no-one will benefit. Because the actual service is intangible, there is a natural tendency to focus on the most immediate tangible object – a person. People are fundamental to the performance of services. When a highly efficient engineer turns up two days late, the fact that he did a good job is often overlooked. The performance of employees can harm any business but services suffer especially in this respect.

It is quite understandable that criticism, and occasionally praise, should be directed at the people who represent the company providing the service: after all, that is what the customer pays for. The 'production costs' of services are manpower costs and goods and other services associated with them in the performance of their tasks. This leads to two particular features, and problems, of service industries. In the first case, the output of people is less predictable and more variable than the performance of machines. Differences between individuals performing identical tasks are almost invariably greater than between the same types of machinery. People usually need more breaks from work and, themselves, break down fairly often. On the other hand, they are capable of exercising initiative, intelligence and adaptability. As the famous sign in the IBM office in Tokyo puts it:

Man – Slow, Slovenly, Brilliant
IBM – Fast, Accurate, Stupid.

In so many service industries, the end-product is identical or almost so. The main joint stock banks in the UK offer the same basic services at the same time and with very little variation between them in price. In cases like these, real differences are found in the highly personal qualities of the people who perform these services: their reliability, helpfulness, honesty and cheerfulness. In many service industries,

25

from banks through advertising agencies to highly personal services like hairdressing, one even finds that personal qualities among staff actually overcome a poor end-product. Research conducted into ladies' hairdressing repeatedly shows that the majority of women complain that their 'favourite' hairdresser 'can't cut hair'. The reasons for continuing to go to that salon were mainly to do with a liking for the staff and especially for a particular stylist.

Highly personal services like that are clearly at one end of a spectrum. At the other end would be mainly industrial services. Preventive servicing is clearly a long way apart from most ladies' hairdressing, although the services of a hair clinic and a trichologist could certainly be classified as preventive servicing. In general, industrial services are bought for one or more of the following reasons:

To reduce cost
Improve profits
Promote and maintain efficiency
To improve morale
Welfare benefits to staff
To comply with laws, codes and regulations

The service industries generally lag far behind the rest of British business in the adoption of the marketing philosophy. The very fact that so many services are personal and the heavy person-to-person involvement in all services has tended to convince them they are in touch with their customer and marketing has nothing more to offer. Although the phrase 'The customer is always right' originated in the service industries, we all know far too many cases where this is patently not practised. There are numerous reasons for this, many of them summed up in the earlier paragraph on the differences between people and machines. One big difference is that machines are indifferent to time. People place an increasing value on their time. From trade union pressure, on the one hand, to the effect of popular media on the use of leisure time, on the other, people want more money for the time they are working to use in the time when they are free. Every business has to face this fact. Service industries meet it head on, for it frequently leads to differences in the value placed on time by the employee and the worth of that time to the customer.

By and large, we are badly out of line in the cost of time in services. It has taken the hairdressing craft many, many years to be in a position of putting anything near the true worth of time into their prices. The do-it-yourself home decorating boom is based on the

26

unwillingness to value a craftsman's time as highly as the house-holder's own. They look at the capital cost of the total outlay on decorating a room and compare it with the cost of materials. Implicit in that decision is a refusal to measure how the cost of the paper-hanger's time compares with their own hourly rate and the omission from the calculation of the cost of their own time. As individuals, we all do this sort of thing all the time.

In a very real sense, the under-valuing of time is one of the major harvests from the ignorance of marketing thinking in service industries. In all services, from hairdressing to service engineering, there have been examples of intuitive marketers (and there most certainly is such an animal) who have been ahead of their time in gauging the preparedness of the market to pay a realistic price for a well-performed service, and have publicized and promoted that service. The alternative, and far more frequent response, has been to excuse the inadequate service and justify that by a chain of logic that says: the service is poor because the staff won't work in an industry that pays less than others and which pays less because customers will not pay the price that good service should cost if the wages were right! That is the sort of thing Joseph Heller called 'Catch 22'. An unfortunate result of that phenomenon is a tendency for providing a service to be looked down upon. When this attitude is combined with the demand for such services at the sort of hours other people don't work and often in conditions that the person who pays for the service wouldn't tolerate (that's why he wants the service), the major problem confronting this sector of business is readily appreciated. The absence of good marketing must bear a large part of the burden of complaint for allowing these attitudes to prevail. It may well take a very long time for the underlying sociological problems associated with them to even reduce to tolerable levels, let alone diappear.

2.4   International marketing

In the bad old days, it used to be called export. The very word is redolent of production orientation: not only is it a case of 'We can make it, go out and sell it' but it is also 'If it's good enough for us, it is certainly good enough for foreigners'. International marketing implies two things: first, that the same consideration is given to the assessment of opportunities whatever the market and, secondly, that there are many goods and services for which the world is truly the market.

International markets are obviously made up of consumer and

27

industrial goods and services and they will not be so very different for being performed in an overseas market. However, when we get down to the reasons for using and the methods of selling, distributing, producing and promoting, then there are likely to be very considerable differences. It is precisely because of those differences that the marketing philosophy and approach is so vitally important. The natural tendency is to look overseas for profitable markets for existing products. Almost inevitably that implies trying to sell in rather the same way, and for the same uses, as in the home market. Because of language problems, above all else, companies are hesitant about creating a duplicate operating unit in the overseas market and usually prefer to operate through agents and factors. In the vast majority of cases, British firms put far less resources behind their products in overseas markets: they are under-represented in the field by salesmen, their distribution is generally less swift and prompt and their promotion minimal. It is a sad reality that the overall quality of selling in overseas markets is well behind that in the UK, both in quantity and calibre.

International marketing, that is the application of the philosophy and techniques of marketing to business in several countries, emphasizes two vitally important points. Each new country has to be examined in just the same way as any sector in a domestic market, and the abdication from many of the component parts of the marketing operation removes many of the strengths of the company and ignores the parts they play in the concept of the total product.

Because of the desperate need for foreign currency, successive governments have continually exhorted businesses to sell more abroad. Among the more dangerous phrases they have coined are:

'Export or die'
'Exporting is fun'.

Both are a very long way from the truth. Exporting is extremely hard work, involving all the efforts of a domestic market plus the many new ones of dealing with different languages, new systems of distribution and operations, laws, regulations, public opinion and international politics. If the hard work isn't realized and done, it can so easily be a case of 'Export and die'. The importance of sound and thorough market analysis cannot be minimized. In a domestic market, it is often possible to conduct fairly minimal amounts of pre-testing, safe in the knowledge that the company is well known and that its reputation will do a great deal for the product when it is launched. Experience in the market enables one to slot the new venture into a known pattern and this in turn gives the company a fair chance of anticipating both customer and competitive reaction. The very opposite is true in new overseas markets. Ideally, one should pre-test the product, then the product with the name of the supplier known and then the country of origin. (The latter is far more important in some countries than others: much as it may be regretted, there are countries that do not welcome British goods, will not buy from Jewish-owned companies, refuse to deal with those who have trading links with political enemies, and so on.) When entering a market for the first time, it is usually necessary to find some way of testing the sales, distribution and servicing arrangements. British industry compares unfavourably in this respect with many of our overseas competitors. The example of the Japanese motor cycle manufacturers is a salutary one. Those who now dominate the British and European markets built up their servicing and spares capability before they started to hard-sell.

In Chapter 1, we saw how a marketing-orientated company would approach the problem of over-capacity. Consideration of international markets is very much of that kind. A sound reason for searching for overseas markets is to utilize existing capacity and know-how or to justify longer production runs to maximize production efficiency. But the question should be 'What overseas markets may exist for the skills we possess, either exactly as they are now or reasonably adapted?'.

Marketing teaches us to take a broad sweep in looking for the skills we have that induce our customers to buy from us rather than from someone else. Frequently, it is something other than the product itself such as the skill of the sales force, the speed of delivery, a rapid trouble-shooting service. When a company with those sorts of attributes operates overseas through agents, factors or contractors, many of those advantages disappear or are out of its control. Often the failure to identify just what it is that your customer is buying from you (in terms of what we might call the total product) starts at home. Failure to perform up to expectation in overseas markets is based on lack of realization.

A division of ICI, manufacturing and selling industrial paints, had been remarkably successful in this country but very unsuccessful in selling overseas. The product was superior to local ones and it afforded significant value in its protective qualities and fireproofing. It was, in fact, careful marketing analysis of the domestic situation that revealed the answer. Although the product claims had always been based on the protective qualities and fireproofing, the product

29

had two other important qualities: ICI produced the widest range of colours on the market and they were able to guarantee almost 100 per cent availability. And those were the very things which could not be provided under the sales arrangements in the majority of the overseas markets.

Marketing overseas is extremely difficult work which is not made any the easier for the long absences from home and the heavy burden of travelling that managers have to endure. The calibre of executives and the rewards they earn (and the two probably correlate closely) are all too often a long way behind the needs of the job. International business epitomizes the need for sound marketing.

The term 'multinational marketing' has gained widespread currency and is often seen as a threat to a domestic economy. Multinational marketing is a special form of international marketing used to cover the situation where marketing takes place across national boundaries *and* where plants and management teams are located in several countries. Whereas international marketing tends to imply that trade develops from a home base, multinational marketing describes a situation in which there are several bases and it may well be that each country (acting semi-autonomously within broad corporate objectives) actually markets different products. Unilever is a good example, marketing different products in Africa from those in Europe; marketing some identical products in several countries; and even using different brand names for the same product or familiar names for different products.

2.5 Small businesses

In a strange way, the small successful business is a prime example of a marketing-orientated business. For every 100 small businesses that fail, perhaps 95 do so for a basic marketing reason. One man on his own finds it hard to undertake the analysis that a large company would require before entering a new market. More often than not, the inclination is lacking. The subsequent failure usually has two major ingredients: either the product as such or the particular quality of product service was not required or, if it was, not at a price that justified the time involved.

Any small business has a very marked affinity with a service industry. Its major resource is people. The capacity to expand is limited by the capacity of people to multiply their own efforts and the lack of funds to employ more people. In the early days at least, personal qualities tend to dominate, even where the final product is the output of a machine. The very personal qualities of reliability, punctuality and honesty are often the reasons why people buy from a small firm rather than a large. The standards set by the owner-entrepreneur are important too, things like final quality, inspection, after-sales service, care and attention. All these things can be instilled into operatives and carefully monitored in a small business.

However, those very qualities lead to two big problems and both are compounded by growth. Either the time to contemplate and plan for growth is severely limited by the need to be continually involved in the setting and maintenance of standards in the business, or growth takes place beyond the capability of the owners to monitor the kind of performance that caused them to grow. How often do you hear 'Now they've got big, they don't seem to bother any more'? Often it is a failure to appreciate what it is that attracts customers to the business that is behind the apparent change of standards. Frequently, the owner of the small business just does not realize what satisfactions his customers are taking from the total service he provides. Consequently, when the business grows, incorrect priorities are assigned and senior people tend to become involved in, say, finance to the neglect of the very skills and qualities that made the company grow. Certainly, the vast majority of ladies' hairdressers in the country regard themselves as skilled craftsmen and recruit staff on that basis. The research quoted earlier shows that women do not see the great majority of hairdressers in that light at all. When a salon owner employs an artistic director who behaves like a prima donna, he may be throwing the baby out with the bath-water; he may be emphasizing a production quality which his customers do not buy, in place of a very different one of pleasant service, which they do buy. Yet another hairdresser will succeed simply because he or she is a talented prima donna. The secret in all cases is to know your market. Often the sheer size of a company enables mistakes and sheer bad practice to be overcome in the market-place. The methods of many big companies would kill the small business. The techniques of marketing will be beyond most small businesses; those they can employ may only have limited use. The marketing philosophy, the constant analysis of what it is your customer buys from you and the questioning of every potential step, in terms of the consequences for the business now and in the future, are absolutely vital for the small business. In subsequent chapters it will be seen that there are some simple guidelines that help remove the major obstacle – time. It is sad that so many pieces of legislation, aimed at curbing the excesses of a very few large companies, hit small businesses particularly badly and cause them to apply that valuable commodity to areas which are more likely to slow the small business down than create the impetus to profitable growth.

2.6   Marketing for all

It isn't easy, as we have seen, to divide businesses into watertight compartments. It is easier to imagine that all businesses fall along a continuum. Some products that seem to be highly industrial, actually behave in ways that have far more in common with what are obviously fairly frivolous consumer products. Others, obviously aimed at consumers in their own homes, have more in common with a nuclear reactor. Actually, an energy authority is far more likely to buy two nuclear reactors at a time than a householder is to buy two homes.

In Figure 1, some attempt has been made to illustrate this phenomenon. The usefulness of the illustration will become increasingly apparent when we refer to particular ways of looking at businesses and even more so when ideas for action and separate techniques are discussed. If your business fits the characteristics of the 'consumer' end, for example, it means that techniques commonly used in those areas will probably be right in your business. You may have thought, say, that because you were selling paint through builders' merchants to the building and decorating trades, you were primarily industrial. The fact that you have wholesale and retail channels, deal with an industry in which there are large numbers of firms, where there are, effectively, no national operators and few large customers among the end users, means that you have to deal with the same kinds of problems that Heinz do when they sell baked beans. One of the routine objections to marketing people is that they want to sell everything as though it were a can of baked beans. If they do assume that all problems are capable of similar solutions, they most certainly are not adopting the marketing way of thinking. What they will be saying if they are experienced marketing practitioners is that a surprising number of different businesses make the strangest bedfellows. People like builders, doctors and farmers act in many ways just like housewives. There are millions of them, they act individually or in small groups, they do not have separate buying functions (only very few of them do) and the bulk of them work from home – just like housewives. All kinds of business have a great deal to learn from each other. Most of what we normally gather together under the heading of marketing is applicable to all kinds and sizes of business. In the rest of this book, that is the approach that will be taken. The reader must continually question how appropriate any particular statement or example is to him or her. Where a particular sector of business has problems or characteristics which are quite different from any other it will be pointed out and examples drawn.

One final word of explanation. A constant criticism of marketing books, lectures and courses is that they are consumer biased. By now, the reason for that should be better appreciated. There is another good reason. Few people work in, say, stainless steel stockholding. Fewer still have actually bought steel from a stockholder. Almost everyone has bought a bar of chocolate at some time. Examples that live and can be matched with experience are generally remembered better than those that have to be taken on trust. Where an example is universally applicable, it is more likely than not to be taken from the everyday experience which most people have as customers. Where that doesn't apply, more specific illustrations will be used.

2.7 Summary

Attempts to categorize industries are doomed to failure. Although distinctions are commonly made, comparison of one's own business against any of the conventional yardsticks will reveal the futility of the definition exercise.

The only validity of definition by industry type is to correlate techniques and methods of approach with product groups and thence to products from other fields sharing the same characteristics. This will often show (see Figure 1) that industries, generally classified one way, behave more like a totally different kind and are more amenable to similar treatment.

There are more similarities than differences in business problems. Although few, the differences may be highly significant, but are more likely to be between competing firms in the same industry than between different industries.

2.8 Checklist

1 Consumer markets:
   a Distance from producer.
   b Number of intermediaries.
   c Frequency of use.
   d Need to create and maintain customer loyalty.
   e Buying decisions often highly subjective.

'Frivolous consumer markets'

———————————————————————————— Highly localized markets ————

—————————————————————————— Short life in use ————————

————————————————————— Narrow product definition ————————

———————————————— Standardized product ———————————

————————————— Large no. potential customers ——————————

————— High frequency ——————————————————————————

—— Fashion content ——————

— Impulse ——

Standardized/Relatively cheap/Wide demand/Frequent purchase

Typical marketing methods:

| Mass media | Consumer offers | Emphasis on packaging | Sales force calling on wholesalers/retailers | After-sales service |

Examples of typical industries:

| Toys | Confectionery | Records | Luxury foods | Staple foods | Necessary consumer durables (e.g. cookers) | Luxury consumer durables |

Examples of problem fits:

| Consumable industrial supplies (e.g. electricity, stationery) | High-frequency ingredients and components | Basic bulk items (e.g. cement, fertilizers, chemicals) | Packaging machinery |

Figure 1 *The marketing progression*

(Note: Each of the attributes named is commonly assumed to have its opposite on the other side of the dividing line. For example, it is normally assumed that no industrial buying decision is ever made on impulse.)

Specialized/Relatively expensive/Narrow demand/Infrequent purchase

Alternative product uses — Complexity of product — 'Heaviness' of product

— Buying decisions by group — Direct contact buyer/seller —

High unit cost —

Derived demand

High cost of mistakes

Buying for stock

Rational buying motives

| iterature, xhibitions, ymposia | Subsidized initial orders | Trade-ins as part of 'deal' price | High-level negotiations | Trade credit, leasing, export guarantees |

Components — Computer systems — Major plant — Factory buildings

| omestic i-fi | Domestic deep-freeze | Larder stock (cooking fat, dried fruit, etc.) | Private cars | Packaged holidays | Life assurance | Houses |

2 Consumer durables:
  a Greater objectivity in purchasing.
  b More 'shopping around' (to compare specifications, performance, price, etc.).
  c Often complex interrelationships in the buying decision.
  d More likely to involve group decisions (e.g. the family).

3 Consumer services:
  a Domestic: applied to the home.
  b Direct personal: one at a time to individuals.
  c Public personal: used individually, provided to many simultaneously.

4 Industrial goods:
  a Technology not necessarily the way to describe the market.
  b Vary from high-value, low-frequency to low-value, high-frequency.
  c Direct contact between supplier and customer more common.
  d Demand is derived.
  e Markets defined by benefits and the time-span over which that benefit is obtained.
  f Markets defined by interdependence; that is, technically linked.
  g Selling efforts affected by the degree of 'branding' or identification of the item.

5 Service industries:
  a To private individuals, companies or institutions.
  b Benefits without a tangible product.
  c May produce a tangible result (often several stages removed).
  d Benefits cannot be stored.
  e Intangibles difficult to describe and measure.
  f People become the tangible aspect.
  g Industrial services to:
    i Reduce costs
    ii Improve profits
    iii Promote/maintain efficiency
    iv Improve morale
    v Provide welfare benefits to staff
    vi Meet laws, etc.
  h Problem of service industries is the proper valuation of the time employed (that is, the customer's valuation).

6 International:
  a Adapting marketing principles across national boundaries.
  b Same techniques, different solutions likely.
  c Difficulties of operating through different and distant channels.
  d Search for markets to use existing skills/capacities or ones those skills can be adapted to.
  e Multinationals may seek completely different markets in different parts of the world.

7 Small businesses:
  a High failure rate due to lack of demand or insufficient demand at the price required.
  b Problems come with growth.
  c Difficulty of maintaining original standards as the business grows.

3

What Shall We Buy?

For those who do not think, it is best at least to
rearrange their prejudices once in a while.

Luther Burbank

Since the sole end purpose of production is consumption, and
because all a business has is costs until it has customers, any
businessman ought to know as much as possible about his customers.
We shall see in later chapters more examples of what has already been
indicated, that customers are often behaving in quite a different way
from the way their suppliers thought. It will help to be aware of some
valid generalizations about the way customers decide to buy before
applying new-found techniques to a particular product or a particular
business.

Obviously, different kinds of customers behave differently in
different kinds of buying situations. But most people are confronted
with very different kinds of buying problems even in the same sort of
situation. Can one really believe that decisions about the choice of
washing machine and the brand of powder to use in it are of equal
value to the housewife? Or that the choice of location for a new
factory is equal to the choice between alternative production
processes and between competing suppliers of paint for the new
factory? Again, there is a difficulty in making clear distinctions.
Where those distinctions can be made and where they are inappropriate is of vital importance. That is what this chapter is about. It is
not necessary to become too complicated; the important distinctions
are between the very broadest categories of consumers and
industrial buying decisions. By and large, decisions about purchasing
services will involve the same sort of considerations as either
industrial products or consumer durables. Other particular examples
(such as the pharmaceutical industry) will be given in the next
chapter.

3.1 Consumer purchases

Although the conventional descriptions of consumer markets allocate a low priority to rational thought, implicit in the way many companies approach consumer markets is a belief that buying decisions are at least made in logical sequence. In fact, most decisions involve far less logic than even the most vociferous detractors would argue.

Most consumer buying decisions are made at a remarkably low level of consciousness. Some are taken with no apparent thought at all. Some involve decisions about money – can it be afforded, should money be spent on this rather than that, which offers better value for money? Others involve considerations of performance, belief, fashion, 'fit' (will it match the curtains, suit my family?) etc. Yet others are inherently more interesting decisions to take and get involved in: deciding on the family's new colour television is clearly likely to rank far higher than deciding between competing brands of butter. Obviously some decisions are complex, involve a good deal of logical analysis and involve considerable financial risk if the wrong decision is taken – a good deal more risk than is involved in a great many buying decisions made in industry.

Only very few buying decisions in the consumer market can truly be equated with industrial purchasing decisions and they are the ones that most closely accord with the principle of decision by a buying unit rather than an individual. Individuals haven't got time for that sort of process every time they want to buy something. Just take a moment to think about all the decisions a housewife has to make every day – decisions about the use of time, amount of money to be spent, what to buy for immediate use, what to buy to cook today, for stock, and so on. If this were reduced to a mathematical equation, every home would have to be equipped with a computer, and a rather large one at that. Nor would the computer be very happy with the data a housewife has at her disposal. It would find that there was far too little usable information (and the efforts of the law and consumerist organizations wouldn't make much difference to this) and there was an enormous number of decisions in any case. If a computer is likely to blow a fuse or two, what about the poor housewife?

She cheats. Without a great deal of conscious thought on the subject, she arrives at processes that make life a little more tolerable. You can check the validity of these little tricks by comparing them with your own behaviour.

First, she allows habit to take over wherever possible. Watch a housewife in a supermarket. It is remarkable how often her arm seems to reach out almost automatically. These habits can become so strong that new information is not merely rejected, it is totally ignored. She always buys Typhoo Tea; what does it matter that PG Tips are 3p off this week? Maybe she does notice but is pulled back by the strength of her husband's habits. Habits can affect buying decisions at both levels, the second involving slightly more thought than the first.

Secondly, she allows her brain to make maps. Some trigger pulls the appropriate map to the forefront of her mind and selection takes place. It is a simple conceptual map of the options available. It could be a map of tea-time: 'Tonight we could have bread and jam, baked beans on toast, cakes or biscuits'. A decision at that level prompts other maps to come forward for attention: will it be plain cakes or fancy; cream or chocolate; from the baker or branded goods from the supermarket? When you refer to a road map and then discover that the road you wanted to take is no longer there, you either make a deletion on your map or make a mental note to be recalled the next time you travel that way. That is what happens with any buying decision involving one of these conceptual maps. They are very susceptible to outside influences. New pressures can disturb them. A price reduction might remind the housewife that the product is very good but normally too expensive. This new information reshuffles the information in her head and quickly produces a new map. Actually, there may be a dozen other items on the map but they all pale into insignificance compared with this new relationship of price to quality: all the others are held constant. This also helps to explain some of the stranger phenomena of consumer markets. There aren't many things that are important enough on their own to justify redrawing the map; if one thing changes, something else ought to be associated with it. If the pack alone changes, it poses questions about what has happened to quality, why the price hasn't changed, and so on.

Thirdly, there are groups of 'family decisions'. These occur where there is a very close link between products. For example, buying a turkey involves a near automatic purchase of stuffing, sausage meat, peas, gravy browning, and checking whether there are enough potatoes and that there is fat for the roasting. Eggs and bacon usually go together; a razor needs blades; a pen needs ink, and so on. This sort of clustered decision is close to the other two in that, in one sense, it is a form of habit-decision whilst, in another, it is a particular type of conceptual map. All three are used to ease the burden of decision making. Whilst they do that, they make the task of promotion more difficult. Ideally, one needs to isolate which of these kinds of decision applies to one's product. Is it the kind that is amenable to promotion? Does it respond to rapid efforts (like money off) or does it need the slow, steady drip of mass media over a long period? Behind so much promotion aimed at the consumer market is a naive belief that all consumers react in similar ways to the same stimulus and that the buyer cares about the product as much as the producer does.

In my young days in the tea business, we used to liken tea to oxygen. If people are stopped in the street and asked what the most important thing in their life is, they will give answers like the family, love, work, sex; no-one will say oxygen, yet one cannot live without it. Oxygen? That's just there; no-one thinks about it. Ask the same people what the most important product in their lives is and very, very few will say tea – or eggs, or butter, or sugar, or any other staple item. They are classic examples of products that have sunk to the lower levels of consciousness.

Yet the 11 items that every grocer knows are the great draw-lines to his store are included in the list of low-consciousness staples. Why? This involves a whole new set of buying decisions about where to shop. Information which is not crucial in one dimension may be quite critical in another. This is an area where it is crucial. In effect, the housewife is saying 'I have to buy these things; I want to push them down to the back of my mind where habit operates best but I must be sure that I can trust my habits to this shop'. The decision about which shop to buy at is a critical one from which a host of other decisions will spring. It is one of the reasons why most women shop at different stores supplying the same goods: one for price, one for range, one for quality, one for 'last resort' purchases (after normal hours, running-out, etc.) and one for 'habit'. The more rational housewife will try to group these decisions so that she optimizes her shopping hours.

There are other kinds of decision that are deferred to others. When one goes into a public house and asks for a pint of beer, it is very seldom that one is asked which brand. At the most, the only question will be about price (expressed in terms of 'Best?'). In cases like this, and also with petrol, the same sort of decision occurs. The usual assumption is that the brand has been chosen before entering the outlet. In fact, there is a great deal of evidence that there is often no conscious brand decision involved in the choice of outlet; the motorist is more likely to need a tankful of petrol than a tankful of Shell petrol. If the decision can be delegated to someone else, it does make life easier. If it can be partially delegated, it helps, too. The

41

housewife asks for a pound of apples; the greengrocer asks whether she wants cooking apples or eating apples and then which kind. A good deal of delegation has taken place. Obviously, it is important to recognize whether a particular product is included in this area. If, like petrol and beer, a good deal of purchases are of this kind, it may well be that the actual position of your pub or petrol station and how attractive it is will be the prime influences in the purchasing decision. On the other hand, there isn't much point in going into a well-sited, attractive confectionery outlet and asking for 'a bar of chocolate' or 'a packet of cigarettes'. A brand name is clearly required.

Another implicit assumption in a great deal of marketing activity (and especially in some of the more complex academic models of the buying process) is that buying decisions are made in logical and consequential order: 'Right now, what I really fancy more than anything is a Kunzle cake, a very sweet, chocolate shell type of cake. It is only a short while since I last ate, so I am certainly not hungry. Not being hungry, I have not gone through my logical sequence of consideration of what kind of thing I would like to assuage my non-existent hunger. Most buying decision models would have me go through a sequence of deciding I would prefer a cake to a slice of bread and jam, a fancy cake to a plain, a chocolate cake to an iced tart, a Lyons Kunzle Cake to a Cadbury's Chocolate Kup Kake. I didn't; I simply fancy a Kunzle cake and if I can't have one I don't want anything else to eat.' That is the classic consumer purchase but there are others far removed from it.

An area of common ground between consumer and industrial purchasing is buying for stock. The importance of buying for this reason is heavily under-rated in consumer markets.

In fact, not a great deal is actually bought for immediate use. By far the greatest number of grocery items are actually bought to release a similar item from stock. This is a fully conscious decision and the reasoning goes something like this: 'I am going to make a meat pie for lunch today. There is one tin of stewing steak in the cupboard. Better get another one to replace the one I am going to use. Flour is a bit low – better get another bag.' Marketing efforts aimed at increasing consumption mean reducing stocks and thus motivating buying. In other words, over a wide range of goods and buying situations, the housewife acts in precisely the same way as a retailer. Awareness of the level of larder stock and the average length of replacement time is as important to a manufacturer of grocery items as it is to a supplier of repeat components to industry. Changes in those levels will equate with new levels of sale. One of the most significant features in times of

42

economic recession is a reduction in industrial, consumer and retail stock levels, not necessarily associated with a change in patterns of use. When the housewife reduces her larder stock cover to one tin of meat, the retailer reduces his stock cover from three weeks to two.

3.2 Purchasing behaviour

Laws are scarce in marketing; generalizations are more plentiful. Experience gives rise to many observations about consumer behaviour and many of them are at variance with the ways in which companies approach the sale of their products. Although the bulk of these observations come from consumer fields, they are applicable to almost any kind of repeat purchase item. The first of these generalizations is a good example. People do not always buy in the manner expected of them. Many products which would appear to be aimed at middle to upper-income families are actually bought by much lower-income groups. The reasons are often to be found in the fact that the lower down the socio-economic scale the measurement is taken, the more likely there are to be several wage-earners in the family. They are less likely to have regular calls on their income (like mortgages, insurances, children's education) and thus have a higher level of discretionary income (the economists' term for cash available for spending). Small families may be heavier consumers than larger ones; small companies often buy more of a given product than larger ones. As we shall see later, the use of standard classifications is a valuable tool in defining and deciding markets and deciding the position a company might adopt in the larger market-place. However, it should not be followed too slavishly. Pareto's Law applies again and a small proportion of total customers will probably account for a high proportion of turnover and profit. Some customers are worth a great deal more than others. Analysis in terms such as heavy, medium and light users is a meaningful addition to other kinds of classification, even where it does not replace them completely. It can be especially useful when deciding on which media to use to contact a target audience; many consumer product companies have been alarmed to discover that heavy viewing of television and high rates of buying of their products do not necessarily go together.

In consumer markets, the realization that the more usual standard classifications of age, sex and class may not distinguish buyers sufficiently has led to a search for other kinds of measurement. One of the more important is psychographics – or life-style research. As the name implies, this is an attempt to discover whether there are

43

psychological characteristics that link people together irrespective of their age, sex or class. Obviously, in almost all kinds of buying situation, there are some people who are more adventurous than others, those who tend to be leaders of fashion whether it be in clothes, hair-styles, cars or new machinery. Any manufacturer of the more expensive kinds of office equipment ought to be well aware that there are many companies who are the first to have new electric typewriters, the first with vending machines, the first with water fountains – and the desire to be a leader often transcends economic considerations.

Psychographic research is expensive and in the great majority of cases it has not come up with any more meaningful classifications than the ones it sought to replace. There is a famous piece of French research which took 18 months to come up with such earth-shattering conclusions as 'Women are significantly more likely than men to crochet'. There have been many cases of most effective use of the technique, but here we are simply concerned with pointing out that the simple ways of classifying customers – age, sex, location, size of unit, industry – are not always sufficient to explain how and why customers buy from one firm rather than another.

One of the favourite phrases of marketing people is 'brand loyalty'. To the uninitiated, it implies total adherence to one brand or company. It seldom happens. Most buyers are willing to accept a substitute at least some of the time. Under these conditions, brand loyalty is more likely to mean the brand they return to most often. Many buyers purchase from more than one company and often in a reasonably short period. What are often seen as non-buyers are, in reality, infrequent buyers. The most successful approach to improving market position will often come from upgrading infrequent users to more regular buyers and this is usually far more attainable than switching non-users.

The followers of brand loyalty often set their ambitions too low. Table 1 shows how this may come about. According to the normal terminology, housewife A is not brand-loyal; she switches about with gay abandon – but she buys Sugar Puffs five times in ten weeks. Housewife B is the opposite; she is absolutely brand-loyal even though she only buys two packets of Sugar Puffs. Housewife C is neither brand-loyal to Sugar Puffs nor a regular buyer – but she does buy more than the brand-loyal housewife. Housewife D is a non-buyer of Sugar Puffs; she is the only woman who is worth less to Sugar Puffs than the brand-loyal housewife! Clearly, it would be better to make housewife B buy with greater frequency even if she

Table 1 *Examples of buying frequency*

House-wives	Week 1	2	3	4	5	6	7	8	9	10
A	SP	R	SP	SW	SP	PW	SP	R	SP	PW
B	SP	–	–	–	–	–	SP	–	–	–
C	R	SP	–	PW	R	SP	PW	SW	–	SP
D	R	R	SW	R	SW	SW	PW	R	R	SW

SP = Sugar Puffs   SW = Shredded Wheat
R = Ricicles   PW = Puffed Wheat

also bought some other breakfast cereals at the same time.

A brand of instant coffee was searching for a form of consumer promotion that would build brand loyalty. My company was asked to put up a scheme. We were supplied with a great deal of research information. It showed clearly that both the frequency of buying and the quantity bought at each purchase were significantly lower than for its main competitor. If a brand loyalty exercise had succeeded at those levels of buying, the brand might well have levelled off at something close to the rate of sale at that time. Instead, by aiming for increased usage, sales were increased significantly. Lack of loyal customers is often seen as an affront; what makes the till ring is the number of users and the quantity they use.

So one major task of marketing activity is to stimulate use as well as buying. Sales can frequently be successfully stimulated by promoting new uses: Kelloggs' emphasis on recipes including cornflakes added usage to the standard quantity consumed at breakfast. Weetabix, again in the breakfast cereal market, extended sales of the product by promoting summer use as well as the more usual winter consumption. Carbonless papers moved beyond order forms into accountancy forms, computer print-outs and other systems uses. Existing users normally constitute the soft under-belly of any market. A person who already knows and appreciates the quality and performance of a product is more likely (other things being equal) to use more than a non-buyer is to change to it. Research conducted on behalf of tea-producing countries has shown that the best potential markets for their produce are existing markets and present buyers rather than taking the gamble of attacking new ones. A man who already drinks three cups of tea a day is an easier prospect for an extra cup than persuading a three cups of coffee man to change the habits of a lifetime and disrupt his family's routine by taking one cup of tea a day.

If we sum up the lessons that a study of buying behaviour teaches, we come up with a hierarchy like this:

Persuade existing users to buy more often.
Persuade them to use more.
Make occasional users into regular buyers.
Increase their frequency of purchase.
Convince them that they should use more.
Increase brand loyalty.
Seek new users from the total non-user market.

However, all this does rather pre-suppose that there is a single dominant buying influence over fairly frequently purchased items. In truly industrial markets, this is seldom the case.

3.3   Industrial buying

It is in the industrial sphere that perhaps the most revealing discoveries have been made over the last decade. Successive pieces of industry-wide research, backed up by product-specific investigations, have shown that there is a clear separation between deciding what to buy and placing the actual order. Over a considerable part of industrial selling, companies had been concentrating their efforts on order-placers without realizing that the people who determined what to order were quite different and much more difficult to gain access to.

The great bulk of industrial buying is dictated by a group decision-making process with final decisions about supplier most frequently being taken at chief executive or board level. The concept of a decision-making group divided from the process of placing an order is so important that it has become commonplace to refer to it as the DMU (decision-making unit).

Unlike many consumer buying decisions, a great deal of industrial purchasing involves a complex operation in which a number of people are likely to be concerned in a number of finite stages. A fairly typical pattern is for a chief executive to commission a thorough examination of a new process or a piece of replacement equipment, or a trial of new components. A project team or some kind of sub-committee under a technically qualified person (or with significant contributions from some such person) will be set up and it will consider literature and specifications, visit exhibitions, study advertisements and possibly even visit other firms using the product or process. It will make recommendations back to the chief executive or the board as a whole and a decision will be taken at that level. It is exceedingly rare for the chief executive to actually place an order: that will be delegated. However, it is also revealed as extremely rare for a purchasing manager to have discretionary limits allowing him to change supplier or specification without reference to some higher authority.

Obviously, the process does vary according to the product or service being considered, the size of the company and often the salary of the managers involved. (A manager earning £8,000 p.a. is far less likely to be given wide powers over purchasing than another earning £17,000 p.a.) Again, certain industries have conventional patterns of behaviour which produce other sequences of buying decision-making. Nevertheless, the complex form is revealed to be widely applicable to British industry. As one would expect, decisions involving major capital items are more likely to be taken at the highest levels. The chief executive, the board as a whole or individual directors will make the decision to buy in principle, possibly leaving the detailed consideration and evaluation to department managers. Final decisions will go back to where the first decision was taken. Needless to say, more delegation occurs in the larger companies than in the smaller: there are simply more people and more who can be trusted with important decisions involving considerable risk if errors are made.

The only significant area which has been revealed by industry-wide research as one where the purchasing manager still has powers of decision over actual suppliers is in the buying of materials. The more typical pattern is for the choice of material to be made at a very senior level but the choice of supplying company to be left to the buyer. Components are treated in a fairly similar way.

Obviously, any company should consider how relevant these findings might be to their area of business. Research does tend to deal in averages and it is always possible for 95 per cent of a business to act one way and for the companies making up the other 5 per cent to each behave differently. If your company supplies one of those in the 5 per cent, knowing how the other 95 per cent act will not be much help. However, the realization that so much of British industry has misled itself for so long by calling on managers with no power of decision may have important ramifications for any particular business. The number of cases where a firm has ceased to call on purchasing managers (or, at least, only with reduced frequency) without any consequential loss of sales is legion – and dramatic confirmation of the automatic nature of a good deal of industrial purchasing. Buyers, too, may use habit as an escape from routine decisions.

There is another important factor arising from the concept of the DMU. It is that the people who have to be influenced may be too widely dispersed throughout an organization to be reachable by salesmen. It may also include people who traditionally do not see representatives. This frequently produces a case for forms of advertising which otherwise would appear to be unjustified.

The overlap between consumer and industrial markets has already been commented on and illustrated in Figure 1. Obviously, a good deal of industrial buying takes place on levels similar to consumer buying and *vice versa*. At the right-hand end of the scale, the really heavy end of industrial marketing, much more considered decisions will be taken. Complex equations will be set for solution, advanced decision theory may well be involved and tendering comes into its own. Any of these methods might well be used anywhere else along the scale – for example, institutional canteens adopt tendering as a way of life, often to the apparent exclusion of considerations of quality.

3.4 Models of buyer behaviour

A great deal of very interesting work has been done in this field. Unfortunately, most of it confirms that buyer behaviour can be very complex and is influenced by many variables. So complex is the decision process and so many the variables, that the models, whilst adequate as descriptors, have very little practical predictive use other than to cause us to carefully consider our actions and the possible reactions to them. For that reason, this section is little more than a 'taster' for some of the theories that have some practical applications or consequences.

The difficulty of using models of buyer behaviour as predictors of purchasing intent is readily explained by the 'Black Box Model' (Figure 2). On the left are the various stimuli — internal ones induced

Figure 2   *The Black Box model*

by physiological needs (food, warmth, protection, etc.); external stimuli are ones taken from the environment (for example, the effect of family or friends, the media, advertising and sales promotion, etc.). To the right (or output side) of the Black Box are the response variables. These are the observable ways in which customers react to the various input stimuli (for example, negotiation, trial, purchase, repeat purchase, loyalty). A big difference between the input variables and the output ones is that the latter are relatively easily measured. Many of the stimulus variables are practically immeasurable or only capable of measurement with great difficulty.

The real problem is the contents of the Black Box. These are entirely individual and personal and extremely difficult to observe and measure. They deal with our perceptions and our beliefs, attitudes and motivations. Although each of these is capable of measurement, the actual *way* in which each individual puts them together in reaching a buying decision is not. The inclusion of a Black Box in any model effectively means 'Something is going on but we don't know what it is!'. Clearly, for some products the Black Box element is of vital importance, whilst for others (generally the more objective purchases) it has far less significance.

One of the best known and widely accepted models of buyer behaviour is the 'Howard-Sheth' model. The actual model is involved and beyond the scope of this book but a simplified version is shown in Figure 3. In this model 'Hypothetical constructs' equate with the Black Box and involve how a prospect sees and receives the stimulus inputs and how he or she constructs them into a learned behaviour pattern that will produce buying responses. However, this model proposes additional external stimuli to both the perception and learning elements. These include how important the purchase is to the

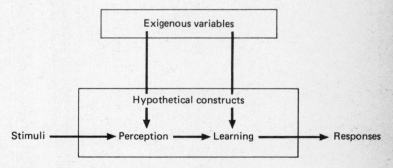

Figure 3   *Simplified Howard-Sheth model*

prospect, his or her financial position, the socio-economic class the buyer belongs to and the influences that class imposes. The full model is detailed, with considerable attention being given to each of the terms used in the simplified diagram of Figure 3. It is worth indicating, in this much-simplified description, the elements of the input and output variables. On the 'Stimuli' side, the originators use both social and commercial inputs. Social inputs arrive via the family, peer groups, reference groups and the dictates of one's socio-economic class. Commercial inputs include price, availability, service, etc. However, commercial inputs may be 'significative' (the actual attributes of the product in the way it is marketed and presented to the customer) or 'symbolic' (the attributes and concepts generated by the supplier and communicated to the prospect in order to influence buying behaviour – for example advertising messages, brand images, corporate identities, etc.).

A characteristic of any effectively descriptive model is the number of 'feedback' loops. For example, you gain an impression that a product you have never used before will be suitable for you. You buy it. Now you can effectively judge its performance and use your experience to make decisions about possible future purchases. Wider implications are shown in Figure 4 which follows a familiar 'hierarchy of effects' pattern. Having first gained the prospect's attention, the knowledge gained is fed into a 'bank' of information about the product category, and comparisons are then made (against target specifications, competitive claims and performances, knowledge of availability, etc.). In that comparative examination, an attitude towards the product is formed. The prospect can now

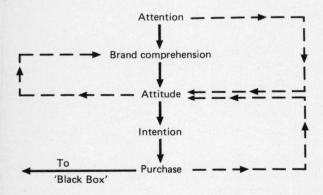

Figure 4 *Output stages of Howard-Sheth model*

50

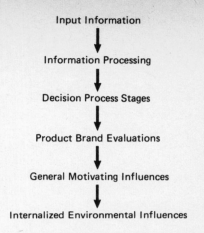

Input Information

↓

Information Processing

↓

Decision Process Stages

↓

Product Brand Evaluations

↓

General Motivating Influences

↓

Internalized Environmental Influences

Figure 5   *The Engel, Kollatt and Blackwell variables*

formulate an intent; negative as well as positive! Often, the response is to include the product on a mental list of those from which a final purchase might be made. The desired result, of course, is a purchase.

Then we see the feedback of the effect of that purchase on the attitudes previously held. They may be completely changed, partially altered or confirmed. However, those changes in attitude will have consequences on 'brand comprehension' by the effect of practical experience on what was previously a conceptual comparative ranking, and even on awareness as a product is recognized as 'my brand' or rejected because the buying experience was unfavourable.

A very similar model is that proposed by Engel, Kollat and Blackwell. Again, the model is complex but, reduced to its simplest form, is based upon five groups of variables (Figure 5). The 'Input Information' stage begins once a problem or need is recognized. A prospect generally starts with stored information and/or a set of perceptions, and reviews these before going any further. If this produces strong, positive inputs, the prospect tends to search for products or suppliers capable of confirming the buying hypothesis he or she has formed. If the information is insufficient, a search begins to fill in the gaps. From here on, the stages of Figure 5 resemble those of Figure 3.

At the 'Decision Process' stages, alternatives are critically assessed and a choice is made. 'Product Brand Evaluations' involve 'testing' the criteria used in the previous stage against the prospect's attitudes and beliefs and the intentions he or she has for the product in use. The major 'General Motivating Factors' are the prospect's individual motives, his or her personality and life-style, and the degree of 'normative compliance' involved.

Normative behaviour is an important buying influence that comes out of several theoretical concepts. A simple definition is 'Not the way I think I should behave but the way *other people* think I should behave'. Its effects can be seen in fashion, 'keeping up with the Jones' and 'buying British'.

Cultural norms feature in the 'Internalized Environmental Influences', as does the prospect's reference group (the group, often the family or friends, against which comparisons are made). The model also adds to this fifth stage anticipated and unanticipated circumstances (these last two are among the 'Exigenous Variables' of the Howard-Sheth model).

A criticism of the two models briefly considered is that they leave out any consideration of the place and role of the supplier. The 'Nicosia' model (Figure 6) actually begins with the firm. Analysis follows the steps outlined for the previous two models. The fundamental differences are, firstly, that buying is seen as an adaptive process in that the actions of one party may influence those of the other; secondly, that purchasing does not result directly from attitudes formed, but that other influences may also be important.

An important element in the feedback process is the concept of 'cognitive dissonance'. It is rare that anyone can make the perfect buying decision; most choices involve an element of compromise. This involves dissonance (or disturbance) because we have had to compromise our standards in some way. We seek to justify our compromise to ourselves, so that we may feel more comfortable with the decision we have taken. The lady who has just bought a dress in a sale can hardly resist looking in all the other sale windows to see if she could have bought it cheaper. Naturally, she hopes she cannot find a cheaper version; if she does, she may well try to justify the purchase: 'Perhaps it is not my size'; 'It looks dirty'; 'I prefer the sales assistants where I bought it'. As an old, once-popular song used to say: 'Accentuate the positive; eliminate the negative'. The theory of cognitive dissonance says that we may reduce our inner conflicts by doing just that for the selected purchase, but concentrate on the negative aspects of the rejected purchase.

Cognitive dissonance is something we should all be able to recognize in ourselves. The purchase of a car is a prime example, even to the extent that readership of car advertisements tends to be higher *after* purchasing a new car than before it! It should come as no

52

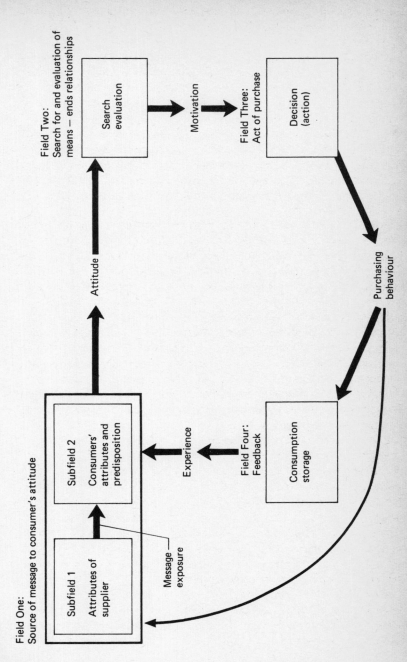

Figure 6 *Nicosia model of consumer behaviour*

surprise to learn that dissonance is likely to be highest when the risk is greatest and the opportunity to buy again, relatively distant. Thus, the purchase of capital equipment, houses, and major items of consumer durables are subjected to extensive pre-purchase examination in order to reduce the likely dissonance to an acceptable minimum.

Before we look at one final, very simplified, model of the buying process, it is worth moving outside the field of models to touch briefly on a major piece of work into attitudes and beliefs.

'Fishbein's theory' employs two equations. In keeping with the level and tone of this book, neither will actually be mentioned. Instead, we will consider the ingredients and the objectives of the equation. The two key elements (one for each equation) are:

A_o or the attitude towards an object;
A_{act} or the attitude towards performing a specific activity.

Each, says Fishbein, is a function of the strength with which beliefs about an object (or brand) or an activity are held; how those beliefs are evaluated; and how many beliefs there are about the object or activity. Imagine a set of beliefs about a camera. We will ask respondents to assign scores to the importance of those attributes. Each is then asked to give an evaluation score about that belief (using a technique known as 'semantic scaling' which broadly equates to a range of opinions from 'very good' to 'very bad'). Normally, five or seven points are used, with the central one representing a 'neither good nor bad', neutral opinion. The scores for 'importance' and 'evaluation' are then multiplied together to give a final attribute score. Table 2 gives an example.

Table 2   *Attribute scores for a camera*

Attribute	Importance	Evaluation	$I \times E$
35mm	1	1	1
Coupled exposure metre	1	1	1
Automatic mode	4	3	12
Interchangeable lens	2	2	4
			18

In this analysis, low scores are the more favourable. A total score of 18 is very favourable (compared with what the maximum could be) but it is very clear that a 35mm camera with a coupled exposure meter is the prime requirement. The interchangeable lens would be quite nice but perhaps does not justify the cost for the limited use the buyer might get from it.

However, the attitude towards a 35mm, coupled-exposure-meter camera will be conditioned by your attitude towards photography. To someone with little or no knowledge or experience, an automatic mode camera might assume far higher importance.

Thus, Fishbein's theory has several important consequences for marketing:

1 To change the attitude towards a product, it may first be necessary to change the attitude towards the activity it represents. The detergent that advertised 'Washday white without washday red' simply drew attention to the fact that hand-washing clothes *could* cause red hands, even though the product claim was emphatically that it wouldn't!

2 To change purchasing behaviour, change the beliefs about the product (although this is seldom easy to do or quickly achieved).

3 Change the way in which the beliefs are evaluated. The desirability of a new airport differs dramatically between householders and local shopkeepers. Harmony of interest could possibly be achieved by stressing the benefits to the community of the increased trade the new airport will bring. Similarly, the use of fully automatic cameras by leading press photographers has quite dramatically changed the way multi-mode cameras are evaluated by keen hobby photographers.

3.5 A simplified model of buyer behaviour

Here is a simplified model that I have used for some years now, which relies upon many of the concepts included in the models we have examined and which has the advantage (together with the consequent disadvantage) of simplicity. It is also rather more appropriate to the industrial purchasing decision than some of the models and theories we have seen.

Figure 7 acknowledges that, for many purchases, a considered weighing-up of rational positives against carefully considered negatives is the main element in the purchasing decision. Thus the industrial buyer may have to arrive at a formula for dealing with the same performance at different prices, with different delivery dates, and with different levels of service. He may also have to take into

55

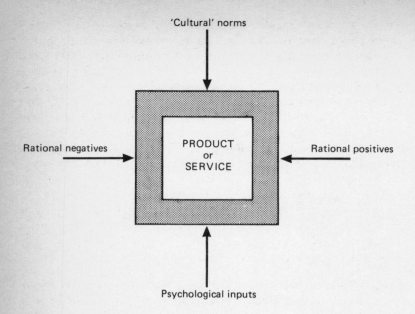

Figure 7 *Simplified buying model*

account the supplier's reputation and experience, the terms on which the purchase is to be financed, plus a number of less objective but highly important factors. He may, therefore, move marginally into the psychological and normative areas.

The marketer of fast-moving consumer goods will be primarily involved with the psychological inputs and effects of cultural norms. But that does not mean that rational negatives will not be considered or that no account will be taken of strong positive factors. The big difference is that the high frequency of purchase of items in this category will mean that detailed consideration will not occur every time, and the purchasing decision will be relegated to the habit area as rapidly as possible and until some new information (or new product) comes along to challenge it.

Nevertheless, even this attempt at a simple and practical model has to include a version of the Black Box to contain the imponderable elements.

3.6 Changes in buying behaviour

There is a dual purpose to this chapter. On the one hand, it prepares the ground for the next chapter and reduces one of its sections to more manageable lengths. On the other, it draws attention to buying processes and attitudes that may seem somewhat surprising to the less experienced in marketing analysis. It is not comprehensive in that it does rather assume that all kinds of buying behaviour can be reduced to two simple umbrella categories. The balance will be redressed later where it has not already been set on record. For example, Figure 1 does draw attention to certain similarities and some unexpected differences in particular product fields. More specific examples will be used to illustrate other headings. However, it is important that it is recognized that people behave quite differently under different changes in stimulus.

There are people who make conscious decisions nearly all the time. They are probably very difficult to live with and they would certainly be wise to stay out of supermarkets. There are probably just about as many who never take a really serious decision about anything. Neither is the normal case. The fact of the matter is that most people make some very serious decisions some of the time about some products and services. Some of them are obvious: house, furniture, cars, certain kinds of clothing. Others are far less obvious. Often, a great deal of the most serious consideration will be given to the change from a 'habit' brand to another, which it is hoped will become a new habit. Housewives often go through a good deal of mental anguish on these occasions wondering if the change will be appreciated by their family. It is a well-known phenomenon in food marketing for a housewife to change a brand unannounced. If no comment occurs, she will go on buying. When she is really sure everything is as it should be, she will announce the change. Then it is relegated back to a habit. On the other hand, if the change is noticed, her reaction is often to deny that any change has been made and quickly return to the usual product.

No-one is obliged to be either consistent or logical when buying things. We do not divide our lives simply into work time and leisure time, and mention has already been made of how they may be expected to overlap and the habits of one period be carried into the other. The industrialist taking an apparently rational and logical decision when considering whether to buy your product is going to call in on the tobacconists on his way home and take a couple of habit decisions and possibly a few others at a very low level of consciousness. Even people who make conscious decisions most of the time often behave in a totally different way in another aspect of their life. Because I have studied the subject of buying behaviour more than most, I like to think that I take rather more conscious decisions than most people. I am also a very keen cyclist and when I am indulging my hobby, I am inclined to be recklessly extravagant. For a start, I never own less than three bicycles, even though I can only ride one at a time. Nearly everyone has these 'blind spot compartments'. The managing director who subjects every other buying decision to computer analysis may behave completely self-indulgently when it comes to decorating his office. It is perhaps highly significant that each major piece of research into how British industry buys has shown that most boards spend a considerable amount of time on the decision about which private cars the company will buy, yet delegate decisions about commercial vehicles!

Our last point provides both a summary of a sort and an introduction to the next chapter. It is usually tacitly assumed that consumers (of all types) seek to optimize their buying primarily in cash terms. This is patently not so. If it were, why would a considerable proportion of housewives have switched from the cheaper packet tea to the more expensive (and usually less satisfactory in strength terms) tea bags? Obviously, they value convenience more than they care about buying at the cheapest rate consistent with an acceptable level of quality. Convenience may rate so high, as it does in this case, as to change the old considerations of quality.

In other words, customers seek to optimize their satisfactions. To be successful in business, we have to discover what those satisfactions are and who, in the buying unit (firm or family), expresses them. What a good deal of available research evidence tells us is that one of the satisfactions that many, many people seek is that of an easier life. Easier not only in terms of convenience products but also in terms of adopting little mental 'dodges' that enable a great deal of complexity to be removed from everyday living.

3.7 Summary

Expressed in the terms of the marketing progression, buying decisions tend to be more conscious the further one is to the right, that is the 'heavy' end of business. To the left, decisions are often reduced to vote and taken individually. To the right, more rational thought is employed and the concept of the DMU comes into its own. In the middle, the two major types of buying behaviour become confused and the role the product or service plays in the life of the individual will largely determine how much conscious thought is given to it. For most people, life is a mixture of habit decisions and highly organized thought about purchases.

Generalizations about the way people buy, especially repeat items, indicate that the highest premium should be placed on the number of users and the amount they use. Looked at from this point of view, completely loyal customers may be less valuable than is frequently thought.

3.8 Checklist

1 Consumer purchases
   a Buyers reduce as much as possible to the level of habit.
   b The use of 'brain maps' is another way of simplifying buying decisions.
   c 'Families' of decisions are built into 'clusters' as an additional means of simplification.
   d Deferred decisions are sometimes used.
   e Alternatively, decisions may be delegated to others, partially or wholly.
   f Buying for stock is important even for domestic purchases.

2 Purchasing behaviour
   a People do not always buy in the way expected of them.
   b Some customers are much more valuable than others (Pareto's Law).
   c Psychographic research searches for patterns of living ('life style') that may influence purchasing decisions.
   d It is important to seek 'brand loyalty' only at acceptable levels of sale.

3 Lessons of buying behaviour
   a Get existing buyers to buy more often.
   b Persuade them to buy more.
   c Turn occasional users into more regular ones.
   d Then increase the frequency of their purchases.
   e Convince them to use more at a time.
   f Now aim for brand loyalty.
   g Seek new users from the non-user potential.

4 Industrial buying
   a Concept of the DMU (decision-making unit).
   b A number of influences are usually involved (although there is usually only one ultimate specifier).
   c It is seldom possible for any sales force to reach all members of the DMU.

d Very often, it is impossible to establish face-to-face contact with specifiers.

e A wide range of buying methods is used.

5 Black Box models
A convention used to position highly individual factors and influences between the input and output stimuli.

6 Howard-Sheth model
   a Introduces 'exigenous variables' into the Black Box element.
   b The output stages use a 'hierarchy of effects' approach.
   c Purchasing produces feedback information that may refine, reinforce or change previously held attitudes.

7 Engel, Kollat and Blackwell model
   a More comprehensive in a descriptive sense.
   b Similar in effect to Howard-Sheth in the output stages.
   c Includes 'internalized environmental factors' to show how external influences are incorporated and adapted to individual motivating factors.

8 Nicosia model
   a A model which incorporates the firm.
   b An adaptive model in that changes by one party may lead to changes by the other.
   c That adaptation will be triggered off by the effects of feedback resulting from purchase experience.

9 Fishbein theory
   a Basic theory deals with attitudes towards the 'object' or product.
   b The extended theory considers attitudes towards the activity the object (product) is required for.
   c The strength of attitudes will be determined by the beliefs held and the way they are evaluated.
   d To change attitudes:
      i Consider the attitude towards the activity.
      ii Change beliefs.
      iii Give reasons to change the evaluation of those beliefs.

10 Simplified model
   a Explains the importance of rational considerations.
   b Rational factors are of paramount importance with high-risk, low-frequency items.
   c Psychological inputs and cultural normative behaviour is

associated with low-risk, high-frequency items, especially where the decision has been relegated to the habit level.

d   Elements of each parameter are present in most first purchases, but their relative weight and importance vary enormously.

11   Customers always seek to optimize their satisfactions.

12   Marketers need to discover those satisfactions and who expresses them (or specifies them) in order to make the most effective sales approaches.

4

Where Are We Now?

I keep six honest serving men
(They taught me all I know);
Their names are WHAT and WHY and WHEN
And HOW and WHERE and WHO.

Rudyard Kipling

Like Kipling, you can learn a lot from the use of these six questions.
Most management consultants and all the good advertising agencies
use some form of questionnaire with any new business that seeks their
services. Frequently, they run into many hundreds of set questions
that require a great deal of internal analysis, as well as formal market
investigations, before the answer to each can be ticked as completed.
Most businesses, if they are honest with themselves, complete such an
exercise with not only a feeling of relief but also with the feeling that
they have done something they should have done years ago. Many
frankly admit that they obtained enormous value from looking at
their own business with fresh eyes and found themselves challenging
many of the ways they had been acting in the past. How much better
to do something of the sort yourself and on a regular basis.

It isn't necessary to answer 500 questions. The replies to only six,
the same ones that Kipling used, will provide most of the benefit any
business will be seeking. As a matter of fact, dealing with only the six
basic questions is often far better. That way, you will be forced to
concentrate your attention on the fundamentals of the business; it is
possible to ask many hundreds of finely detailed questions without
actually answering the really crucial ones. It is all too easy to confuse
a data book, a single volume which provides as much information as
possible about the company, with business analysis. The data book is
an excellent idea: it provides newcomers, inside the company and out,
with all they need to know to be able to take up a new role in the

minimum time. But it isn't designed to question the very basis of the business.

The self-analysis questionnaire which will be developed in this chapter is intended to be a searching examination of where the business currently stands, what it is all about and how it got there. It means questioning many old company customs (a far more dangerous and virulent beast than the famed Spanish Customs). If such things are really to be probed, the questions must be treated in a creative way, looking behind the raw statement for hidden meanings. No book can answer the questions for your business. What it can do is to look at each question in turn, pose some of the subsidiary questions that have opened doors in other businesses, and give examples from a number of fields to illustrate the points, and suggest the kinds of things others may be wise to look out for. That is what each of the following sections will be aimed at achieving.

4.1 What?

The traditional, and proper, starting place is always 'What?'. Carrying the tradition on, it is rephrased to ask:

'What are we selling?'

Remember what was said in the very first chapter about the sole end-purpose of all production? Obviously, the marketing mind needs to turn the question round and ask:

'What is the customer buying?'

That in turn prompts an ancillary one:

'Are they the same?'

And again:

'If not, what business are we really in?'

From that will stem a number of very pertinent and vital questions for the business to ask itself – if they aren't the same, with whom are you really competing? Are you properly geared to be in this new business? Is the new business being maximized or are new opportunities presented? – and many others like these.

If this is the first time any businessman has come up against this kind of talk, he will be appalled to think that other businessmen don't know what market they are in. If, on examination, he finds himself in the same boat, he will be in very good company indeed. Experienced marketing men like myself used to be surprised at the differences we all found between the markets we thought ourselves appealing to and those that market research revealed. Nowadays, those same people would probably be even more surprised to find that any business's first shot at defining a market position for itself was right. Customers of all kinds have a perverse habit of deciding upon quite different uses for a product from those its creators ever thought of.

A couple of examples were mentioned in passing in Chapter 1. The hand-cream company thought it might have much greater potential in the future by promoting into two 'new' markets for which it thought its product well-suited but which it had neglected in the past. In fact, they discovered that those two markets were already accounting for the bigger shares of total sales. Johnsons, on the other hand, had discovered that their sales of baby powder and baby lotion were far greater than could be accounted for by mothers using the correct dosage on babies of the right age. The discrepancy was such that it suggested either the mothers were using several times the reasonable amount at each occasion, supplemented by bathing the child in the lotion and possibly even feeding him or her with it in their bottles; or that babies up to the age of 14 were still having it applied to the appropriate part of their anatomy. There was, of course, a third alternative – someone else was using it. In short, the products had become general cosmetic items. A number of complementary factors had caused this positioning. Women had reasoned that a product good enough for a baby's delicate skin would be good enough for theirs. It was cheaper than most of the products on the market and, very importantly, it was in far wider distribution than most other branded cosmetics.

The next step in the Johnsons saga is very important, for it is a classic example of how to move from the sort of finding they had happened upon. If you ever discover that you are in a completely different market from the one you had aimed at, it is vital that you do two things very quickly:

Redefine your market carefully.
Analyse the strengths that put you there.

In other words, be sure you don't make the same mistake again and be sure you understand why the customer put you into your new position. Johnsons put themselves into the skin-care section of the female cosmetic market. (Much later, they acknowledged another change and spoke directly to the many thousands of males who were discovered to be using the household tin or bottle of Johnsons.) And they decided that their strength was in the word 'baby'. Alternative copy appeals like 'Cheaper than most' or 'Available at Boots, Woolworths and all good chemists' were clearly less effective and far less strong in basic appeal than the description 'Baby Lotion' and the distinctive labels with the baby on. Appeals were variants of a theme based on 'Baby yourself: be a Johnson's Baby'. Instead of being in a market of roughly 1.5 million children, Johnsons found themselves in a market made up of those same children, their mothers and big sisters and any women over the age of about 15 – a much larger market.

Lyons launched Ready Brek as the 'instant hot porridge'. Initial sales produced one of the steepest sales curves ever seen for a new grocery product. Almost before the sales force could achieve a reasonably euphoric state about their early success, sales dropped back alarmingly – clear evidence of that dreaded phrase 'no repeat sales'. Panic measures were introduced, including a good deal of the research that ought to have been done before the product was launched. The investigations showed two things very clearly. First, confirmed porridge eaters did not like the taste and texture of Ready Brek. Secondly, it clearly had a very effective television commercial based on a superb product claim that had produced a high level of initial trial by porridge eaters. (The television commercial had used the claim: 'Now! Porridge you can make in the plate. No more messy saucepans'. A very appealing claim for any housewife who has experienced a saucepan of porridge bubbling and festering on the stove for an hour every morning, producing a skin that almost required a blow-lamp to remove it from the bottom and sides of the pan.)

Hardly had Lyons learned why Ready Brek wouldn't sell than it became clear that it was picking up and looking quite promising. A consumer diary panel was consulted. (At this stage it is enough to know that this is a technique which enables the user to see not only what type of housewife buys his product but what else she buys and with what frequency.) This research confirmed what earlier investigations had led Lyons to expect: porridge eaters did not eat Ready Brek after the first trial. Those who did were those who belonged to what is described as the variety cereal market. A large number of products in this category may be bought by the same household (Table 1 was an example from this field) and all sorts of reasons may be behind the changes. Paramount among them are the simple factor of taste boredom (not everyone likes eggs and bacon or Kelloggs Corn Flakes every single day of their lives) and the offers in or on the pack

65

appealing to children – this is very much a market conditioned by the presence of children in the household.

That was where the plot became complicated. There were now two clearly distinct variety cereal markets: one included Ready Brek, the other didn't. Why? Children seemed an obvious answer, but both markets were shown to have similar proportions of children in them. Eventually, the research company was asked to ascertain the actual ages of the children in the different households, for the basis of the definition of a child had been up to the age of 14. That was where the difference was – Ready Brek was being served to children by their mothers, not asked for by the children. In most cases, the children were too young to express any real opinion other than outright and spectacular rejection. Mothers had decided that if Ready Brek could be made in the plate by simply adding hot milk (or water), clearly its consistency could be controlled. Besides, everyone knows that oatmeal is good for you. Ready Brek was both a post-weaning food and a way of giving a child the nourishment it might not seek from its own choice.

At this point, Ready Brek had two competing directions it could take. It could become an out-and-out baby food or it could aim for a wider child market. In fact, it chose the latter path. The product description was changed first, to the instant hot oatmeal breakfast. Like Johnsons before, Ready Brek was basing its product claim on the qualities the consumer had identified, even though Lyons themselves had promoted others. The second move was to change the pack, from a very adult red to a beautiful golden colour with pictures of children on the front. The whole aim was to produce a pack that mothers would readily identify with and want to pick from the supermarket shelves. To complete the change, the advertising was changed to a direct appeal to mothers to give their children the best possible winter start to the day under the banner of 'Central heating for kids'.

Ready Brek has been one of the most successful new product introductions in the cereal market in the last 25 years, yet it was so nearly a failure. Indeed, the porridge market into which it was launched was in decline at the time and went on falling for several years. Lyons were fortunate in that their customers chose to promote Ready Brek to a place in a growing market.

The same sort of thing can happen in any kind of business and does with at least the same sort of frequency. In mid-1975, I did some pioneering work into the market for hairdressing services in the UK. When I tried to answer the question, 'What real satisfaction do women obtain from a visit to the hairdresser?', I discovered that these could be grouped in sets, thus:

Cut, shampoo, blow-dry, set.
Beauty, confidence, excitement.
Relaxation, rejuvenation, relief.
Health, treatment, cure.
Ambience, attention, care.
Personal attention, friendly staff, familiarity.

Notice that only the first set contains any reference to the basic craft of hairdressing. Most of the others have to do with atmosphere and satisfaction in the truest sense of the word. That underlines the key to this sub-section: we have to discover the satisfaction customers take from our service. In the case of hairdressers, the list outlined above caused women to look on their hairdresser in three different lights: as an artist, as a craftsman and as a hair care expert (a sort of hair doctor). In ranking, the artistic craftsman, the traditional way the trade has always looked upon itself, is the least important. Nine times out of ten a woman doesn't want artistry, she wants a quick, efficient service. Emphatically, she does want healthy hair all the time. Here was a clear opportunity area for hairdressing that all but the most go-ahead had failed to discover under their very noses – and of course hairdressing is a trade where the customers literally are under your nose.

Think of what financial services such as banking and insurance companies offer. The very same package can offer different things to different people. What is a cautious investment to one family can be a piece of speculation to another. Where one man is buying security for his family if any disaster overtakes him, another is buying a guaranteed sum of money at the age of 65. The same policy will give them both the same things; if the family security-conscious man survives to 65, he will benefit from the lump sum; if the safety-first investor dies before he can cash in, his family will benefit from an assured sum. These two men will buy for different reasons and need to be sold to in different ways. Certain approaches, different publications, other salesmen will succeed in one case and fail in the other. The whole image of one company can be for one thing, whilst its competitor provides an exactly similar package yet has a totally different reputation. As we saw earlier, all the main joint stock banks provide basically similar services at similar hours. Yet people choose between competing banks on the same high street. How? Why? – two of the questions to be considered later but vital to answer if the business of any one bank is to prosper at the expense of any other.

It is frequently assumed that the more rational buying motives of industrial marketing offer a reasonable guarantee of an effective and early reconcilation between buyer and seller. It is certainly true that the more logical nature of a good deal of industrial buying does reduce the number of examples as dramatic as Johnsons and Lyons. But the parallel with hairdressing is very close in industrial services and in a good deal of component supplies. Remember the ICI paint example quoted earlier; they thought they were supplying qualities of fireproofing and effective life; their customers were buying the length of the range, the speed of delivery and the ready availability of that wide range of colours. They were buying two qualities that ICI had hitherto ranked as extras. The additional qualities were, in fact, the prime ones; the others were unnecessary to the great majority of their customers.

Some of the most dramatic examples of mis-identification of the basic business actually come from industrial markets, a fact not entirely disassociated from the general lack of early market research and the late adoption of the marketing concept. The problem stems from the very nature of industrial marketing. Where demand depends upon customers who are several stages removed from the first transaction, the possibilities of error are multiplied. The natural tendency is to go along merrily meeting the direct demand without making it your business to attempt to assess the true nature of the derived demand. If your customer has misinterpreted his market, yours will suffer too. A company supplying machinery for making carpet in rolls of standard widths collapsed with dramatic suddenness. It had defined itself as being in the fitted carpet business: more properly, it was in the floor-covering field. Even if it had not opted to stay out of linoleum it would still not have been prepared for the fate that did overtake it – the advent of carpet tiles which could not be manufactured on their machinery.

There are two things an industrial company must be careful about in the overall context of the question 'What are we selling?'. Firstly, it has to continually look beyond the immediate market and consider the real nature of the ultimate demand that its goods and services contribute to. Secondly, just like any other business, it must continually assess the real skills that provide the satisfaction the direct customer is buying. Suppose the key is prompt delivery and supply of rush orders within 24 hours. Perhaps there are other unnecessary 'benefits' the customer is not really buying; perhaps these could be dropped with a consequent improvement in profits. Once you realize that it is efficient delivery services that have put your company where it is, perhaps this will lead you to consider what other types of business you could supply that you don't do business with now. When you are in the efficient delivery section of a business it is time to look for those companies who ought to be putting a premium on those very qualities.

A good example of an industrial company who found considerably greater market potential from examining these two points is Black and Decker. The first electric drills were very much industrial products used in other industrial companies. It quickly became obvious that the qualities offered by these drills could provide benefits to a large number of occupations. Just how wide the appeal could be did not really strike anyone until they really got down to answering the question of what business they were in. Their strengths lay in the speed and efficiency with which Black and Decker drills bored holes. The deferred demand was essentially for different kinds of assembly and construction job. They weren't selling drills; they were selling to people who wanted $\frac{1}{8}$ inch holes. That size hole takes just about the most commonly used screw and is therefore required for an enormous range of jobs about the home. The rapid growth of home ownership led to an ancillary market for attachments (sanders, circular saws, polishing buffs and so on), and a demand from industry for heavy duty drills with larger and longer bits, and thence to a range of heavy duty attachments.

Not every company is going to be able to come up with something as exciting and novel as being able to go around saying 'We are in the $\frac{1}{8}$ inch hole business' but then no one should be looking for something exciting to talk about; the desire is to find something that will produce a more profitable and secure direction for the business. There is often a danger that businesses will end up with one of a number of almost cliché-type definitions. Words like 'transportation', 'entertainments' and 'communications' have been grossly over-employed. Eventually they become meaningless and competitive advantage is then scored by the company who best defines a position within the more global view. A former employee of mine went so far as to define jellies as being in the entertainment business on the grounds that a jelly has no real nutritional value but just sits there and wobbles. On a more practical note, the (then) Thomson Organization (now International Thomson) broke out of the broad business definition of 'communications', an otherwise reasonable word for what was then a newspaper, magazine and book group, and looked for the area within publishing that they were best at and which afforded them most profit. The answer was 'advertising'. That redefinition led to the successful launch of a number of new magazines and newspapers and the launch in the UK of *Yellow Pages* with the Post Office.

Just to round off this important section and give a few more examples of the sorts of definition that may be helpful in your business, here are a few examples of some of the ways very different businesses have defined their area of enterprise and skill.

1 *Sealants* A company manufacturing sealants and 'O' rings redefined its business as 'selling containment'. It then examined those areas where leaks could happen and where they would be disastrous if they did. As a result, they now concentrate on the containment of hazardous chemicals and the aeronautical business: two areas where premium prices and healthy profit margins are available to companies who meet the needs of those industries.

2 *Computers* The generally accepted and broad business definition has been 'information storage and problem-solving'. However, this has been challenged by two major developments: the widespread use of micros and personal computers and the development of 'user friendly' software packages which permits sophisticated use without programming knowledge. Data processing departments are rapidly assuming the characteristics of threatened species! As a result, computer manufacturers are segmenting the 'information storage and problem-solving' market into software applications. In short: define the business need; develop software to meet it; produce a computer with the capacity to run the programs.

3 *Cosmetics* Rather like the previous example, conventional definitions have changed. 'The beauty business' may be suitable as a broad definition but a more sensitive one is necessary to cope with the segments. As the market has developed into ever younger sectors and broadened into male cosmetics, the definition has widened to the 'health and beauty business'. Now it can include skin care, allergy treatments, fashion, hair care, etc. Some are exclusive to each other; others are highly competitive. Selling cosmetics has been described as 'selling hope', but different people have different hopes and each provides a clear business area.

There is enough in these three examples to indicate that most areas of business suffer both direct and indirect competition, often from

70

apparently unrelated sectors. The UK package holiday business rates its biggest competition not as holidays in the UK but as painting the house (which takes up the holiday period), or buying a new car (which takes all the family's discretionary income). Obviously, in one real sense, everything is competitive if it absorbs the time or the money of a potential customer. The trick is to identify the really relevant competition. That is often the clearest indicator of the market you are really in.

It will become increasingly obvious that some of our six questions can be answered from existing sources and personnel in the company; others require independent analysis. Experience shows that what managers believe to be the reason for their success, and thence the definition of the business the company operates in, is more likely to be wrong than right. Getting at the real satisfaction a customer obtains from a company or its products is something usually only discovered with any accuracy by independent research. Nevertheless, using the examples to take a really good, long, hard and creative look at what the business might be selling can often give a surprising stimulus to an enterprise.

4.2   To whom?

Kipling paid more attention to scansion than to business logic: a fairly logical corollary to *What* is *To whom?* We shall see that all the questions interrelate and that the answers to any later question may well cause some change in the way an earlier one has been treated. What a customer is buying may often depend on who it is doing the buying; a managing director may put a much higher premium on financial stability and company reputation, whilst the purchasing manager may rate prompt delivery and efficient invoicing more highly. However, just as the first question taught us to avoid the superficial, so the replies to this second one again require considerable care. What we want now is not the person who places the order or hands the money over the counter but the person who influences the purchasing decision.

In consumer markets, the answers to this second question are usually rather easier to discover than with other types of business. There are still the odd surprises, though. Most people would readily recognize that many breakfast cereals are bought according to the dictates of the children of the household, and that housewives frequently buy according to the known tastes of their husbands. A relatively high proportion of razor blades is bought by women, but we know that the brand is determined by the husband for whom she is buying. Marketing effort, therefore, continues to be directed at men. Men's underclothing, on the other hand, is almost entirely a female purchase, with a high proportion bought without any prior reference to the man of the house. Brand-name promotion to men is of little value in cases like this; availability at shops where women normally buy is far more important. The whole point of this question is to ensure that the right kind of marketing effort is being directed into the right channels and to the most appropriate target audience.

In consumer markets, it is often possible to talk simultaneously to both decision-maker and purchaser; a particular attribute of mass media is its wide coverage which inevitably means picking up rather more people than simply the prime targets. In industrial markets, as we saw in the last chapter, the purchasing decision often involves several people at different levels. Since, in total, they usually amount to considerably less than a consumer market, individual approaches may be required. We have already noted the importance of the formal DMU in non-consumer markets. In fact, the position can be even more complicated than we have discussed so far.

Industrial markets have a number of potential influences over any buying decision. There is a good deal of far more sophisticated print machinery available than is actually used in British print rooms. The DMUs have reached their decisions, boards have approved expenditures and trade unions have refused to accept the plant – clear evidence of a very potent buying influence in the print industry. We can simplify the very considerable problems that industrial companies can face by the use of a diagram. In Figure 8 some of the more frequently encountered buying influences in industrial markets have been set out under four headings: formal and informal, internal and external. Then they have been cross-tabulated. The first block, the internal formal influences, corresponds to the DMU which has already been identified. However, that DMU will have to take into account a number of very significant external formal influences in reaching any decision. One of those is the policy of trade unions. It is arguable whether this is more correctly an internal influence; strictly speaking, a branch or chapel decision might be internal whereas official union policy might be regarded as external. In the case already quoted of print unions, the companies concerned are dealing with official union policy – the decision on whether to allow the installation of a bank of vending machines instead of half a dozen ladies with tea trolleys might well be a local branch decision. Laws, regulations, codes of practice and the growing ranks of Government

72

	Formal	Informal
Internal	Specifying technologists and managers Purchasing Manager Project Committee Chief Executive Board	Operatives Salesmen
External	Laws Regulations Codes of Practice Industry Standards Government Inspectors Trade Unions	Customers Final end-users Public opinion Local Government Contacts in other companies

Figure 8 *Typical industrial buying influences*

inspectors also come into this very significant category.

The informal influences can be every bit as potent. Operatives can express their opinions in other ways than through official trade union action. Typists are more often than not consulted about the choice of a new machine (indeed, one wonders whether certain typewriter manufacturers might not have defined their business as selling personal status or providing welfare or moral benefits). Salesmen get about a great deal and pass on solid information about products and companies as well as gossip. They are often asked to glean what they can from customers about the performance of a machine, piece of equipment, components and so on. And on the outside are customers. If the company to whom you supply is, in turn, in a derived demand situation, they must take notice of what their customers may think about their product incorporating yours as an ingredient. (The extent and importance of this will depend largely on the sort of parameters examined in Section 2.2) To your company, that will be an external influence of considerable magnitude if it applies. Any industrial goods supplier will have the final end user as an ultimate external influence, very much in the sense discussed in the preceding section.

Public opinion can be another potent influence, either expressed directly, through the media or through the agency of local government. A company buying a new fuel for its factory will have to consider what effect it might have, if any, on the pollution of the air in the neighbourhood, whether deliveries will inconvenience local residents, and so on. Finally, industrial marketing companies should never neglect the value of contacts in other companies. At the investigatory stage, visits to other firms using the items under consideration will be high on the list. Good salesmen know this and use existing customers to help sell for them, by arranging demonstrations. It does, of course, asssume that those customers are satisfied users.

Service industries tend more often than not to be involved in some sort of group decision-making process; services to industry meet up with the formal DMU, whilst consumer or family services have to convince a family group. A characteristic phenomenon in service industries is the way the identical service can mean very different things to only marginally different people. In the case of a hotel, the same person may require different things depending on whether he or she is making a business or private booking. A package tour to Greece may appeal to the student of ancient history as well as to the sun-seeker. Financial services, especially those comprising personal investment factors, may have to deal simultaneously with sophisticated and unsophisticated investors, reckless and cautious ones, convenience-first against rainy-day, nest-egg investors. If those are then tabulated by demographic characteristics (age, sex, class, location, etc.) one might well find that each group looks surprisingly alike. This might be a case where life-style is far more important and psychological factors may override sociological ones in some cases. Many decision-making groups may contain more than one of these types. Insurance salesmen know this phenomenon well. The wife may be looking for security should anything happen to her husband; he believes he is immortal and places a much higher value on future benefits in terms of cash. Alternatively, he may be so concerned with the possible need to get at his money quickly that he would prefer to put any spare cash in a Building Society rather than give his family the protection his wife requires for them. That particular decision-making process jumps across product fields and into a quite different business – but only from the point of view of the definitions of the businesses themselves.

The most difficult field in my personal experience, in terms of identifying the ultimate buying influence, is that of ethical pharmaceuticals. (For those who have not met this terminology before, ethical pharmaceuticals are those sold only to the medical profession on prescription and to medical institutions.) One part of the problem is the existence of hospital management committees and buying committees. Where the latter exist, they perform a role similar to that of the industrial purchasing manager. However, in the institutional field, these committees may well be made up of lay people so they will rely heavily on the expert advice they are given.

For most ethical pharmaceuticals, the equivalent of the buying manager is the pharmacist: he is the man who holds the stock on which the doctors draw. But the doctors may prescribe something the pharmacist doesn't have; one is going to have to convince the other. It is generally even more complicated. The ward doctor makes a preliminary diagnosis and a corresponding prognosis. Blood samples may be sent to the pathologist who makes a final prognosis and prescribes treatment. In a case like this, there are three distinct and seperate people who can influence a buying decision by insisting on a particular treatment. If they are in harmony, all is well; if not, someone, somewhere is going to be unhappy.

In cases like this, it isn't really at all surprising that old company customs spring up and there develops a vested interest in not disturbing the water too much for fear of what might be stirred up. A company supplying surgical sutures made a remarkable discovery whilst researching the effectiveness of a journal they produced for consultant surgeons. Earlier research had revealed that the journal was well-received and widely read. Constant efforts were made to keep the list up to date by requiring surgeons to nominate themselves every 12 months. In a new piece of readership research it was decided to throw in an odd question: 'Which brand of surgical suture did you use in that last operation?'. (The interviews took place in the ante rooms of operating theatres.) Over 90 per cent replied 'Ask the theatre sister; she looks after those things'. Subsequent research revealed that the theatre sisters did in fact 'look after those things' but they never specified a brand. In most cases, the suture was supplied on tender to the hospital management committee. There are many cases like this. Kleenex value the influence of nurses so highly that a great deal of their marketing activity for paper sheets and pillow cases is directed at them. Now nurses do not buy things for hospitals. But if they keep on at the matron, the matron will get at the management committee and linen bed-clothes may well be changed for paper.

Any kind of business can build a pattern similar to that in Figure 8. For many, the very same words will suffice. Nurses are operatives in this sense and the final users are the patients. Matron and her nurses may well be convinced that there are substantial advantages with paper bed-clothing in keeping bacteriological infection down, but if the patients find the sheets harsh and uncomfortable, the linen may well be restored. Public opinion may well be in favour of clean linen and that, too, will have to be taken into account in marketing action.

Finally, on every type of list there is always one ultimate negative decision-maker – the man or woman who controls the purse strings. The closer you are to those people, the easier the task of convincing them of the value of your goods or services. The next question is to consider why they might choose you rather than some other company.

4.3 Why?

Why do people buy from your company rather than some other? What are the strengths that attract them and, of course, the weaknesses that put others off?

The first place to look for the clues to the answers – if not the answers themselves – is in the replies to the first two questions. What you really are providing in terms of customer satisfaction and to whom you are giving those services will be prime determinants of the reason why. But there is more. Often the revelation of what you are selling is really only the tip of the iceberg. A good example, and one which shows how the three questions come together, is to be found in the sale of advertising space in certain quality newspapers – such as *The Times*, *Guardian* and *Financial Times*. A first shot at what is being sold would say something like 'Advertising space in a quality newspaper'. A more refined description would add something about the kind of reader: more businessmen and civil servants, say, than any other general daily newspaper. The 'why' and the 'to whom' come very much together when it comes to getting down to considering the decision-maker for advertising of this kind. Daily newspapers like *The Times* do rather badly in terms of the numbers which media planners in advertising agencies like to use; thus, a good deal of space is sold by direct appeal to the top management of the advertiser. A considerable advantage in doing this is the very high probability that the man being sold to is either a reader of the paper or very sympathetic towards it. That is a very strong reason why so many very large companies choose *The Times* to carry their advertising, or advertisements of a particular kind.

Often the reason why is to be found in areas other than product performance. Service, delivery times, consistent quality and performance, reliability in service areas, helpful staff, few errors in invoicing – these, and many more like them, can be the deciding factors in the choice between close competitors. A few examples may help make the point clearer. When Lyons acquired control of Symbol Biscuits, the sensible thing appeared to be to sell biscuits through the grocery sales force and deliver them with all the other grocery items. It appeared that the new organization would be able to offer quite significant advantages over the old; for a start, five times as many salesmen would be selling the lines and they would also be calling on a larger universe of shops, and with greater frequency. In fact, it didn't work out that way at all. Symbol were very small in a market dominated by two great biscuit companies (United Biscuits and Associated Biscuits). With the exception of a few small to medium turnover speciality biscuits, they were heavily out-gunned by the big two. Yet they sold to particular stores on a regular basis and to a constantly changing set of larger stores, including some of the leading supermarket chains. Why? Apart from certain regional strengths based on a combination of tradition and acquired taste for a different biscuit formulation, the reason lay in speed of delivery. A high proportion of their biscuits were ordered over the telephone and delivered within 24 hours. The giant Lyons grocery organization had a regular salesman's call-cycle and an associated delivery frequency. Incorporating a 24-hour delivery facility in that would have been uneconomic, yet sales of biscuits could not stand the lack of that particular service. Writing as the man in the middle of that exercise, we had placed too high an emphasis on quality (even though that was allocated considerably lower status than the previous management had given) and far too much on the qualities that had provided a reason-why for selling tea.

Quality can be a very important attribute. However, quality is a word that is only meaningful to a customer. The tea trade always talks about 'quality' tea. It has assigned a fairly arbitrary price level to a group of teas and called those below it 'popular' and 'cheap'. The housewife has a slightly different vocabulary; she substitutes the word 'funny' for 'quality'. The quality of tea she gives her family is the arbiter of taste. Compared with that, the more expensive teas taste different – peculiar enough to earn the description 'funny teas'. Symbol Biscuits, when I first became associated with the company, had been selling 'the best chocolate couverture in the world'. The consumer thought quite differently; to most of them it was the worst. Now there is nothing at all wrong in adopting such a strategy. A number of firms in the confectionary market have taken a similar stance and been very successful. The key is that they have geared all their efforts to sustaining that position in the market-place. The critical mistake, and the one that Symbol had made, was to try to impose that positioning on an organization catering for a mass-market operation. It is well-known in the confectionery field that

77

artificial fruit flavours are generally preferred to real fruit flavours. If you want to compete with Mars Spangles, you would be well advised to take note of that evidence. If you want to sell the purest, freshest fruit sweets on the market, you will need a much smaller factory, a smaller sales force, carefully selected outlets – and you probably will not be able to advertise effectively due to the problems of reaching your target market.

People can be vital. It is often assumed that this applies only to service industries, in depth, and only to salesmen, in particular, in other fields. Most salesmen can tell you of the order they almost lost because of unsympathetic handling of complaints, being left hanging on the end of a telephone and complaints about the handling of invoices. In so many fields, there is a wide variety of acceptable substitutes. The concept of the total product, including its price, after-sales service, competent handling of complaints, discounting procedure and so on, becomes vital in such circumstances. The company which performs best over the field, or the one who offers the longest list of desirable attributes, can so easily score. People can hold business too, and often in cases where the product has fallen below par. We saw earlier how a large number of women expressed discontent with their hairdresser. When they were asked why they didn't change, the vast majority of reasons were to do with the personal relationship built up over the years with the stylist: 'She's very sweet and always nice and friendly but she can't cut hair' sums it up. Most salesmen have come across the buyer who readily admits that the competitive product he is buying is inferior but 'They've always looked after me and I don't like to let them down when they've never done it to me'.

A company that adopts the marketing concept and promotes it at all levels throughout the company is less likely to fall into these errors than one that has a divine faith in the superiority of its product and treats the buyer as extremely fortunate to be allowed to do business with them. Some companies have evolved little promotional tricks that have greatly helped in creating good staff attitudes towards customers. If, like Avis, you pick up the telephone and answer 'Avis; we try harder', you are not merely keying in to what was a very effective advertising campaign but you are also forcing yourself into an attitude of being helpful. If, like El Al, you answer 'Shalom', it isn't too easy to pick a fight. Make a point of noticing how your own staff answer the telephone to you, handle your complaints, talk about customers; that is the time to do something about it.

If the first two questions have been tackled with the proper degree

78

of objectivity and creativity, it should be much easier to make frank and honest lists of competitive strengths and weaknesses. There will be rather less need to go outside the business to find answers, but you may well find that many of the responses you need now will correlate closely with answers to the first question; this particularly applies to things like quality and performance. Be prepared to listen objectively to those in regular contact with customers. And that may well include telephonists and invoice clerks, van drivers and service engineers. These people often have to put right the mistakes of other links in the chain. Many a service engineer bears the brunt of the anger of the victim of a glib salesman; the girl at the switchboard could know more about your sales force's lunch-time habits than anyone in Head Office, simply by answering calls about the late arrival or non-appearance of salesmen. It is not easy to distinguish between excuses for poor performance and real problem areas that could affect customer relations, but this is the question that should prompt a realistic examination. A full and complete list of reasons why you are or are not selling and, thus, of why your customers are or are not buying, will overlap almost inevitably with the question of how you sell and how the customer buys.

4.4 How?

There are a number of ways this question can be tackled. Most companies will want to use them all.

First, there is how customers get to know about you and what you have to offer. Is it by promotions, media advertising, exhibitions, personal recommendation or simply waiting for customers to come in? A very large part of business is conducted by simply waiting and hoping that personal recommendation will speed things up a bit. How do your competitors do it? You don't have to follow the leader; it may well be the right thing to do to go in a completely different direction. You must consider what satisfaction you are both offering and to whom, before you can decide whether your different way of doing things is a competitive strength or a weakness. Try to find out what the competition is doing and make efforts to understand why: why at that time of year, why in that media and so on. Has he discovered a new market opportunity at a different time of year or is he simply doing what so many large companies do, starting every new campaign at the beginning of the new financial year? Why does he use that particular medium for selling his wares? It could indicate a significant change in his strategy, for most alternative kinds of approach to potential customers do tend to reach different target groups and often very significantly different groups. If a manufacturer of electric drills suddenly changes his approach from selling through builders' merchants and advertising in trade and technical magazines to selling in electrical shops, department stores and every retailer that will take them, whilst, at the same time, using television to promote drills, it ought to be a reasonable assumption that he is trying for a completely different market.

Businessmen often complain that they would drive themselves mad trying both to monitor all competitive activity and to fathom out what the reasons were and how they might respond to a counter-attack. On the other hand, the most usual reasons for business failure (after cash shortages) have to do with not knowing how the competitor achieves his success and failing to estimate his possible reactions. If the six questions are tackled in the order we are going through them, by the time you reach this, the fourth, you will have a much closer idea of who you have to worry about most and which areas are likely to be critical. The overall task should be considerably reduced in that way.

Secondly, it is worth devoting a good deal of attention to the physical act of selling. If there is one area where information is lacking it is this. Not long ago, a company in the grocery field discovered exactly how large one of its competitor's sales force was. They had always estimated it at around 30; it was over 600! When this was revealed at the annual sales conference, it turned out that many of the salesmen were much closer than head office to the truth. The trouble was that their estimates of around 800 seemed so wildly exaggerated that no-one took the difference seriously. Sales forces often know a great deal about the size, location and calling patterns of competitive sales forces. One of the characteristics of modern sales forces is that they work from home. Unlike my early days, they seldom meet at depots every morning and night. Instead they meet perhaps once a month at area sales meetings or less frequently at specially convened conferences. They very often see more of their competitors than they do of their own colleagues; they meet in the same shops, the same ante rooms and the same cafes and pubs. Even if no confidential information is exchanged, a great deal can be gleaned from piecing together the number of times any salesman runs up against the same guy from the competition and how often he sees different salesmen on his territory. It may produce nothing; it may give you ideas for improvement or for seizing comparative advantages. Good communication between field and head office is essential: it will be more pointed when salesmen know why they are passing on information and they can see the results.

Thirdly, there is the aspect of the complete terms of business between you and your customers. In the carbonless paper field in the UK there is an important distinction in the way the three largest companies do business. One offers no discounts but fairly lengthy credit; another does it the other way round with generous discounts for quantity and prompt payment but is exceedingly tight on credit. The third strikes a fairly conventional balance between the two. Under conditions in which the final user may have considerable difficulty in recognizing any one from the other, his printer might well choose a brand according to the trade-off in his firm between the need for cash discounts and the desire to hold cash in his business as long as possible. 'Long credit terms' may be the how of selling for Company A and the why of buying for its customers. In the computer industry, training can be the equivalent. Engineering firms frequently offer free servicing for a contract period or a marked degree of subsidy. Kleenex, we saw, paid a great deal of attention to an influential group of non-buyers. Brooke Bond tea attribute a great deal of their continuing success to the influence of the tea cards inside the packet in creating awareness which is carried on through life and into a purchasing situation. All these 'ancillary' marketing devices go towards the concept of total product and help answer the question 'How do we sell; how does our customer buy?'.

4.5   Where?

Once again, the same format has to be adopted: Where are we selling? Where is our customer buying? You will find that the answers divide two ways; those concerned with geographical location and others concerned with sales through outlets.

One of the standard demographic breaks used by most business firms is area. In most cases, the Registrar-General's standard regions form the basis. Sometimes, another standard might be used, such as areas described by certain research companies, groupings provided by firms providing selling data (usually called 'sales bricks') and, very frequently, the company's own sales or distribution areas. Companies who rely heavily on mass media may well use television transmission areas.

More and more companies are finding benefit in the ACORN analysis ('A Classification Of Residential Neighbourhoods') which works on the very tenable assumption that people tend to choose to live among others with similar life-styles, or that they adopt those habits when they move into a neighbourhood. Twelve ACORN groups are used (such as agricultural areas, multi-racial areas, poor quality older terraced housing), and 39 ACORN types (including areas of farms and smallholdings, multi-let big old houses and flats, private flats with single pensioners). These classifications are also of enormous benefit to companies using direct mail as part of their promotion or selling.

Obviously, there is considerable advantage in using a generally accepted standard, so that use can be made of a great deal of ancillary data. It is, for example, very difficult to establish the population in one of your own sales areas; it is far easier to make a sales area conform to a standard region.

Not every company will find important distinctions in geographical break-downs. Many are local to start with and are more interested in individual customer records. That does lead to an important point. It is necessary to establish which is the dog and which the tail and which wags what. In the grocery field, for example, there are very few national supermarket chains. Leading supermarket operators like Tesco and Fine Fare have marked regional strengths. Because they also have considerable buying power, companies selling to the customer through those outlets try to make favourable deals, with the frequent result that a particular store group may have disproportionate sales of some products. It is by no means a rarity to discover that a brand which is number two or three in the country as a whole is brand leader in one particular group of stores.

Now, if that group has a marked regional basis, it could well appear that the supplier does very well in that region whereas, in reality, its strength is due entirely to one store group. There are several vital lessons to be learned. Firstly, success in one area may not be repeated in others, simply because the conditions which created success cannot be duplicated. Not only may it be the case that the store group which has supported you is not in the new area, but it may also be a fact that its biggest competitor is strong there – and will not accept your product at any price. Secondly, it may well mean that the scale of your marketing efforts should be entirely different from area to area, based on customer strengths not pure regional ones.

On the other hand, there are marked regional preferences for certain products, particular brands and individual companies. The eating habits of the Scots are very different from the English. Scots tend to eat less meat but pay more for it. They eat rather more chocolate biscuits per head and drink more soup. Particular brands may be better suited to certain areas. Teas and soap powders have one thing in common – they perform in different ways according to the water in which they are used. There is a good reason why Horniman's tea should have established such a strong foothold in South Wales – the blend was particularly suited to the water there. There was a quite different reason why Black & Green's tea was so strong in the outlying districts of Manchester. It was a local company which established a marked for a 'gift tea' (one where labels could be exchanged for goods like cutlery, crockery and linen), by selling in the local markets around the edge of Manchester. If you were a company like Horniman, the next move ought to be to other soft water areas where your blend might be especially suitable. When Birmingham started to draw its domestic water supplies from the Welsh valleys, it provided a splendid natural development for Horniman's tea. Black & Green had no such advantage; they would have to look for other parts of the country where their selling method and strength might enable them to repeat the success around Manchester. Throughout this chapter, we have been looking for those areas of activity that could offer the greatest competitive advantage – we are still looking for the same thing but now we are trying to see whether that could arise from some geographical characteristic.

The same basic considerations of geographical location will arise in international marketing. The fundamental strengths of a company in international markets will be remarkably like those of the two tea companies in the example quoted above. Additional factors include exchange parity, exchange control and availability of currencies, political stability, local laws and regulations, and so on. The equivalent to Horniman saying 'Where else is the water similar to South Wales?' could be asking in which other countries are the laws similar to those in the markets where the business is already a success.

The other category of answer has to do with customer strengths. Most of British industry took a very long while before it realized that recognizing that some customers were worth considerably more than others could pay handsome dividends. A great many companies have still either not recognized the fact or have failed to take any action. Nowadays, the conditions deemed necessary to justify a very large sales force calling regularly on the vast bulk of the distribution network for any product are high volume and value, high frequency of purchase, and perishability. Even medium-life products are not considered worthy of regular physical contact with the numerical bulk of the retail trade.

It means that the basis of measurement should change. One should be concerned not with the physical numbers of customers but with the value they represent. That old 80:20 rule will almost certainly rear its head again. A small number of customers will account for the bulk of the trade in any given product, service or commodity. What we should be looking for is which stores account for the highest proportion of the grocery trade; which bank's current account holders have the highest number of transactions; which socio-economic groups buy most life assurance; which countries have the highest *per capita* consumption of Scotch whisky; which farms have the highest consumption of fertilizers? This kind of consideration gives rise to a most useful concept known as 'sterling weighted distribution'. Normal distribution checks might well tell you that your soap powder is stocked by 60 per cent of the retail grocery trade. That is a fairly meaningless statistic unless you have some measure of the importance of those stores. You could well find that the 40 per cent your company is missing accounts for 60 per cent of total sales of soap powders. Your distribution figures begin to look a little sick now. What any business ideally needs to know is:

1   What proportion of the total business do your customers account for?
2   What proportion of the specific product field do they command?
3   What proportion of your sales do they account for?

The first will ask, for example, what percentage of total retail food business, what proportion of total motor manufacture, what share of total packaged holidays booked? Moving on, the question will be refined to enquiries such as what share of total soap powder do those stores have (soap powders do tend to be more highly geared towards large supermarkets than all grocery items taken together), what proportion of tyres do the manufacturers account for, how much of the all-inclusive tour market to the Costa Brava do they account for? In each case, the aim is to refine the information as closely as possible to useful, actionable data for the specific business. Thus, it must lead to the most meaningful - and that means the most actionable - information directly comparable to facts about the company's own business.

We saw, in Chapter 2, how important different categories of buyer could be and how essential it was to isolate the heavy user from the light. 'To each according to its worth' should be our credo for maximum profitability. We shall see more evidence of the value of this dictum as we progress through the other sections of this book. In particular, we shall see that there are many emotional barriers to be overcome in making the most sensible allocation of resources; it never comes easy to any salesman to be forced to consider which customers he is prepared not to supply or even to consider how often he is willing to allow them to be out of stock. On the other hand, it is easy to contemplate the impossibility of calling on and delivering to every customer precisely when they want it. The optimum will be somewhere between the two. The reconciliation will be costs and profit, and this is the first of several opportunities to say that the sooner regional profitability summaries become a way of life, the quicker profitable rationalization and exploitation of real opportunity areas will happen. Ironically, most companies still measure geographical sales when, often, those analyses have become relatively meaningless. At the same time, they make all their profit calculations on a global basis which assumes that a head office located in London exerts the same influence on Glasgow as it does on Birmingham, that Glasgow actually requires the back-up of a London head office and that the effect of an advertisement in the *Daily Telegraph* is the same throughout the country. Customer records are needed for virtually all the most meaningful forms of marketing analysis and forecasting. Most businesses would be all the sharper for backing them up with profit calculations made down to the smallest practical unit.

When the customer strength is recognized and recorded, we need to know one more thing: when are we selling; when is he buying; have we got these in harmony?

4.6   When?

It is natural for any manager to think only of aspects of seasonality under this heading, but there is more. A real understanding of regular fluctuations is a considerable aid to effective sales forecasting, whilst a completely different but nevertheless vital consideration is which periods afford the best opportunities for selling.

Obviously, the time periods chosen for consideration may vary dramatically according to the business being considered. If, for example, your business is selling porridge, the difference between October to March sales and those for the rest of the year will be critical. If you are a hairdresser, you will be much more concerned with days of the week (Mondays are traditionally poor) and Bank Holidays (when women like to look their best for planned events). The first step is to recognize strengths and weaknesses by day, week, month or season as each affects your business. Then consider what you might be able to do about it.

Several of the breakfast cereal manufacturers have promoted summer uses for products previously served mainly with hot milk during winter. They had discovered that a very high proportion of people used cold milk in winter in any case. Additionally, some were able to promote the use of their products as ingredients in other meals and in cakes, whilst most have successfully developed uses at other meals. Meals can be important under the heading of 'When?'. The great strength of tea in the UK is first thing in the morning, often before breakfast; in coffee-drinking countries, coffee assumes the same role. Many hairdressers have made Mondays their day for children, old-age pensioners, even models. If you are doing no business at all at certain periods, it can make sense to consider marginal costings; things that may not be worthwhile in good times can be very beneficial in poor periods.

Sometimes it is necessary to recognize that there are times when no amount of effort can produce a sale. Closing day is an obvious example. Certain industries close down for annual holidays; parts of the country have annual holidays (Wakes Weeks, extra days at Bank Holidays, etc.) and these affect your effort. There are two things you can do about this kind of situation. Firstly, you can stop wasting effort. Perhaps this is the time for your own annual close-down to take place. Certainly you can plan for these periods in sales forecasting and production scheduling. Secondly, this may be the time when a valuable service can be provided for customers. Whilst no selling takes place in the average supermarket on early closing days, a great deal of merchandising of stock goes on. A considerable amount of goodwill is created by giving this kind of assistance at precisely the time when the store needs it most. Industrial companies may send in their technical experts and service engineers at the time when their client company is shut down for annual maintenance. Not every off-season for selling is a problem; many present opportunities.

It will be noticed that the discussion has gradually narrowed down from the more obvious days, weeks, months and seasons to any regular occurrence. This can be vitally important when it comes to both sales forecasting and the almost inevitable inquest into why sales did not meet the budget. These are matters which merit fuller consideration later but it should be said here and now that, on the one hand, a technique that analyses the value of regular fluctuations is the beginning of most of the more scientific forecasting techniques whilst, on the other, managers do have an alarming tendency to produce budgets which ignore the fact that Easter is in a different month the following year, that Christmas falls in such a way that many factories will close down for a week, and completely forget about works closures and local holidays.

Almost every question that has been asked forces us to look back at the replies to a previous one and consider, firstly, how the earlier answer affects the present question and, secondly, whether the response to this one forces some reappraisal of the earlier. 'When' is no exception. If not at the beginning of the sequence, then certainly now, you will be forced to consider whether your product or service provides the same satisfaction at all times during the year. Take fountain pens. They come in all shapes, sizes, qualities and prices. They can be considered as necessary writing instruments, gifts, expressions of a person's personality or an outright status symbol. A 22-carat gold pen may write no better than a plastic-barrelled version costing only a tiny fraction of its more status-conscious fellow. A necessary writing instrument can be a 50p pen picked up off a rack or one costing 20 times as much chosen from a counter with the skilled help of an assistant. All that comes under 'What?'. But it also comes under 'When?'. By far the greatest proportion of all types of fountain pen are bought at Christmas. Even the very cheapest sell more at that time, for they provide a useful, much appreciated, cheap gift. Nevertheless, those pens do a far higher proportion of business at other times of the year than solid gold ones. The degree of effort, the timing of promotion and selling and the kinds of appeals made either through media advertising or at the point of sale will vary considerably by the time of year. If a fountain pen manufacturer asks the question 'With what are we competing?', he will find that the answer changes by time of year. A fountain pen for personal use bought at any time of the year will probably compete primarily with ball-point pens and felt-tip versions. The same pen at Christmas is more likely to compete with a cigarette lighter, the item most often paired with a fountain pen as an alternative gift for a man.

As the timing changes, so the opportunity differs. One of the most significant clichés in marketing (and one that has already been implied several times) is that marketing is concerned with opportunities, not problems. What every businessman should be looking for is when those opportunities are greatest. For example, a knowledge of the depreciation policy of major customers can be a great help. Depreciation allowances run out in time and no further claims can be made to offset corporation tax. As that time comes closer, boards of directors become increasingly concerned with knowing if the plant is to be replaced, with what, when and at what cost. It becomes even more vital when, as is usually the case, there is no actual cash reserve which represents the annual depreciation. If the plant is to be replaced, the money has to be obtained from somewhere. If reserves are not available, borrowings will have to be increased. It is obvious that senior management is going to be very concerned as capital equipment nears the end of its scheduled life. This is obviously the time for sales approaches to intensify, to change from simple contact to hard-selling.

A very different example comes from the field of national daily newspapers. In the sense that most people use the word, newspapers are not seasonal. They tend to behave a little strangely around Christmas; a characteristic of the British is that we like to have a house full of reading matter at Christmas. Probably because the whole family is sitting down together, most families buy extra papers and magazines. Depending where Christmas falls, either daily or Sunday newspapers may receive a very short burst of sales. However, between the wars, there was a sharp drop in sale during July and August. People went on holiday and cancelled their newspapers. (The UK has two unusual characteristics in the newspaper field: it is the only country in the world with truly national newspapers and it enjoys a higher level of home delivery.) One enterprising circulation manager noted the number of people sitting in deckchairs doing nothing and thought how much better it would be if they bought his newspaper. He reasoned that if only he could devise a scheme that would get them to sample his paper, a good proportion might stay with it when they went home. Even if they didn't, his overall sales would increase substantially. He also thought that cancelling a newspaper and escaping, as it were, from what was going on in the world, was all part of being on holiday. On the other hand, by about the first Tuesday of the holiday, Dad would be fretting to know the latest cricket scores, which footballers had been transferred to whom and what the favourite was for the three o'clock at Ascot. He could salve his conscience by not buying his usual newspaper (because he was on holiday) but trying a different one. And perhaps his wife would like one too; after all, she usually only got to read the paper after her husband brought it home from work, if at all. That was the beginning of all the mystery men and women who produce largesse when correctly identified – provided that the challenger is carrying a copy of the right newspaper. It heralded the now-familiar beach games sponsored by newspapers and a host of other activities at popular holiday resorts. That instinctive assumption by that circulation manager was absolutely right: summer holidays were not a problem to the industry – they presented real opportunities. Under normal everyday circumstances, people do not like to change from a familiar newspaper; here was a situation where the very same people, of their own free will, actually wanted to have a change.

There is a relatively simple set of criteria for distinguishing between problems and opportunities and we shall come to it later. The moral of this section and of the examples given is that every business should seek to recognize regular variations, question why they happen and decide whether they represent a problem they cannot solve, and thus should adapt to, or an opportunity to be seized.

There are many more examples of the sorts of events that offer opportunities. For the sake of brevity, here is a list which should give enough examples to allow most businessmen to translate one industry's experience to their own field.

Announcements of engagements to marry.
Marriage announcements.
Birth announcements.
Starting school (which can be calculated from the date of birth).
Starting at university (students receive their grants in lump sums and may need help in budgeting).
Job promotions (life assurance and investment scheme opportunities).
Building new factories.
Acquisitions (especially where one of the firms involved is already a customer).
Life of plant or consumer durables (last new car bought three years ago; children should be growing out of the bunk beds bought four years ago; plant superseded by new methods, etc.).

All of these present new concepts of time but fit quite properly under the heading of 'When?'. They are examples of times when customers are open to suggestions for new goods and services and, in several of the examples, are themselves making fundamental changes in their buying and behaviour patterns.

4.7   Repeating the exercise

It will be fairly obvious that answering this set of questions and the associated subsidiary ones that arise will be a demanding task when approached for the first time. Many aspects cannot be answered without outside and independent help. If market research is outside the budget (or possibly inappropriate to your business), it can be extremely useful to involve an experienced consultant for a couple of days to do no more than act as a catalyst. It is often easier for an outsider to ask apparently naive questions (but which are often the most searching) than it is for an insider – especially when that person is a subordinate.

It gets a little easier each time the exercise is repeated, for now the examination is concerned with identifying changes that could prompt fresh initiatives. Mention has been made before of the fact book or data book. Although, as we saw, the primary function is quite different from this self-analysis questionnaire, recording each fresh new fact and decision in that book can be extremely useful and every management group using the six questions will find it useful to have a completely updated fact book of some kind.

Personally, I believe that the annual repetition of this six-question analysis is more valuable than the formal annual plan, for the latter can so easily take place without the necessary preliminary analysis of what the business is, where it got to and where it wants to get. I have been fortunate in working for companies where senior management has taken itself away from the business for a week at a time and stood back to look at the wood instead of concentrating on the trees. Businesses do change. Often, however, the sheer momentum of the day-to-day operation keeps top management's nose so firmly to the grindstone that they fail to notice what is really right under their nose. The tea business in the UK denied the possibility of a viable tea bag market on the grounds that the product was inferior and the price too high. Many of them were still denying the possibility when tea bags accounted for 10 per cent of the market. Now the industry is concerned with calculations of when tea bags will account for 75 per cent of the total UK retail tea sales.

One final note of caution. It can too easily be implied that success is only for those who follow the herd. History is full of examples of men and women who have succeeded by backing the trends. The reason so few do it is that the risk is high and the investment often beyond individual capacities. It is so easy to get the timing wrong too; the Xerox machine was around for some 30 years before anyone with sufficient courage to market it could be found. The reason for this kind of analysis is to enable a business to decide what position it wants to take up. It may just as well choose to operate in a narrow section on the fringe of a large market as opt to be in the mass sector. If the basic ingredients of a perfume cost only 5p per ounce, it could be marketed in one guise for 15p, or in another for £5.00. The choice is yours. The strategies are entirely different and the tactics by which each strategy is achieved very different.

4.8 Summary

Six simple questions will provide a searching analysis of any business field and any product or service within it. Confining the exercise to so few questions can actually provide a sharper definition than asking for too much detail. The keys to success in this form of analysis are:

1 Complete objectivity.
2 A creative approach to the questions and their answers.
3 Being prepared to obtain independent information rather than relying on what the business has always believed *or* obtaining the help of an outside catalyst.
4 Recording all new facts for future reference.
5 Acknowledging that all businesses change over time and the implications of change must always be considered.
6 Repeating the exercise at regular intervals under conditions which emphasize its importance to the continuing success of the company.

4.9 Checklist

1 The key business question is 'What are our customer's buying?' and this is a matter of identifying the ultimate satisfaction the customer derives.

2 Identifying that satisfaction and the competition for satisfying that need is the way of correctly answering the question 'What business are we in?'. Until that question has been satisfactorily answered, the business has little effective control over its destiny.

3 Those involved in industrial marketing have to look not only at the satisfaction their direct customers seek but also go beyond that to discover, on the one hand, what satisfactions the ultimate end-users derive and, on the other, what part their product plays in that ultimate satisfaction. The greater the part (for example a Rolls Royce engine in a Boeing aircraft) the higher the price that can be commanded.

4 Care must always be taken to identify the benefits your customers seek, rather than to catalogue the features your product or service provides. A feature only becomes a benefit when someone needs it.

5 Next, a business has to ask itself 'What am I selling to whom?' and 'Who is buying what I sell?' Buyers are not always decision-

makers. Specifiers can be groups or individuals (although it is usually possible to identify one key specifier).

6   However, ultimate purchasing decisions are often affected by 'influences' – ultimate users or consumers of the product or service. Workers, children, families and nurses are all good examples of powerful influences on certain buying decisions.

7   Frequently, different segments of the same market have both different specifiers and influences. People involved in the same purchase may have entirely different viewpoints. (To the alcoholic, a bottle is half-empty; to the moderate drinker, it is still half-full!)

8   Why people buy from your company is usually an amalgam of what you are doing right and what your competitor is doing wrong. (The opposite can also apply!) A continuing, absolutely objective, analysis of comparative strengths and weaknesses is necessary – related always to desired customer benefits and satisfactions.

9   How you get your product or service to its market is as important as what your market is. It is an exceptional product that people are prepared to search for. Why your competitor may be doing better than you may be because he has the 'how' right: that is the right product at the right price at the right place at the right time.

10   The way sales are spread amongst potential outlets and customers is also vital. Two concepts apply. The first is that of customer location and identifying the best way to reach the most businesses most effectively and profitably. The second is that of sterling-weighted sales and distribution; selling to the customer groups and through the outlets that account for the bulk of the available business (unless, of course, you opt for a smaller, more specialized, market sector).

11   There are two aspects of timing involved in the question 'When are we selling?'. One is the question of seasonality, using the word as market researchers do to describe any regular variation, however short. The other is the identification of periods when the need to buy (and thus the opportunity to sell) is greatest.

12   Whilst analysis based on the six questions posed is a worthwhile exercise, it is also time-consuming and may require expenditure on independent research, analysis and, often, advice. It becomes

92

increasingly valuable if the exercise is repeated annually. It will not be necessary to repeat everything every year. Look for significant changes and search for the new opportunities they present.

5

If It's Living, It's Dying

Tempus edax rerum
(Time, the devourer of things)
Ovid

It is an old adage that nothing can last forever. Some things appear to go on for so long that it is easy to fall into the trap of believing in immortality. Just think, however, of the household names of your youth (even the young can do this) and consider how many have disappeared. Famous companies, old-favourite sweets and toys, fashions that were all the rage – many have gone forever. Others have come back. Old people are apt to decry long-haired youth, completely forgetting that their parents shocked their elders by cutting their hair short and creating a fashion that even a century of life makes only a dash on the graph of male hair styles (which have been traditionally long).

Personal experience and memory should convince anyone of two things:

Nothing goes on forever in business.
Some things do seem to come back again.

These two statements come together in a theory known variously as the 'Product Life Cycle' or the 'Demand Life Cycle'. Sometimes they are used interchangeably; at other times the demand cycle is used to describe the role of an individual product or service within a total product group. To avoid confusion with the many other books that make some mention of this concept, the terms will be used in this chapter in the latter sense, giving each a specific role.

5.1 Life-cycles in business

If you really think about a straight-line sales increase, you will realize that each step represents a smaller percentage gain than the preceding

94

one. Equal percentage gains would be represented by a steadily rising rate of slope. Whilst the straight-line graph will represent a 100 per cent increase from one unit to two, it will be only a 5 per cent gain from 20 to 21. By the time the slope represents an increase from 1999 to 2000, the percentage gain is only 0.05 per cent. In a sense, any sales curve contains within it the seeds of its own destruction.

A study of large numbers of product histories leads to the conclusion that there is a generalized shape of sales histories. It cannot be said too clearly that what follows is a generalization; there is no rule that says your industry, or your company within it, will follow the shape which is described in Figure 9. History shows that there is a very high likelihood that it will, but the time period could be very, very long or quite short. The use of coal as a source of energy, for example, provides an example of an extremely long life cycle but, nevertheless, one which exhibits all the classic signs as other sources of energy become more widely used. At the other end of the scale, certain transistorized components have been replaced by more efficient ones so quickly that the down-slope is almost vertical and the time-span often not much more than six months from launch to demise. Later in this chapter, we shall see that there are actually enough well-known variations to merit some alteration to the basic shape in certain circumstances.

Life-cycles will be treated at some length and with rather more detail than is usually given in books of this type. There are four reasons for this.

1   A study of life-cycle theory may answer some of the questions arising from the self-analysis questionnaire and will certainly make the next stage of business analysis more meaningful.
2   A number of quite experienced marketing practitioners question the concept.
3   At the same time, leading academic marketing people have provided a great deal of confirmatory evidence from fields as diverse as transportation and soup, at one end of the scale, to men's beards and the ratio of skirt widths to women's figures. (It appears that men's beards grow longer as women's skirts correlate more closely with their figures!)
4   This is an area where a little knowledge can be an exceedingly dangerous thing and a temporary fluctuation can be interpreted as the beginning of the end. (In which case, of course, it will be – if you act as though it were.)

It is strange that there should be this simultaneous praise and condemnation of an important concept. It is even more strange when it is one of the very few areas in marketing theory where fact can be used instead of opinion and vague generalization. The most detailed of the criticisms that have appeared all endorse the theory and thus confirm the danger of inadequate assimilation and definition. So let's get the definition right:

> The life-cycle concept describes what will happen when the natural forces present in a market are allowed to have free play, that is, what will happen unless you do something to prevent it.

Unless you do something – that is what the critics appear to forget. A well-documented rebuttal was presented by the marketing director of a leading confectionery company in the UK. It purported to show that one of his products had been in long-term decline and had been, accordingly, abandoned by the previous manager. The product was revamped, heavily advertised and quickly moved into growth and profitability. There were two elements in this story which actually confirm the concept as stated. Firstly, his had been the only product in decline in a growing sector. Secondly, he had done something about it. The point is worth making, not simply as a rebuke to a well-intentioned view, but as essential emphasis on the totality of the theory before we immerse ourselves in the necessary detail of individual elements.

Figure 9 is a comprehensive chart which ties together a number of separate components of the theory and its associated activities. Note that it is a composite chart, that is it uses the same scale (left hand) for both volume and value. Look at the shape of the volume curve. This is the generalized curve that comes up so frequently. Fairly flat in the early stages, the curve assumes a momentum before flattening off. Often, this flat top can be very long indeed; in other cases, the peak occurs at a single point of time. Products like tea and biscuits have had long plateau periods; tea in the UK has gone beyond and into decline, biscuits haven't. On the other hand, to take an example used in the first chapter, saturation for ceiling tiles occurs when every ceiling is fitted with tiles. Since that is unlikely to happen on one particular day, the combination of new houses being built, the last few old houses being converted and some replacements for old tiles will combine to keep the top flat for a short while, but not for very long. Thus, frequency of purchase becomes an important element in the life of a product. With any cycle studied to the end of its life, the shape is almost certain to be an elongated 'S' curve – not the normal distribution curve (a statistical concept of a curve with equal

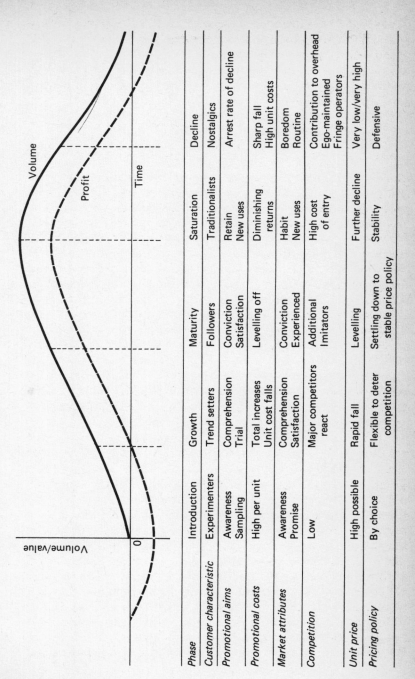

Phase	Introduction	Growth	Maturity	Saturation	Decline
Customer characteristic	Experimenters	Trend setters	Followers	Traditionalists	Nostalgics
Promotional aims	Awareness Sampling	Comprehension Trial	Conviction Satisfaction	Retain New uses	Arrest rate of decline
Promotional costs	High per unit	Total increases Unit cost falls	Levelling off	Diminishing returns	Sharp fall High unit costs
Market attributes	Awareness Promise	Comprehension Satisfaction	Conviction Experienced	Habit New uses	Boredom Routine
Competition	Low	Major competitors react	Additional Imitators	High cost of entry	Contribution to overhead Ego-maintained Fringe operators
Unit price	High possible	Rapid fall	Levelling	Further decline	Very low/very high
Pricing policy	By choice	Flexible to deter competition	Settling down to stable price policy	Stability	Defensive

Figure 9 *The product life-cycle concept*

proportions on each side). Not only does the curve have a slow beginning, it also has a very lengthy tail. A characteristic of most markets is that a number of buyers will go on taking the product until the supply stops. (These are traditionally referred to as 'the lunatic fringe' – the adjective may be far more appropriate as a description of the suppliers than it is of the customers.)

Profit assumes the same general shape but it is stepped in relation to the volume curve. For quite a long time no profit is made. Until a business has customers, all it can have is costs. As sales increase, these costs will first be covered and then past investment will be recouped. Real net contributions arrive after that stage (alternatively known as the 'break-even' or 'pay-back' period). Note another characteristic – profit starts to fall before volume declines. There are few businesses that can escape the ravages of the law of diminishing returns. It is usually possible to find more customers to service but the unit cost of doing so almost inevitably rises. The only chance of escape is the possibility of making realistic differential charges for the service. An illustration that makes the problem clear is to consider selling Heinz tomato soup. The product is nationally known and priced the same throughout the country. Suppose that Heinz distribute their soup to 95 per cent of grocery shops throughout the country; the missing 5 per cent are in the Scilly Isles, the Orkneys and the wilder and more remote hill country of Scotland and Wales. The travelling time of the visiting salesmen and the long distribution hauls would almost certainly result in a loss. One useful result of appreciating the life-cycle concept is the prevention of too large a gap between peak volume and peak profits.

THE INTRODUCTORY PHASE

The customers most likely to buy in this phase will be the experimenters and the fashion leaders. As we have already noted in previous chapters, fashion leaders can arise in any type of business. Equally, even the most frivolous of consumer markets contain a good proportion of people who never buy new products until they have been on the market long enough to 'get the bugs out of the system'. The more technical the product, the greater the likelihood of attracting the more solid kind of customer at an earlier stage. In consumer markets, there does appear to be a certain proportion of housewives who try all new domestic products as soon as they appear. This almost guarantees initial sales but it also makes true estimates of running levels of demand much more hazardous.

Promotion during this period will be aimed at creating awareness

98

of the product and inducing trial. Promotional means, such as free or subsidized samples, may be one way of achieving this. However, whichever way it is done, the trial period involves high unit costs of promotion and this will last until sufficient volume has been created. To make the potential market aware of the new product or service and induce the necessary trial, some promise – in the form of a customer proposition – has to be made. This subject belongs properly to the study of advertising, however it is clear that some means has to be discovered of explaining to the prospect what the product will do and why it is right for the potential customer. In most cases, competition will be low and that will be an asset – unless the new product is being launched against an established competitor or into an existing market currently serviced by a different type of product. With a completely new product, the initiator has the opportunity to set his own pricing policy and the chance to adopt a strategy of high initial price which will afford him the opportunity of price reductions when competition appears, or to price the product very low in order to obtain rapid penetration of the market.

Obviously, this is a high-risk phase with the possibility of enjoying quite high levels of sale without the opportunity to reach repeat levels that will enable past investment to be recouped, let alone break through into net profits.

THE GROWTH PHASE

From the very beginning of a second phase, product-line costings will be showing profit contributions. It may take some time before these are sufficient to achieve a pay-back situation, but at least the slope of the sales curve offers encouragement that it is only a matter of time now. The trend-setters and pace-setters in the market become the buyers now and these are the ones who are likely to stick. They've taken a little time to make up their minds but now they are certain. The first ones in have a 'bell-wether' effect on the others and this is the time when everybody seems to want your product and shortages can arise, which make it easier for competition to enter. Major competitors are hardly likely to pass up this opportunity of getting into what now seems to be a significant new market.

In promotional terms, the market is undergoing its comprehension period. Advertising, if appropriate, has to explain more than it may have done when the primary objective was to create awareness. Although actual budgets for promotional purposes may still be rising, unit costs should be coming down rapidly; if not, either the promotion is wrong or you shouldn't be promoting in this case. Price

99

could well become a major promotional tool at this stage, especially if the first company in has been able to accumulate a little profit 'fat' in preparation for defending its position later. The concept of total product/total price (including service aspects, training, and so on) may well be the means of achieving a price advantage over new competitors.

MATURITY

The followers have now moved into the market and the slope begins to become less steep. As a compensation, however, this is the period of real profit and one you will want to prolong. Buyers are, by now, pretty convinced about product performance and enjoying satisfaction from it. Each succeeding use of the product or service is likely to confirm that satisfaction, so that promotion can be held at a reasonable level. The main task of advertising will be to hold your customers against the counter-claims of competitors.

A new kind of competitor is likely to appear at this stage – the pure imitator whose products are frequently known as 'me toos'. Often, they behave as parasites, living off the reputation and promotion of the leading companies and usually competing on different grounds, such as sheer availability, price, discounts and service. Obviously, several of those are alternatives; heavily discounted goods are not usually backed up with high degrees of service, either at the time of buying or in the form of after-sales service. Where goods are in short supply, there is little point in providing them cheaply – often they are more expensive, depending on how badly customers need them. Several firms have created and maintained a healthy profit record out of never being a market leader but always following and taking advantage of the maturity phase of a life-cycle.

Every aspect of this stage tends to be characterized by levelling off. Promotion has to be watched carefully or higher unit costs will come about. Prices settle down for, by now, customers are well aware of what the product is worth to them and what acceptable substitutes and alternatives are available; the buying mix can easily be distorted by changing price.

In Figure 9, profit is shown as turning over into decline just at the end of this third phase. It may be delayed into maturity but it has been shown at this point simply to emphasize that, as sales begin to level off, the greatest temptation to pursue volume aims exists and this can easily lead into the situation already described whereby diminishing returns set in.

SATURATION

This is the point where all those who are likely to buy are buying. It is the point where profit decline is most likely to begin to show real acceleration not only on the grounds of reducing returns per unit sold, but also through such things as the reluctance of existing customers to accept inevitable price increases, the desire for novelty and the factor of obsolescence. For all these reasons, the prime marketing task is to hold on to existing customers. At the same time, for reasons which will become much clearer when we look at some of the reactions to the saturation point, manufacturers may be looking for new uses to promote. Habit plays a very large part in the sustaining of a saturation level and it could be just a little too late to be making changes for some people. On the other hand, the cost of entry for new competitors is likely to be prohibitive and not very attractive in any case.

What happens to price will largely depend on two things: the initial pricing strategy and the degree of freedom to act (either for competitive or government reasons). There is a general tendency for actual price to fall; discounting often begins to take the place of other forms of promotion even though list prices do not change. In the case of service industries, additional service elements may be added. Pam Am had an interesting case of what to do when an aircraft has reached saturation point but, owing to the multiple pricing structure in existence, full-fare businessmen were sitting alongside half-fare, advance booking, tourists. Their answer was to designate sections of the aircraft as 'Executive areas' and provide extra and appropriate services. In the same way, many American insurance companies have added counselling services so that bereaved beneficiaries can receive good advice just at the time when they probably need it most.

DECLINE

The typical market brief for this period is:

> 'Hold the rate of decline to less than that of the market as a whole' *or possibly* '. . . to that of the market as a whole.'

'Nostalgics' is an appropriate description of the buyers in this stage – they tend to get older and more nostalgic as the years go by. Many markets continue to 'humour' these buyers for quite some time. Where the production process or the servicing routines allow this, there may be little harm. Sometimes, another area to be investigated in more depth later, it is necessary to maintain items in this stage

101

because they complete a range; the ethical pharmaceutical industry provides a number of prime examples.

Promotion usually falls dramatically during this period and faces a constant battle to avoid drastically increasing unit costs per sale. Price is frequently the prime weapon in the armoury and manufacturers are continually looking over their shoulder at what the competition is charging today. They may have to look hard at what the competition is giving away today; buyers have fallen into a routine and boredom has set in – they often need a sharp jolt to arouse their interest. Giveaways, buying incentives and various types of incentive programmes, are frequently used at this time. Price itself could be very low or very high. Where it is vital to keep machinery turning (or people gainfully employed), prices may be slashed to minimum contribution levels in order to achieve those objectives. Wherever possible, companies will prefer to charge prices that reflect the true costs of providing the service to a minority market, on the assumption that anyone who wants it badly enough will pay for it.

It has been said before, and it will no doubt have to be said many times more, that marketing is like a circle and you can break into it almost anywhere; the danger is that it is necessary to refer to concepts and ideas that have not yet been described. So it is with the concept of contribution to overheads. In the last paragraph, reference was made to accepting minimum contributions. Every company has overhead costs – certain expenses necessary to being in business – and these have to be paid for whether anything is sold or not. The larger the company, the larger these overheads are likely to be. They become the first charge on the gross profits of the enterprise; not until they have been offset will the company be able to begin to measure real net profits. Since these costs simply have to be met (in the short term at least), many companies are prepared to continue selling goods and services under situations where they produce no more than something towards the costs of being in business. Hence the term 'contributions'. In the decline stage, many products will continue to be sold simply to provide a valuable contribution to total company overheads. Thus, a product may be maintained on the market long after it appears to have served a useful life.

Of course, that is not the only reason why products may continue to exist long after their prime market has disappeared. Sheer ego may be the reason, especially with a product which was the reason for the company's existence in the past. There are even circumstances under which products may actually be launched into the decline stage of a product life-cycle. There is usually a viable market on the fringe of

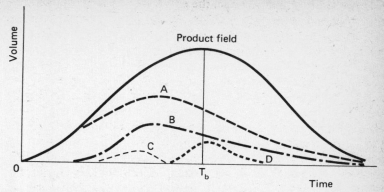

Figure 10 *Products within product field*

any large one. Often, when a market has reached the decline period, the intensity of competition slackens; companies who previously would have been quick to respond to a new competitor may not retaliate but may actually welcome an alternative source of supply which could allow the now-declining brand to be withdrawn or reduced in scale.

CYCLES WITHIN CYCLES

So far, the discussion has been global in the sense that no particular reference has been made to the position of brands within the life-cycle of a product field.

In a one-brand market situation, the two are one: so are they in the final decline stages when only one is left.

In Figure 10, an illustration is shown of the varying cycles which might exist within a market. Product A is first in and has kept going almost to the end. Product B was a follower but a very close one. Although never quite matching A's sales, B's market share has grown as the market has declined. C and D have both had shorter lives, D obviously deciding to launch only when C had withdrawn from the market.

If you try to draw a market profile according to the five phases we have defined, you will find that only D reaches brand saturation at the same time as the market does; indeed, it is quite possible for market saturation only to be attained after each individual product has reached its zenith. This is important to understand. For all sorts of reasons, the products of different companies are not always perfectly acceptable substitutes. There may be simple physical reasons like distribution, availability, service, and so on. There may be far more attitudinal ones which decide certain people in favour of some companies and against others. Thus, early answers to the following questions must be obtained – What is happening in the market? What is happening to me? Why should I be any different? What can I do about it? Back you must go to the analysis of competitive strengths and weaknesses. If, perhaps, you have been wondering why such an important concept – and one which could clearly account for the market position you currently occupy – was left until after dealing with the six questions, here is the reason. In looking at an individual life-cycle, it is absolutely essential that you compare with the right market. When the UK tea business was preoccupied with its own life-cycle it made little impact on the situation. When it learned to take more account of the life-cycle for hot beverages, it took far more notice of the threat of instant coffee. From one of the strengths of instant coffee – convenience – came an attack through the medium of tea bags, plus emotive appeals to the young who were being wooed by the modernity as well as convenience of instant coffee. The decline hasn't been halted but it has been considerably slowed. Advertising appeals were discovered that could produce dramatic effects (but cost more than the industry was able to subscribe on a continuing basis) and the increasing share of total trade taken by tea bags allowed the packers to improve their profits despite falling total tea volume. A look at the tea life-cycle now would show a slight decline in total tea, a steep decline in packet teas (with varying degrees of decline according to price) and a very steep increase for tea bags. Indeed, Figure 10 has elements of similarity with the UK tea market throughout the 1970s and into the 1980s, with tea bags growing (like product D) but not yet at maturity.

The biscuit market is one which has undergone terrific change in the same period. Taking a section of the life-cycle from 1900 would show a very smooth, free-flowing upward curve gradually flattening out in classic pattern and looking, in 1974, as though saturation may have been reached. Unusually, profit and total value had expanded because of a switch from the lower-priced biscuits to the more expensive; in particular, the proportion of chocolate biscuits in the total had accounted for a considerable part of the growth of the market value. When times became hard and housewives sought better value for money, the share of chocolate biscuits in the total declined rapidly. However, biscuits have in the UK assumed the role of staple products in the domestic market. The result was for the housewife to replace the more expensive biscuits with less expensive, chocolate-coated with non-coated varieties, assortments with plain, sweet with

104

dry. The total market volume curve appears static; this time the value curve has fallen. This is another useful lesson to carry forward for possible future use.

Depending on the product field, one may have to take account of quite a number of different cycles. Banks and investment houses, mortgage brokers and insurance agents may have to take much more account of the normal economic trade cycle. (The word normal is used in hope; although the frequency and relative regularity of the boom/slump cycle is well documented, the economy is surprised by the cyclical changes roughly every 22 ½ months.) Investing in shares as against local authority loans, Government bonds as against long-term bank deposits, current accounts versus Building Society shares – all these have had cycles against which any particular scheme could be measured and where it might be positioned. Examining these cycles may well show which is the most propitious moment to launch, and into which market. Lyons were very fortunate with Ready Brek in that the consumers chose a market that was growing; Lyons themselves had chosen a market in the latter decline stages – indeed, they had chosen the only sector of the breakfast cereal market that was declining at that time.

Figure 9 deliberately combines a summary of the characteristics of each stage with the generalized profile. Consider the two together always. In the Ready Brek example just quoted, entering a declining market should have meant high unit costs of promotion, encountering defensive pricing strategies from competition and overcoming the boredom of the aging nostalgics in the porridge market. Compare that with the characteristics of a growth market which was the phase of the market Lyons actually found themselves in. The marketing strategies required, quite apart from the chances of a long and successful life, are completely different.

ATTACKING THE PROFIT CURVE

One mistake that is often made by those with some familiarity with the life-cycle concept is to believe that profit inevitably follows volume trends. It is quite possible to improve profits even though volume is in decline. This is where techniques of value analysis are so important.

Basically, there are three things a company might do:

1 Produce the same product at a lower cost with no increase in price.
2 Produce the same product at lower costs and pass all (or some) of the benefit to customers in the form of lower prices.

105

3   Improve the product at no increase in cost (with options to keep the price unchanged or increase price by a sum lower than the extra value offered).

Clearly, value analysis offers several alternative marketing strategies. It is, thus, unfortunate that so many companies regard cost-cutting exercises as divorced from marketing decisions. Particular care must always be exercised to ensure that the customers' view of cost-reduction outcomes agree with those of the manufacturer. Many years ago, Symbol Biscuits (then an independent company) decided to improve the quality of its biscuits by a system of central pumping of pure animal fats to all products. Moreover, this could be done at a significant saving over the older system of different fats for different products. Unfortunately, consumers were 'trained' to like vegetable fats, which was what the competition offered, and the decline in sales of the more popular lines vastly offset the anticipated economies.

The moral is clear – there are two roles for the marketing department in all cost-reduction exercises:

1   To ensure that the customer's concept of standards is maintained (that is, products provide the same mix of 'satisfactions' as they formerly did).
2   To consider whether the changes offer new marketing strategies or tactics.

In other words, in the ideal situation volume and profit trends should be considered together.

ALTERNATIVE SHAPES

The dangers of this concept have already been indicated. A classic example occurred when I spent a couple of days with the sales force of a leading UK company and we went through the six questions and the life-cycle concept. Unfortunately, time was too short to do full justice to the life-cycle. In the syndicate exercises that followed, the consensus of opinion was that four products were in such a state of decline that they should be abandoned; two of them were the company's biggest selling lines. Now it is not inconceivable that they could have been right. In fact, what had happened was that their product field had been heavily hit by Customs and Excise Duty increases. The prospect was well-known and there had been heavy stocking-up at both retail and personal levels. The size and the rapidity of the decline convinced the sales force that these products would not pick up again. This example highlights two things:

106

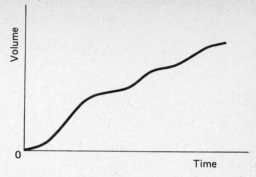

Figure 11 *Natural re-cycle*

1 The concept shows what might happen if you do nothing. (The following day, the sales force were shown what the company intended to do about it – and they were very successful.)

2 The conventional smoothed shape conceals short-term movements which can be misleading if they are unexplained.

This second factor is important and largely unremarked upon in standard texts; it is especially important in industrial and semi-industrial markets, where quite different shapes of curve are encountered and over a sufficient time-span to convince one that a new stage has been reached from which there is no escape. Not all the examples are industrial but that is where the problems are usually greatest.

NATURAL RE-CYCLE

This is shown in Figure 11. The product seems to have been enjoying a perfectly conventional cycle and has begun to show signs of tailing off, when suddenly, and without any impetus from the manufacturer, sales take off again and repeat the early shape. Usually, the later phases are smaller versions of the first; sometimes they are much larger. It all depends on how right the manufacturer was in positioning his product in the first place compared with what the customer wants to use it for. This is a characteristic of markets where future growth depends on finding new applications. Any market for systems is a good example. Computers were extensively used in the first instance for such tasks as payroll and invoicing. Then came sales records and analysis and it quickly became apparent that combining sales orders, records and invoices was leading to the need for a total information system. Carbonless papers have experienced a natural re-cycle growth curve as customers have discovered new uses, not

107

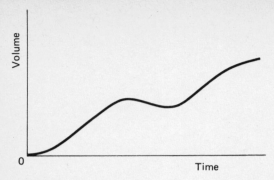

Figure 12 *'Humpback' cycle*

necessarily ahead of the suppliers but in a different order of priority.

To guard against the dangers of anticipating a decline that may not be coming, close contact must be kept with customers and all new uses rapidly communicated back to Head Office so that they may be assessed and promoted if worthwhile. Similarly, newly arising needs from customers should be analysed in terms of the capacity of present products or services to meet them, rather than automatically assuming that a new product is required.

THE HUMPBACK

This one can be even more misleading for it actually seems to go into decline before staging an apparently remarkable recovery (see Figure 12). This situation arises most often in industrial markets with new processes and materials. Buyers often place trial orders. Perhaps the use of the new product will be confined to one section of a plant. For this reason, the order may last a long while; in the meantime, the buyer goes on placing larger and regular orders of the item meant to be replaced. What is happening, of course, is that users are gaining experience and evaluating the product. Until they have completed their trials and formed opinions which probably have to be confirmed by the DMU, no further orders will follow. When everything is fine and approved, the product takes off. Some trialists will drop out; others will replace them.

There is a very close parallel in consumer markets. We referred earlier to the problem of the experimenters who try everything. There is a well-known generalization in new product launches in high-frequency-of-purchase markets that follow-up sales tend to average around 65 per cent of peak sales. This is an average of the number of once-only buyers likely to be present in the peak levels attained in a

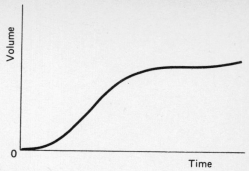

Figure 13 *Plateau cycle*

test situation. One might expect that the follow-up 65 per cent level would be flat. In high-frequency markets, it is the amount used that dictates the slope of the curve, not the number of buyers: remember that those who dropped out were once-only buyers.

We shall look more closely at problems of estimating one's position in a life-cycle a little later in this chapter. However, it should be clear that one must maintain close relations with customers whilst trials are going on if a false position is not to be assumed. Additionally, the reality of any down-turn must be assessed and a business judgement made as to whether it will continue or be a short-term phenomenon.

THE PLATEAU

The title is self-explanatory even without Figure 13. One aspect worth noting in the diagram is the way this particular plateau has a slight up-slope to it. This is an aspect of real life that is easily ignored; in most markets stability means growth in line with the economy. It is actually arguable that quite a sharp rise is needed annually to keep pace with inflation and anything less implies a real loss.

The plateau normally arises in situations where nothing better is available. The very flat life-curves of energy products (wood, coal, horse power) are due to this factor. The obverse side of this pleasant long life is the possibility of rapid replacement when an acceptable substitute is found. Interestingly, when one is announced, it tends to have a humpback shape and the sudden upsurge corresponds with a dramatic fall in the product being replaced. It is by no means uncommon for the decline stage of a plateau product to be sheer. That can be particularly unpleasant for those unable to change their product – many plateau products are commmodities and raw

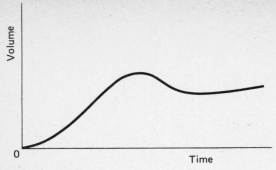

Figure 14 *'Rampart' cycle*

materials and the majority of the producing countries involved do not have resources of the replacement.

Figure 14 shows a life-cycle that seems to fall between a humpback and a plateau. It also appears to have something of the running level of consumer sales after dispensing with the once-only buyers.

In fact, it is almost two life-curves in one: the first for major markets and the second for subsidiary ones. What it shows is that there are still sectors of the market where the product is preferred but the main markets have gone. Supplying the secondary ones is possibly still profitable and it is often profitable enough to attract newcomers, especially if they no longer have to fight the big boys. A good example would be printing machinery. There has been a tremendous change from letterpress and silk-screen printing to offset and web-offset. The curve in Figure 14 could well represent the market for letterpress machinery. The really big suppliers of the old days are no longer solely committed to one form of printing – they are looking to the bigger print companies and their use of the newer methods. This actually produces an opportunity for smaller scales of enterprise to manufacture for those specialist printers who confine their work to letterpress (still the best method for certain jobs under particular conditions) and for replacements and spares for the companies who perhaps feel it is too late and too expensive for them to change.

Markets do not always die in one fell swoop; they often change their whole nature and scale. The same effect can often be created by design by arresting a decline by promoting new uses that may appeal to a minority of users but which may increase their usage.

110

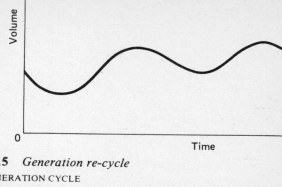

Figure 15 *Generation re-cycle*

THE GENERATION CYCLE

This is one which interests me particularly for it has been ignored in other texts and, indeed, specifically denied in some American ones. Yet it undoubtedly exists. Figure 15 shows a stylized example; what it cannot very realistically do is indicate the time scale. Hence the description 'generation cycle'.

This kind of cycle arises from cyclical changes in taste and frequently contains a considerable amount of rebellion against the past. For example, if one were to draw a perfectly conventional life-cycle curve for tea in the UK, the shape would fit the market profile for almost any developed tea market in the world. The positions would change, however. Writing in the 1980s, the UK would be just beyond saturation and with a clear indication of decline. Australia would be well into decline. France would show encouraging growth turning to an early maturity as competition from herbal teas ('infusions') increased. The USA is well into the growth stage. The interesting thing is that in most of these markets, coffee is going the other way and represents almost a mirror image. (In the USA, although coffee is the mirror image of tea, coffee is a hot drink whilst tea is basically consumed as an iced one; this is its competitive strength.)

What is far more interesting in some of the cases is that the present cycles are merely repetitions of what has gone before. The UK was a coffee-drinking country; so strong did the habit become that drinking coffee in public places was banned because of the interference it caused with the nation's business. The USA was a tea-drinking country (remember Boston?) which has now reverted. The resurgence of what might almost be called the traditional beverages of two countries has been the result of fundamental changes of habit among

111

young people. By and large, in both countries, it is the older people who have not changed; the younger who have. As one with a long-term involvement in both tea (world-wide) and coffee (UK and USA), it has been interesting in both cases to observe the young expressing preference for a drink not very often served at home, buying it when out, serving it to young friends, their mothers believing it the right thing to serve to young people and, finally and inevitably, serving it themselves as first choice beverage when they have homes and families of their own.

Fashions, we noted earlier, come back too. Builders who once tore out the fitted cupboards of yesterday are now busy building them back; a whole industry of whitewood do-it-yourself self-assembly kitchen and bedroom furniture is testimony to a fundamental taste change. Four-poster beds are the current height of fashion; divans are for those furnishing deliberately in 1930s style. Earrings are in for men; granny prints for ladies' dresses. All these are consumer items. The more considered the item, the less room there is for the dictates of fashion or the sheer aspect of rebellion. Where such swingeing changes do happen in non-consumer markets they occur because new uses have been found, new reasons for using have been discovered (such as health, ecology), or simply because supplies of the replacement have run out or are temporarily in short supply. There was, for example, a sudden upsurge in demand for 'old-fashioned' Kraft paper for outer protection of products, during the petrol crisis of 1974, from all those who had switched to shrink-wrap packing using Saran Wrap, a product relying heavily on the availability of oil.

The interesting question which emerges from looking at these alternative shapes that crop up from time to time is how they might be anticipated and whether such changes can be promoted. In the last two sections of this chapter we shall look at what action might be taken to prolong the life of a product and how one can best attempt to estimate the position of a market or a product within a market on its life-cycle curve.

5.2 Re-cycling products to prolong life

The product life-cycle, we saw earlier, is what might happen if nothing is done to prevent it. Often, a great deal can be done and it appears as if the product goes on increasing its sale for ever. At other times, the market forces are altogether too strong for any successful remedial action to be taken. Products like Lyons' Individual Fruit Pies seem to have successfully withstood the ravages of time; in fact, they have changed dramatically over the years. The flavours have changed, the ingredients have been altered and the shape has gone from round to square and back to round. Along with changes in packaging and new advertising appeals, these efforts have all been aimed at giving a new impetus to sales to offset many of the characteristics (especially boredom) which afflict buyers in the maturity phases of life-cycles. Liquid coffee, on the other hand, seems to be a market capable of withstanding all attempts to re-cycle it. It is, moreover, a classic example of the creation of a life-cycle in a reasonably short period.

Before the Second World War, liquid coffee (or coffee essence), sold in bottles, represented by far the greatest volume of coffee consumed in the UK (measured in actual cups consumed). After the end of the war, that situation continued for a few years and then the unmistakable signs began to appear. The younger housewives were turning to the new instant coffees with bland flavours particularly appealing to those brought up on tea. Since then, hardly any significant quantity of new young buyers has come into that market. As the average age gets older, so inevitably some die, others fall out and no-one comes forward to replace them. Liquid coffee is a case where tastes and what might be termed fashion (coffee essence lacks a modern image) appear to be too firmly against the product.

Planned re-cycling follows the example of Lyons' Individual Fruit Pies. Figure 16 shows how such an attempt might appear if successful.

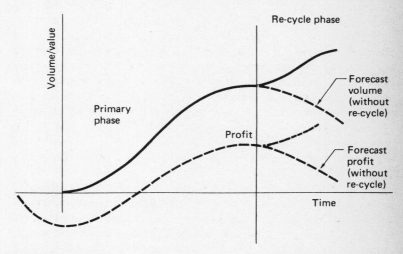

Figure 16   *Policy re-cycle*

113

The natural growth curve of the first cycle is called the primary phase; this is what happens as a result of the initial positioning of the product and the efforts put behind it. There are many ways a re-cycle may be achieved. Product improvement is one of the obvious ones. Changes in promotional appeals may be less obvious but can account for really dramatic changes. Oxo had been at the plateau stage of its cycle for many years. (Indeed, the three most obvious 'humps' in an otherwise flat sales graph correspond to the two World Wars and the Depression. At one stage, it appeared that only starting another war could move sales.) A new advertising agency started looking hard at the situation and came up wih two major strategic planks. One was whole-hearted concentration on using Oxo for gravy-making (instead of promoting Oxo as a nutritious hot drink) and the other was to emphasize the role that Oxo could play in giving flavour to cheaper cuts of meat. It was reasoned that in times of hardship – the times when sales had risen of their own volition – housewives were using Oxo almost as a meat substitute. The only thing that was changed was the product positioning. Advertising set out to teach young housewives how to make use of cheaper cuts of meat to make attractive, warming and healthy meals; the slogan 'Oxo gives a meal man appeal' became the theme of one of the most famous and longest-running television commercials in advertising history (the 'Katie' series). Subsequently, as even that re-cycle began to lose steam, other means were used to jack up a falling sales curve. Flavoured Oxo ('Chicken' and 'Curry') were launched and a 'super', even meatier, variety ('Golden Oxo') was added. Product variants provided not only a degree of excitement to a market in danger of becoming blasé, they also provided the means of achieving new aspirations among those whose cooking habits had been changed by the message of the theme advertising. Eventually, even 'Katie' gave way to new advertising appeals.

You can find yourself in a re-cycle purely by chance. Often, it is by grace of a competitor who has made a mistake and left the field to you. Sometimes, especially in smaller markets, a new form of competition can give an impetus to the older market. The heavy promotion behind lawnmowers using the hover principle gave a big boost to all forms of lawnmower. Users of hand mowers wanted to look at the new machinery. Many found that the new mower was not suitable for their problem; many found that the lack of roller did not give the familiar swathed pattern of the traditional English garden and turned to a petrol mower. Even more decided that it was time they bought a new mower in any case – even a hand one. And the phenomenon of the two-mower family (ostensibly for different purposes) came about. A major attack by Qualcast on the hover market (using the advertising slogan 'It's more bovver with a hover') created a reverse situation, with owners of hover mowers adding a cylinder mower to their stable.

Many companies have benefited from another's action; even more might have done so (or done better) had they been able to identify more rapidly with what was happening and had they treated the preliminary stages of the re-cycle (even though not of their making) just as they would the introductory stage of a new product.

Do not confuse new products and re-cycles, although it is easy to do. A re-cycle for a brand is a change of formula, price, distribution, availability and/or market position. Re-cycling company profits when they near the peak of a cycle may require moving into completely new areas of business. We shall see later that it is always sound advice to stay close to businesses that are well-known and understood. Thus, it always makes sense to consider what might be done to regenerate profits from existing brands before moving into new fields where the company lacks experience. Often both go together and the marginally improved profits of a revitalized product can often be enough to offset the investment stages of completely new items and companies.

5.3 Finding out where you are

The great problem with the life-cycle concept is the difficulty of correctly gauging whereabouts a particular company or product is on its cycle in time to do anything about it. Success and failure in business are difficult to identify when they are happening. They are essentially comparative terms: business can be good compared with last year and lousy measured against the year before. Success is often like good health: you don't know you've got it until you lose it. There are also the problems that were illustrated by the alternative shapes that crop up from time to time. The biggest problem, however, is the almost natural tendency to treat a life-cycle profile like any other sales curve and attempt to make conventional sales forecasts. With a life-cycle, it is necessary to go back further, to consider the sound marketing reasons that put you where you were, and what has got you to where you are now, and to consider if those factors can be changed to your advantage. From the welter of evidence that is likely to be available, the prime task is to isolate the most important causal trends.

In this sense, actual sales history is only the symptom; the reasons for the malaise have to be found. The key area is always going to be buyer behaviour. Look for possible reasons for any changes. What could cause them to buy less than they did?

1 *Do they no longer like the product or service?* What do you know about present opinions? Have any new competitors, direct or indirect, appeared on the market? What other factors might affect consumer habits in your market (legal, interest rates, hire purchase, different machinery etc.)?

2 *Has the nature of the consumer changed?* Are they aging? Are all your customers long-standing loyal ones with few new buyers coming into the market? Is there a real danger that the market may simply die on you for lack of customers of this type? Has the composition of buyers changed in any other way? Has the socio-economic structure changed? Has the size of company buying altered? Do customers still come from the same areas? If not, why not; what has happened to change things? Do you have to accept those changes as inevitable?

3 *Is it harder for customers to get your product?* Are fewer shops or agents handling your lines? Where and why? Have stock levels changed? Have the terms of business made it more difficult for customers to buy, or purchase in the former quantities?

4 *Are buyers using as much and as frequently?* What has happened to the frequency of buying and the regularity of use? What has happened to the size of the average order – from the final end-user, to intermediaries in the distribution network?

5 *What has happened to your competitors, direct and indirect, in similar areas?* Does this explain your trend? Can anything be learned from them?

A simple sales forecast can be very wrong for predicting the future curve of a life-cycle. Sales forecasts rely heavily on extrapolations from the past. The past is too heavily weighted to events that are not likely to recur. If more weight is given to the most recent events, there is the danger that insufficient regard will be given to factors which might be capable of reversing the trend. There is also the acute danger of not using a long enough period to avoid the risk of mis-reading one of the alternative shapes. It is the reasons for sales, the break-down of customers by relevant characteristics and the knowledge of their buying habits and the uses they make of the goods or services they buy that allow intelligent action to be taken. If this section has done no more than impress on businessmen the crucial need for adequate customer records, it will have achieved a great deal. Even among those who do take some notice of the life-cycle concept, there is a tendency to read it like a sales graph and react to the immediate phase without understanding the underlying reasons for getting there. There is also a good deal of neglect of any consideration of what the competitor might do. It is really remarkable how many otherwise detailed marketing plans make the glib assumption that competition is willing to sit back and be hammered and that most of them lack the know-how and guile of the planning company who, thereby, can expect a clear run at the market.

Because, in most markets, buyers enter at different times, even a market which fails because people buy no more than once can exhibit all the classic signs of the life-cycle and fool many in the market that they are in the growth stages when, in fact, they have almost reached saturation. If the same companies had looked at customers they would have realized that they were not repeating; they were selling to customers who weren't coming back. Identification of any of the stages of the life-cycle, whether for a market, a product field within that market, or a brand within the product field, is far more precise when considering the questions outlined in this section; look at who is buying, when, how often, where, what they are using the product or service for and why from you? In other words, use the six questions in a slightly different, rather sharper, context and you stand a very much better chance of not only knowing where you are but also why you are in that position. Then you are in command of the situation and can take positive action.

5.4 Summary

The life-cycle concept is a generalization that describes what happens to a market when no positive steps are taken to change direction. Certain market conditions can give rise to other shapes and a general study of all the possibilities throws considerable weight behind knowing your market well enough to be able to take positive steps to control the destiny of your goods and services. Deliberate re-cycling of a product – by improvements to the basic satisfactions offered, by price changes or by changes in market position – can give new life to a flagging sales curve. However, it can be fatal to treat the life-cycle as simply another sales curve to be projected in the same way as a sales forecast. An understanding of the underlying buying behaviour which has led to the present picture is a far more positive way of identifying where one's product stands on its relevant life-cycle.

The word 'relevant' is a reminder that the life-cycle concept must always be considered in the light of the six-question analysis and the use of the six questions, suitably sharpened to deal with aspects of buying behaviour, will provide a better chance of reaching the right conclusions.

5.5 Checklist

1   Businesses are like people; they gestate, are born, grow – rapidly at first, then more slowly – reach a stage of maturity, go into decline and finally die. These stages describe the 'life-cycle' concept.

2   Two types of life-cycle are recognized:
   a   The product life-cycle that describes an individual product or brand.
   b   The demand life-cycle that describes a market.

3   The life-cycle concept uses a generalized shape and describes what will happen, eventually, to any market *unless steps are taken to change the situation.*

4   In the introductory stage, probable buyers are the experimenters and the fashion leaders. Creating awareness of the new product or service will be the major aim, and resulting promotional costs will be high per unit sold. Depending upon market conditions, there may be a choice between launching at a high price to ensure rapid profitability, or at a low price to ensure rapid penetration and a quicker pay-back of initial investment costs (as well as possibly deterring new entrants).

5   The growth stage attracts the trend-setters and promotion aims more at comprehension – of product qualities, uses, applications, etc. Prices may be flexible, depending on the launch decision. If a high price was set, this may be lowered to deter or attack newcomers. If already low, promotional prices will be used rather than a further reduction in nominal price.

6   Maturity can be very short or very lengthy. In general, the longer it is, the more changes in the profit cycle are likely. Volume is usually easier to hold static than are profits (as costs rise). By now, all the likely 'followers' will have been attracted into the market. Promotional costs should be at the optimum and advertising will concentrate on convincing users of the wisdom of their choice (and thus resisting the blandishments of compe-

titive advertising and promotion). By now, a stable price policy (and the relation between list prices and promotional prices) should have been established.

7   Decline brings the options of holding the decline to that of the market as a whole, trying to out-pace the market by declining more slowly, or getting out. A policy of 'milking' is usually the most profitable. This is done by reducing the costs of selling to the minimum. The real 'nostalgics' will make efforts to continue to buy and this often maintains a low level of profitability for longer than anticipated when the strategy is set.

8   Products may be sold even though in marked decline, providing they continue to make a significant contribution to company overheads. This may become especially significant when a more profitable product shares resources with one in decline.

9   Each product should be examined from the standpoints of its own product life-cycle and the demand life-cycle for the market or product category in which it sells. Different products have different shapes within the overall demand life-cycle. It therefore becomes important to decide whether the demand cycle influences the individual product shapes or if it is the other way round. Products that follow fashion or technological trends tend, as a rule, to be influenced by the demand cycle. However, even these can be influenced by a major, late introduction. One suspects that the entry of IBM into the personal computer market will become a classic in this respect.

10 Five alternative shapes of demand cycles were identified (Figures 11 to 15). These occur more frequently, but not exclusively, in industrial markets. Perhaps the most dangerous, because of the possibility of complacency, is that described as the 'plateau' shape. It is perhaps safer to regard a plateau as a sign that customers cannot find anything better . . . but if they do they will change to it. *+ rapidly*

11 Ideally, the decline stage will be prevented by re-cycling the product; that is, revamping it in such a way that new and additional customer benefits are perceived and volume and profit increased. Obviously, this is not always possible and a company will then be forced to consider completely new products with growth phases that offset the decline stages of older products.

portfolio management.

12 The profit cycle can be considered separately from the demand curve, and it is often better to attack the profit curve rather than attempt to increase profits from volume efforts. There is usually a cost associated with attacking volume. However, it is dangerous to consider profit without thinking of what alternative marketing strategies and tactics might be appropriate.

13 Of particular importance is to measure very carefully whether customers' views of value analysis changes agree with your own. The standards of judgement applied are very often markedly different.

14 It is not easy to recognize the shape of a life-cycle before you have passed a turning point. Rather than look at a life-cycle curve like a normal sales graph, it is better to look at the underlying causes of the curve. What is happening to the number of buyers, the amount bought and the frequency of purchase? For many companies, the age of the buyer will also be important. If older buyers who die off are not replaced by younger buyers, sales will fall. It isn't necessary to wait until they die to find out. When the average age of the Guinness drinker was recognized to be 68, it didn't take much thought to realize how many would be left in 20 years' time! The same considerations can be applied to numbers of purchasers, average quantity bought and changes in frequency. If there are fewer buyers, sales will fall unless they buy more at a time or the same amount more often.

15 Although often denied, each denial adds emphasis to the value of the life-cycle concept and can be said to prove its existence. Of all the concepts in marketing, this one has the greatest amount of validation.

6

The Marketing Mix

It ain't what you do, it's the way that you do it.
That's what gets results.

Popular song of the 1940s

Although, in Chapter 2, we considered different types of marketing (consumer, industrial, service, etc.,) in reality there are probably more similarities than differences. After all, customer satisfaction is the key ingredient of all types of marketing. They all use the same basic tools, too. It is the number of those tools and the degree of emphasis with which they are applied that make the real differences. Even different companies in the same market may compete by using different techniques and in varying amounts. The way these techniques are put together into a whole and the amount of weight, together with the proportions of each to the other, are called 'the marketing mix'.

6.1 Definitions

The simplest definition of the marketing mix is 'the four Ps':

Product
Price
Place
Promotion

These are certainly the key elements for most companies and each is reasonably self-explanatory, with the possible exception of 'place'. That one word has to cover where the goods are made available, the channels through which they reach customers and intermediaries, and the physical methods by which they are delivered. Another objection is the omission of selling. Proponents of the four Ps explain that selling is part of the promotion of the goods or services.

The four Ps provide a simple and easily remembered definition but it does nothing to suggest the peculiar characteristics of the marketing

121

mix concept. Moreover, its omissions simply suggest longer and more complete lists. In fact, there is no general agreement on what should be included in such a list.

Although less memorable, a more accurate definition does not attempt to name the ingredients but refers to:

> **Those elements capable of manipulation and variation in order to improve the effectiveness of marketing programmes, the way in which they are planned and combined, their relative importance and the proportions of each used to produce a desired effect.**

Look at the key elements of that definition.

1 'Manipulation and variation' You can change the order of importance, vary the money spent, make short-term tactical changes or long-term strategic ones.
2 'To improve effectiveness' Each company should strive to discover its optimum mix, which might be defined, simply, as the least amount of money and effort needed to achieve profit objectives.
3 'Planned and combined' Few of the mix items are complete substitutes, thus how they are used together is all-important.
4 'Relative importance' This can be divided into the long-term and the short-term. For example, in the long-term, price activity may play no part. However, in the short-term, tactical bursts of promotion may be more important than, say, advertising.
5 'Proportions . . . to produce a desired effect' This is where the differences between competitive companies really show. Usually, the major differences between different types of marketing are explained by the fact that certain elements of the marketing mix are not available, not appropriate or simply don't work. Even within the same industry, these conditions may apply, reflecting the different strategies chosen by competing companies.

6.2 The elements

It should be obvious that even the simplest list (the four Ps) is capable of enormous expansion. 'Price', for example, could include credit terms, cash discounts, prompt payment allowances, etc. What is perhaps less obvious is the inclusion in many lists of items like marketing research and product development. In an attempt to overcome the difficulties of what to include, I have divided the longest lists into three:

1 Direct   2 Ancillary   3 Indirect.

The 'direct' category includes all those items that I believe fit the definition completely.'Ancillary' items (like discounts, etc.) are assumed to be included in the 'direct' ones. Finally, the 'indirect' items are the ones which, used properly, lead to decisions about the marketing mix. Market research, for example, is useless on its own; it is the *use* to which it is put that matters.The same is true of new product development, long range planning, and research and development – three items quite commonly included in longer lists.

Thus, in the list that follows, we will only consider items that could be defined as 'direct'. We will assume that all the relevant 'ancillary' elements are subsumed under the appropriate 'direct' heading. 'Indirect' elements would be used to set strategies, decide tactics or redefine tactics already in use, and lead to changes in the way 'direct' mix elements are applied.

PRODUCT AND PRODUCT PLANNING
The actual product or service is the 'direct', variable element (such as different performance factors, different target market sectors, etc.). 'Indirect' elements (like market research and research and development help specify the product performance and the appropriate target markets.

Key factors under this heading will be identifying, anticipating and satisfying demand; the use of the six questions; portfolio analysis; naming decisions, etc.

PRICING
Overall pricing strategy (premium, middle of the market, low; stable or flexible; one price or price differentiation?). What does 'price' include (terms, discounts, deals, etc.)? Trade margins (conventional or new?).

SALES CHANNELS
Direct or indirect? How many levels (single intermediary – e.g. distributor – or several – e.g. wholesaler, retailers)? Selection of channel members (qualifications; purchase/service levels; exclusive, franchised, open to all?).

PHYSICAL DISTRIBUTION
Methods; schedules; stock-holding policy (how much/where?). Customer satisfaction levels.

PERSONAL SELLING

What is the sales force to do (take orders, deliver, influence orders)? How many salesmen? What form of management control? How will the sales force be paid (salary only, commission only, salary plus commission)?

ADVERTISING

How much? To whom? How often? Trade, customer, end-user? Dealer/distributor support. Media. Objectives. Relationship to other promotional methods and to personal selling?

PROMOTIONS

Role in the mix. Relation to advertising and personal selling. Customer, end-user, trade? Objectives (e.g. loyalty, trial, stocking, moving stocks). Frequency (continuous, regular, spasmodic, as the occasion demands?). Offence or defence?

PACKAGING AND DISPLAY

Practical aspects (protection, convenience, identification). Design and materials. Trade, end-user. Role and importance.

SERVICE LEVELS

How important? (The more similar the product, the more important service is likely to be – more important with technically complex products). To whom? By whom? Where (customer location, factory, service depot)? Time taken – pre-sales, during installation, after sales? Service on spares – who pays? (Full cost, free, subsidized?)

PUBLIC RELATIONS

Role and importance. Definition of the 'publics' to be serviced (customers, trade, shareholders, City institutions, workforce?). Activities and levels (depends on the answer to the 'publics' question). Timing and frequency. Reporting levels.

One may well question the separation of advertising, promotion and public relations, especially if yours is a company (or a college) that prefers the word 'Publicity' to 'Promotion' in the four Ps. Leaving public relations to last may also seem questionable. Advertising, promotion and public relations are separated here because they are treated that way by perhaps the majority of companies. Vast numbers of companies who, for very good reasons, find media advertising inappropriate or ineffective still rely heavily on press releases to influence customers, and trade promotions to influence stockists. As for public relations, one ought to make a distinction between product and corporate PR. The first is clearly a form of promotional publicity and obviously a 'direct' element. Corporate PR has more in common with the 'indirect' elements. I have put PR last because it is the one area where product and corporate aims are frequently confused, usually to the detriment of the product requirements.

6.3 Why mixes vary

Different businesses and different companies enjoy different marketing mixes for three reasons:

1 Market
2 Company
3 Personal.

Ideally, mix decisions are *defined* by market reasons (who buys, where, how often, through what channels; competition – direct and indirect; threat of new entrants) and are *conditioned* by company ones (strengths and weaknesses; resources; traditions and conventions; attitudes).Unfortunately, personal reasons often prevail.

There are three particular personal reasons that emerge over and over again:

1 Managerial background, training and discipline. (For example, a manager with a financial background may distrust advertising because of the difficulties of predicting results.)
2 Beliefs about the effectiveness of mix ingredients. (Salesmen often prefer to reduce prices or use give-aways rather than follow-up media advertising.)
3 Attitudes to change and risk (often prefaced by statements like 'In an old-established business like ours . . .'. 'That hasn't been done in this industry for the last . . .'. 'It might work for soap powders . . .').

6.4 Typical mixes

Figure 17 shows typical marketing mixes for six different types of business. For each, it considers whether each possible element is of high, medium or low importance. You will notice that the diagram doesn't quite tie up with the list of 'direct' elements in Section 6.2. An

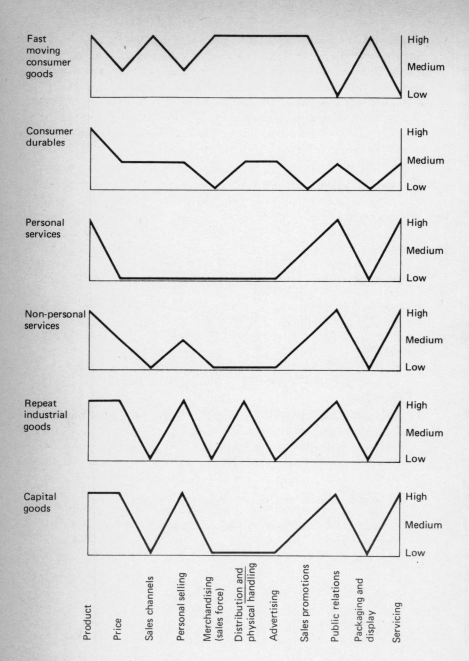

Figure 17 *Typical marketing mix patterns by industry type*

extra item, 'Merchandising', has been added. Strictly speaking, this is an 'ancillary' item (ancillary to personal selling), but it is such an important element in the mix of fast-moving consumer goods (FMCG) that the diagram would be quite misleading without it. 'Personal selling' is not highly important in the FMCG category but 'merchandising' is, and that is what explains the often very large sales forces employed in companies in that sector. The diagram is largely self-explanatory. A few words of explanation are necessary for a few items.

1   Sales channels are of high importance only in the FMCG category. They are of medium importance to consumer durables only because that heading covers a wide range of goods which may vary from those for which sales channel decisions are of prime importance to those which are supplied direct to end-users and thus do not need other channels. Although shown as low for personal services, many such services are, of course, provided in retail outlets.

2   Personal selling is highest where sales are direct from manufacturer to customer. Again, personal services are the exception. Suppliers of those services cannot create the *need*; the customer normally seeks out the provider of the service when he or she needs it.

3   Physical distribution is the more important, the more often the product is purchased and the more sales channels it has to pass through.

4   Although packaging and display rate highly only for FMCGs, this is an area where many industrial companies have been able to produce significant benefits by packaging and clever identification (such as colour coding for drugs in hospitals).

6.5   Manipulating the mix

According to our definition, the ability to vary the mix is the prime function. There are three ways the mix might be manipulated and each is expressed in relation to the kind of shape outlined in Figure 17.

1   Choose a different shape from your competitors. If you do this, it must not be a case of difference for difference's sake; it must be relevant in a way which benefits your customers. In long-established markets with traditional patterns, it may be better to stick with convention.

2   Keep to the same shape but do better. Again, the improvements must be in areas your customers rate highly. This usually means

that you have to try to improve in an area where your competitors already do well. If you are behind in this aspect, this is where you *must* improve.

3. Keep to the main shape but make changes to specific elements. If sales channels are of great importance, are there new ways of getting your products to your prospects? Think of the way you buy things now compared with 10 and 20 years ago and you will realize how even strongly-entrenched conventions can be attacked.

Remember, the key to successfully manipulating the marketing mix to improve profitability is to improve in areas that will produce significant, recognizable benefits to your customers, and to reduce or eliminate efforts that do not produce such benefits.

6.6. Summary

The marketing mix concept is the key to the profitable employment of the technique areas of marketing. It accounts for differences in the marketing tactics employed in different industries as well as those adopted by competitors in the same market. However, varying the mix will only be valuable if it results in significant customer benefits, improves the cost-effectiveness of supplying those benefits, or reduces or eliminates expenditure on activities that do not produce rewarding benefits.

6.7 Checklist

1 The simplest description of the 'marketing mix' is the four Ps: product, price, place and promotion.

2 A more meaningful definition refers to controllable and variable elements (without defining those elements) and the way they are combined and planned to produce desired results.

3 Opinions as to what elements should be included vary. It helps to classify them as:
   a Direct: the controllable, variable elements.
   b Ancillary: those that represent extensions of the first category (for example, discounting can be regarded as ancillary to pricing).
   c Indirect: elements which are not really items in the marketing mix but whose use leads to decisions about the way the mix is assembled or varied.

4 Mixes vary for one or more of three reasons:
 a Market
 b Company
 c Personal

5 In an ideal world, personal reasons would be unimportant.

6 The marketing mix should be selected for market reasons but may have to be conditioned by company reasons (for example, strengths, weaknesses, abilities, resources).

7 Typical marketing mixes for a range of industries are shown in Figure 17. In each industry, a company's market mix may be manipulated by:
 a Choosing a different mix from competition.
 b Using a similar mix but performing better (in one or more areas).
 c Maintaining a similar mix but changing one or more elements.

8 Although we have considered only the elements that might be included, the amount of money put behind the use of particular resources, or the manpower devoted to others, can be decisive factors in selecting a successful marketing mix.

7
Where Shall We Go Next?

'Would you tell me, please, which way I ought to go
   from here?'
'That depends a good deal on where you want to get
   to,' said the Cat.
'I don't much care where . . .' said Alice.
'Then it doesn't matter which way you go' said the Cat.
                                              Lewis Carroll

Anyone who has stayed the course this far is presumably very
interested in where they go next. This chapter follows logically in
work sequence from the answers to the six questions. Discussion of
life-cycles formed a bridge and will clarify some of the statements that
have to be made in this chapter.

Practically, the very next step after completing the six questions is
to compare what is essentially a verbal description of opportunities
with an analysis of actual results and profitability. There are several
alternative conclusions that could emerge from such a study. Results
may be out of line with potential; this would force consideration of
whether the day-to-day figures had concealed the real movements in
the market or whether the results of the self-analysis had been
altogether too pessimistic. It is not unknown, as an earlier example
showed, for short-term events to cast too long a shadow on estimates
of the future. Revisions, in either direction, might be called for. From
a combination of the two kinds of analysis of the same goods or
services, a multi-product company will be able to produce a listing in
order of both present and potential importance, which will highlight
what kind of company it is now and provide strong hints at what kind
it could become in the future.

7.1 Straightforward products

Nothing in business is ever all that straightforward. Nevertheless,
some areas are simpler to examine and deal with than others. Two of

the five headings to be considered under this general topic are specifically related to the life-cycle; one may well be, although there could be other explanations; two are quite separate in this respect.

PRESENT PROFITMAKERS

These are the lines which, however they are measured, are current profit contributors. More than that, they have some clear and continuous history of profit behind them and they are short of the saturation point on their life-cycle. In all probability, candidates for this position will be towards the top of the growth phase and into maturity. It is difficult to be absolutely precise about the position on the cycle; in short-life products, a present profitmaker may only come about in the maturity phase; with a very long-life one, it could happen well down the growth phase. The important thing is that one feels safe with products put into this category. Efforts will be made to maximize market share and profits and maintain that healthy position for as long as possible. In all other respects, the analysis of the latter states of the cycle portrayed in Figure 9 will apply.

FUTURE PROFITMAKERS

This time we are looking at products that have earned their spurs, as it were, but have not yet sufficient track record as profit-earners to justify the highest ranking. Again, the length of the life-cycle will determine the actual stage on the curve where this phase begins and ends. However, it is most likely that it will commence into the growth phase. A look back at Figure 9 will show that a product is unlikely to have fully paid back past investment much before mid-way through the growth phase. To qualify for this second group of profit-earners, a brand must have demonstrated its ability to break out into the clear and have a sufficiently strong volume growth record to instil confidence in the continued growth that will bring forth the profits.

Together with the present profitmakers, this is where the company's immediate prosperity will come from.

PROFITABLE SPECIALS

Few companies can resist the temptation to move, at least marginally, away from their main stream of activity. Frequently, the use of common resources (and especially where common plant is used) can fool the company into thinking that it is still on the well-beaten path. For example, products like a very expensive blend of fine teas packed in small wooden chests for sale through a handful of stores and bought by a tiny number of discerning tea drinkers; life assurance offices which provide cover for ballet dancers' injuries; bolts in odd sizes (and, presumably, non-metric threads). To qualify, they should be low-risk by-products of main-stream activities. If the special blend of fine teas falls flat, the write-off of materials is unlikely to amount to much – the machine time released may well be easily absorbed by other blends but, even if it is not, the extra overheads will not be a crippling burden on other brands. These factors provide essential qualifications for inclusion in this category.

There is another highly desirable qualification. Worthwhile, profitable specials should earn an extra profit margin. Although it is always assumed that no special and additional efforts are being put behind these lines, in fact it is almost impossible to be sure. Someone's enthusiasm put them into the range in the first place and when that person is a senior manager, others may assume (and often rightly) that these lines are not to be deprived of attention. The actual time taken selling them can be much more than was ever anticipated and, thus, the real profit is much less than that assumed, especially if the time could have been used for other products. The oil companies are good examples of firms that have found the profitable specials taking up more and more of representatives' time. They started by providing items like stationery and overalls as an additional service to their site-owners. Over the years, the time spent on those items has grown to take up the greater proportion of many an oil representative's call-time. A safety margin is a good idea as a safeguard against the difficulty of correctly costing the resources employed, the 'nuisance value' often entailed and the dangers of misallocation of scarce resources.

PRIORITY DEVELOPMENT PRODUCTS

By the time a business has torn itself apart in the ways suggested, it may well begin to feel that it has not only been going in directions that are not as good as others it might have chosen, but also that its plans for future development have been on the wrong lines too. At this point, it should look very closely at products in the pipeline. On the one hand, there is the danger of wasting investments of time, resources and money. On the other, is the possibility that continuing the developments may lead to new problems later. In between is the possibility that the turn-round time to the 'new' company it wants to become is too long to be covered adequately by the profits of present products. The latter is a high probability in most companies and a good case for pushing ahead with priority projects. This may be the

132

time to upgrade some development items in line with the new directions emerging from the marketing re-examination.

It is, of course, assumed that any project that has got this far along the line has been adequately screened and researched and all the bugs have been ironed out. It has no place in the line-up if this is not so.

FAILURES

It may seem strange to regard a failure as a straightforward product. But if it has taken this long to identify the line as an irredeemable failure, then it really is time that positive action was taken.

Businessmen fear failure. So much so, that they are often reluctant to admit it even to themselves. Yet business history is full of disasters compounded by that very action and successes due to the rapid excision of problems. Tesco Supermarkets is a very good example of the latter. A store that doesn't come up to target within a (short) defined trading period is mercilessly closed. How many people remember the stores that closed after six weeks – how many more remark on the stores from other groups that are near-empty most days of the week? There is a lesson in that.

Associated with the fear of failure is a worry about loss of face that even the Chinese would regard as excessive. Courageous action never lost face; what can be disastrous is when your customer recognizes before you admit it that your line is a failure. This is never more true than with items selling through retail stores, wholesalers and distributors. Nothing disturbs them more (for they live by stock-turn) than 'sleepers' – lines that just sit on their shelves and never move. Rapid action often earns the opportunity of going back to the same store or depot with an improved version and getting a fair chance on the shelves again. Companies with such a reputation find the launching of new products easier; the ones whose new products are greeted with questions about what is to be removed from the shelf to make room are not the ones with a reputation for courage.

Good money can easily be poured in after bad and there is a strong case for withdrawing unprofitable lines as early as possible – once one is certain that nothing can be done to effectively redeem them. However, as we shall see later, there may be circumstances where it can make some degree of sense to maintain an unprofitable line whilst, as we saw in the first section of this chapter, it may be necessary to retain products for what they contribute to general overheads until other lines come along to replace their contribution. Thus, the only real safeguard is to have sufficient new sources of profit at various stages of both development and life-cycle to make it

133

possible to make swift excisions when and where these are necessary.

At the beginning of this section on the straightforward group of products, the statement was made that two fitted the life-cycle curve readily, two did not and one might or might not. The present and future profitmakers obviously come right off the life-cycle curve. A failure might well do so, too. If it is too far down the curve to be re-cycled or if there is such a change in buyer characteristics and behaviour (age and usage patterns, for example), then it can be said that the concept explains the lack of profit. On the other hand, products can fail even within an otherwise healthy growth curve because of inherent lack of profitability, wrong pricing strategy, high cost of sales, rank bad management and so on. All these things can easily happen quite early in the life-cycle and it may be necessary to take the decision to withdraw even though the sales curve holds out promise of further growth. If a market is miscalculated right at the outset, it is all too easy to attain a position where volume can only be achieved at uneconomic prices. In recent years, many businessmen have come to refer to this as the plastic pipe syndrome. Plastic piping for the building trade found it could only achieve sales at prices that did not justify making the pipes. There are many other less-vaunted cases in British industry.

7.2 Problem products

The dividing line between the straightforward and the problem product is a thin one; the bottom of the 'straightforward' list begins to merge with the top of the 'problem children' category. A failure is obviously a problem that has been allowed to go too far. The specials can so easily become problems if they are not watched very closely. The four classifications in this sub-section represent some of the more difficult areas of business, and situations where effective marketing can really come into its own and provide the means of allaying the worst effects.

CONTRIBUTORS TO OVERHEADS

This situation can reach most disturbing proportions. As a marketing manager at Lyons, I once had to face the problem of a high volume brand which showed me a 'net contribution loss' of £9,000 – after contributing £600,000 towards the cost of a £1,000,000 sales force. That was by far the largest single contribution and could not have been replaced by other brands if the biggest one had been withdrawn.

Halving sales force costs would almost invariably have had dramatic effects on sales of other products handled by that sales force.

The problem usually comes about at the top of the life-cycle for a particular brand. It is a prime example of the case of diminishing profit returns even though sales volume may still be increasing for a time. Often it can be exacerbated by the efforts to stave off the phenomenon. In theory, sales will be pushed until the extra cost of generating them is exactly equal to the extra revenue gained (where marginal cost equals marginal revenue). Unfortunately, theories of equating marginal elements in business are exceptionally difficult to actually use. What is a marginal unit? A can of baked beans? A case? Where the units can be so small, it would seem better to regard the marginal unit as something like a day's production, but that quantity could be dispersed over a very wide area, nor can one accurately identify the marginal unit for one day's production when it will almost inevitably include replenishment stock for long-established customers. Of even more importance is the fact that the additional costs are incurred before it is recognized that they relate to the marginal sale. Because of the enormous difficulty of accurately forecasting the turning point of a sales curve, managers are reluctant to reduce, let alone abandon, effort too early. Even when decline sets in, the immediate reaction is likely to be to put extra effort behind the line to remove what everyone is usually convinced is nothing more than a temporary problem.

It is not easy to overcome this stage; the chances depend on whether it is the beginning of long-term secular decline or simply the result of over-reaching in the market. There is normally a strong case for regarding it as the latter, at least initially. Deliberately pruning low volume and low frequency customers is often the way to reduce the cost elements and achieve a higher profit per unit, albeit from lower total sales. Possibly a contributor to the problem is the fact that promotional costs have become too high. Dropping back to a previously acceptable level, probably associated with a lower, but more profitable, level of sale will often solve the problem. In the example taken from Lyons, the solution was to stop trying so hard to achieve sales that had proved extremely expensive to gain. By doing that, sales fell back but the sales curve grew again from the lower base, more slowly and with lower final ambitions, but the problem was solved.

In many cases, however, and in every case of gathering momentum of the decline stage, the only real answer is to have products in each stage of the life-cycle (including products under development) so that each decline is offset by a new profitmaker replacing the contribution. For these are yesterday's profitmakers – a widely employed alternative description.

PATCHWORK PRODUCTS

In marketing, we are always looking for opportunities – not problems. A 'patchwork product' is one with nothing but problems and solving one is followed immediately by another, and another and so on. It is natural to worry about problems yet, so often, there is nothing that can be done about them or, alternatively, the cost is out of all proportion to the benefits. One major problem that every businessman in the UK has wrestled with in recent years is inflation. No government in the world has succeeded in solving that one, so no one business will have much chance. It is better to look for the opportunities within that situation. There are some. For example, a steady flow of new products is one very effective way of countering inflation; each new product is more in line with current conditions than the one before it. There is a tendency for inflation to give products relatively short but much more profitable life-cycles.

Perhaps the best way of describing the patchwork product is by analogy. It can be likened to a hole in a dyke; unfortunately, the trouble with this dyke is that the water pressure behind it is such that as fast as you block one exit point, another appears. The example I have always used is that of the punctured tyre, for it not only illustrates the situation but also helps prescribe the rules for distinguishing the problem that is amenable to solution.

Imagine that you go to your bicycle one day and discover that a tyre is flat. You pump it up but still it goes down. You take out the inner tube and immerse it in water but there is no sign of escaping air. You replace it, pump it up and everything seems to be fine. Next morning when you go to it, the tyre is flat again. A few mornings like that and, in disgust, you throw the inner tube in the dustbin and buy a new one. Along comes the dustman and sees what appears to be a good inner tube so he takes it home, puts it on his bike – and the tyre goes down. He immediately examines the valve rubber, finds there isn't one and replaces it at a minimal cost. For practically nothing, he has a sound inner tube.

This particular dustman is an honest man and he tells you of his good fortune – you have learned a lesson. Next time your tyre is flat, you replace the valve rubber, pump up the tyre – and it goes down. You've got a puncture. You mend it, put the tube back – and it goes down again. You have another, and another; not until you have spent a whole afternoon putting patch after patch on the tube do you realize that you have wasted an afternoon trying to repair a perished inner tube.

The key to this kind of problem is to identify the 'valve rubber' case from the 'perished inner tube'. If there is one single problem that, if you could solve it, could be turned into an opportunity, then – and only then – is it really worth tackling. One of the very best examples of this comes from the field of ladies' hairdressing. There were two major problems: inflation had made hairdressers realize that what they were really selling was time, and their price levels meant that they were inadequately rewarded for that scarce commodity whilst, at the same time, their clientele was getting steadily older. They had a classic life-cycle look about them, with profits falling well before peak volume, but a decline in sales also setting in.

Age was the fundamental problem. The older women were used to the low prices for the skilled services; hairdressers used to think that the basic cut and set had to be low in price or women would not come into the salon, where they might be persuaded to buy a more profitable service. However, young people were not going into salons; they wanted long, straight, natural styles that were totally foreign to those their parents came home from the salons with. The problem seemed insoluble. Fashion gave the answer. A few hairdressers began to offer precision cutting and blow-styling at what seemed to be outrageous prices. The fashion magazines took up the styles, the young people went to salons to ask for them and, to their surprise, were often turned away. The hairdressing trade, by and large, convinced itself for some time that it could not afford to offer blow-styling which was a time-consuming operation and for which they didn't have the staff.

To simplify a rather long story, blow-styling now accounts for the biggest single part of most hairdressers' trade, almost 50 per cent of total profits. Not only did the young come back but they came back with the realization that what they wanted took time and cost money. Young people have entirely different attitudes towards paying for time than their parents do. If you can remember a £1 haircut, it comes hard to pay £3. If the first price you pay is £3, it is not so unreasonable when that goes up to £5. Almost by accident, ladies' hairdressing had found the opportunity that sprang from their biggest problems. There were even significant spin-off benefits. For example, the answer to 'who will do it' turned out to be some of the more senior apprentices or even those whose skill with the scissors wasn't what they had hoped. However, the young people having their hair styled in this way *wanted* to believe that it was a highly skilled operation. The regard in which they held the local hairdresser, or a particular stylist, or the promoted junior, went up by leaps and bounds when they could get what they wanted at prices they expected to pay.

The acid test of any problem is: 'If I succeed in solving this one, will there be others? What sort of opportunity will the solution present me with? Can I be sure it will bring profit rather than possibly increase volume at the expense of profit?'

There are other considerations that can be used as additional checks to make sure that good money isn't going to be thrown after bad, in trying to improve a situation defined as a problem. The problem product should have:

1   An existing and sizeable volume of sales.
2   A high probability of exceptional benefits if the measures succeed.
3   Substantial growth opportunities.
4   A clearly defined problem.
5   One that is relatively easy to correct.
6   Possibilities of high returns on low risk.

Where all these things come together and one is sure that the defined problem is one that is either depriving the product of immediate potential or threatening to reduce its future potential, then the problem is probably one that will repay the efforts to correct it. In the majority of other cases, the efforts will not succeed and will simply use further resources that would be better employed behind other lines.

We shall find that marketing men are seeking opportunities in all areas of business activity and seeking to avoid problems altogether. Whenever, for example, the temptation exists to put extra promotion behind sales in a poor area, the question should always be posed as to whether there is still further potential in good areas that deserves backing first. If that way of thinking is applied to all cases of competing uses of scarce resources in the business, fewer patchwork products will be created.

UNNECESSARY, UNPROFITABLE PRODUCTS
Make sure those two qualifying words go together. There are cases where it is necessary, if only in the short run, to be unprofitable in certain areas. When Gillette first gave away razors in order to sell the blades which would obviously be the bigger long-term market, they were dealing in a necessary, unprofitable product. Looked at in that way first, the whole concept becomes clearer. When a pharmaceutical

company is selling one item in a range of treatments at a loss, it isn't doing so in order to set the price of others in the range, but it is doing it to hold customers. This is a field where it is frequently necessary to provide a whole range of treatments or equipment, and examine the profitability of the range as a whole, even where some items may be unprofitable. Service industries, too, often find it necessary to provide 'extras' in order to both obtain and retain customers.

All this is fine, so long as the situation is watched continuously and carefully. There is a tendency for the eye to be taken off the ball long enough for the loss to escalate beyond reason. There is a similar tendency for other items to join the category without questioning whether it really is necessary to supply an unprofitable product. What this section tells you to be on the look-out for is the unnecessary, unprofitable product. These can easily happen. They frequently arise from the selling stage of a company's development, when the sales force starts saying things like: 'We already call on builders' merchants with nuts, bolts and screws; they also buy hammers, why don't we supply those, too?'. So it goes on until you have a range of products, some of which may be a long way from your basic concept of business and outside your real strengths and competence. There is a danger that another company will start at the other end of the scale and end up selling a similar range of products to your own. Now the buyer may look at the total range available from each of you and the price and service he gets from each. And he may conclude that, although your nuts and bolts are superior to the other guy's, there isn't enough in it to justify foregoing the lower prices and the higher discount across the range that your competitor offers.

In cases like this, salesmen frequently are convinced that products A, B and C will not sell unless you carry X, Y and Z. Events seldom bear this out and the type of exception was outlined at the beginning of this sub-section. It is also often argued that the situation portrayed above would happen in any case if the competitor extends his range to your end of the scale. It might, but it doesn't actually happen all that often without provocation. There are two acts of provocation in that example. The first is that to the other supplier you have attacked. The second, and the most important, is to the buyer: if your range hadn't matched so closely with your competitor's, he might never have made the comparison he now makes.

So many companies have been staggered at the ease with which they have been able to take unprofitable products off the market when necessity has forced them to practise range-reduction, that it obviously makes considerable sense to question whether any line should ever be allowed to fall into this category. The time to deal with it is before it has actually crossed the line from profit into loss. And since range-reduction is one of the classic starting points for profit improvement for ailing companies, one should question very carefully any suggested extension at any time.

INVESTMENTS IN MANAGEMENT EGO

Perhaps the most important single reason for 'specials' appearing in ranges is the whim of an individual manager. Many, many successful products have been created out of such whims; most companies grew up out of one man's conviction that there was profit to be made out of something he found enjoyable to do. The problem starts when the individual's belief is allowed to over-rule all objections and independent analysis. Examples quoted earlier in this book were very much the result of management ego; the magazine that failed was launched against every shred of evidence from the market; the new form of roof insulation had been progressed much further than caution would have dictated from a logical analysis of market requirements. Many life-cycle problems are compounded by the refusal of managers to believe the evidence before them. No-one can pretend it is ever easy for a business which has been highly successful in one area to admit that its future now lies so completely in another that the first must be put out of everybody's mind – including that of the founder of the business.

Most people will be able to identify this situation, so examples are almost unnecessary. What fewer are ready to admit is that they, too, are guilty of the same thing. Although most managers are not in the position to launch new products against the evidence of the market-place or push water uphill in attempts to justify their own faith, they are frequently guilty of another form of ego-exhibition – showing favouritism to products or customers and giving disproportionate amounts of time and resources to those sectors. Practically every salesman has a favourite product and, left to his own devices, he would try harder on that than any other. Salesmen often are left to their own devices and disproportionate amounts of sales effort may be given to the favoured product. We all have things in our business lives that we enjoy more than others. I freely admit that I am guilty of this syndrome, even though I write and talk about it practically every month of the year.

What this last sub-section of the product range analysis tells us is that there is absolutely no point whatsoever in going through a long exercise aimed at defining our business and its opportunities as

objectively as possible, if there is a current of management ego
running through the business all the time, and if we are not prepared
to maintain the same high standard of objectivity at all times. What
we have really done is to emphasize yet again, and it cannot be done
too often or too strongly, that whatever you do, for heaven's sake
make sure you know why you are doing it and understand what the
ramifications and implications of both doing it and not doing it are.

With the results of the six questions and the range analysis,
combined with estimating the positions of our products on their
life-cycles, it is now possible to examine what type of company we are
and begin to make decisions about the kind of company we would
like to become. Then positive plans to achieve that ambition can
be made.

7.3 The Boston Grid

An alternative analysis is that proposed by the Boston Consulting
Group and generally known as the 'Boston Grid'. It is also known as
portfolio analysis. Although it presents another way of looking at
where a company is and what it should do next, there are close
similarities with the model already examined.

Figure 18 illustrates the concept. Four categories are distinguished
and these relate high and low market shares to high and low rates of
market growth. Each category is given a name. Thus category 1 is
named 'cash cows', combining a high market share with a low market
growth. This should not be confused with what was earlier called
'milking'. A cash cow is one that provides vital funds for the
development of new products and support for growing ones. The
'stars' (category 2) are those with high share and a high rate of market
growth. However, a star performance in volume does not always equate
with similar profit performances. More often than not, there is a
heavy cost associated with reaching and maintaining such a position.

Categories 3 and 4 represent the problem areas. Category 3 is, in
fact, called 'problem children'. Their difficulty is that the market
enjoys a high rate of growth but the brand or product has only a low
share of that market. Finally, category 4 is called 'dogs' – low share,
low market growth.

Compared with the earlier analysis, this shorter description ties it
up in this way:

'Cash cows = today's profitmakers.
'Stars' = tomorrow's profitmakers.

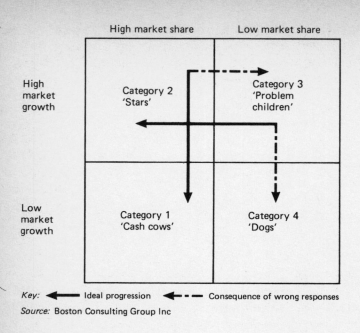

	High market share	Low market share
High market growth	Category 2 'Stars'	Category 3 'Problem children'
Low market growth	Category 1 'Cash cows'	Category 4 'Dogs'

Key: ◄——— Ideal progression   ◄— — Consequence of wrong responses

Source: Boston Consulting Group Inc

Figure 18   *The cash quadrants*

'Problem children' = either tomorrow's profitmakers or
yesterday's profitmakers

The lines on Figure 18 show both the ideal progression and the consequences of getting things wrong. A 'problem child' ought to be made to grow into a 'star' and ultimately develop into a 'cash cow'. However, if not given development time and funds, or if promoted wrongly, it could easily fall back to become a 'dog'. The ultimate destiny of a 'dog' is failure and withdrawal.

A 'cash cow' is hardly likely to revert to a 'star', unless there is some substantial re-cycling of the demand life-cycle of the type, caused by users finding new uses for the product. It is all too easy, however, for a 'star' to fall back, by losing share, to become a problem again.

In a very real sense, the Boston Grid reformulates an older principle for examining market position by a simple combination of sales growth, market share and the important aspect of profitability. This is set out in Table 3

Reference 1   A happy position but one likely to attract competition, especially if there is room to enter at lower prices or competitors

142

Table 3   *Product ratings by sales growth, market share and profit level*

Reference No.	Sales growth	Profit level	Market share
1	High	High	High
2	High	High	Low
3	High	Low	Low
4	Low	Low	Low
5	Low	High	High
6	Low	High	Low
7	Low	Low	High
8	High	Low	High

prepared to take lower profit rates. Sales will not grow for ever, so the important thing is to maintain both the high market share and satisfactory profits.

Reference 2   Failure to secure a high share in a period of rapid sales growth combined with high profits means one of two things. Either the low share is consistent with marketing strategy or the company is greedy and could make its position safer by investing in share growth. The present position is likely to be attractive to competition.

Reference 3   Good growth, everything else low. The danger here is of building a high share at too low profits. This could be a market that will never generate good levels of profit. Investment in this situation requires careful watch over all three elements to prevent any one advancing at the expense of the other.

Reference 4   Everything is wrong with this one! Milk it or get out fast.

Reference 5   Profits are good and share is OK but there appears to be little or no market growth. Looks like a life-cycle plateau. Use the profit to protect share, for life becomes tough and highly competitive under these circumstances, especially if there is over-capacity in the industry. Look to opportunities to segment the market or produce different products for different market segments. The long-run answer is new products ready to take the place of the present one.

Reference 6   Examine the reasons why profits are high despite low sales growth and low share. If it is a developing market, it would make sense to employ the profits to build share and push sales faster than they are at the moment. It may be that the situation indicates the product has found a small but highly profitable market niche.

Reference 7   With no sales growth, any fall in market share will further reduce profits. Share must, therefore, be maintained. Mature products often come into this category.

Reference 8   An almost certain indication of a product that has 'bought' its way into a market. Because there is apparently good market growth, any fall in share need not lead to a fall in sales (the product will simply not be growing quite as fast as competition). It has a high share which normally indicates reasonable buyer loyalty and that should make it less risky to build profits, which must be the major aim for a product of this kind.

We have looked at three different but obviously overlapping types of analysis that help plot the way forward. It does not matter a great deal which you use; what is important is to use one regularly.

7.4 Summary

A contribution test looking at the various ways products might contribute – or not – to the welfare of the company will impose a useful and necessary discipline on the answers to the six questions, and link up with life-cycle analysis to provide the basis for categorizing a product range. Products can be listed as:

Present profitmakers
Future profitmakers
Profitable specials
Priority development products
Failures
Contributors to overheads
Patchwork products
Unnecessary, unprofitable products
Investments in management ego

Now a decision about what type of company you have can be made and, from this, a direction for the future can be chosen. The fundamental choices are between horizontal and vertical integration, on the one hand, and marketing or technological centred organizations, on the other. Although the conglomerate style and the multi-faceted verglomerate will not be for many companies, every businessman ought to consider a strategy of leverage to secure

144

economic advantages as a possibly viable alternative to any other possibility.

7.5 Checklist

1   After any form of largely verbal analysis, it makes sense to examine the figures carefully to see if they are in line with the opportunities identified. If they are not, either the analysis is faulty or past marketing efforts have not maximized the opportunities. If the latter, re-examine both the fundamental strategy and the way the marketing mix has been applied.

2   One way of looking at opportunities and classifying products within a total mix is to divide them into 'straightforward' and 'problem children'. At the top come those products clearly making enough profit to provide dividends for shareholders and fund the development of new products and the growth of younger ones. At the other extreme come those products that perhaps should never have been launched plus those that have had their day and now absorb undue amounts of time, effort and money.

3   From time to time, it may be necessary to continue to market a product that otherwise would be a candidate for withdrawal. The best justification for such an action is when it provides necessary support to other lines in the range or otherwise contributes significantly to company overheads. However, it could indicate that the company has got way behind with new product development. Giving support to declining products is not a long-term objective.

4   When tackling problem products, there must be a clear indication of sufficient potential in the market to turn the product into a winner.

5   The Boston Grid shows how easy it is for a product to fall back from a more successful category to a far less happy one. 'Cash cows' are necessary to the success of any company. Always remember that it is today's successful products that pay for tomorrow's successes. Unless sufficient attention is given to those, there won't be any new products tomorrow.

6   Alternatively, analysing a product range by combinations of sales growth, market share and profit levels produces eight categories, each with its own appropriate action.

7   Which model one uses makes relatively little difference. It is more a function of management style which one is likely to work best. With sophisticated management, the Boston Grid is capable of far more development than its treatment here suggests. With companies relatively new to marketing analysis, the 'straight-forward'/'problem children' analysis usually works best and easily develops into the format explained in Table 3.

8   What is important is that every company adopts some systematic method for continually analysing its position and assessing the relevance of its marketing strategies and activities to the positions revealed.

8

Plans are Nothing, Planning is Everything

This very remarkable man
Commends a most remarkable plan:
You can do what you want
If you don't think you can't,
So don't think you can't think you can

Charles Inge

Anyone who has actually achieved a forecast has either had luck on his side or cheated. The odds against precise achievement of a plan are far too high. Cheating is far too frequent. Soon after joining one of the companies I have worked for, I became involved in a detailed investigation of every part of the business to attempt to track down the reasons for profits failing to meet the target by just over £1 million. We were near the end of our search and had only found some £30,000 of the deficit when we were about to leave the office of one of the chief executives. 'I know where the missing million is' he said. A year earlier, the chief executive of the group had rejected the first forecast of the division and asked for another £1 million. The sum was built into the budget and the division achieved its original forecast: the difference between the two was just about £1 million. Whenever I have told that story, I have received dozens of similar examples back.

It would appear that plans are flexible but in one direction only; if the first figure isn't good enough, it is frequently changed for a higher one even though nothing in the original plan is changed. Any effective planning system ought to be able to take account of a situation that arises so frequently. On the one hand, there is the ideal plan whilst, on the other, there is that which will achieve a pre-determined objective. In the process of planning we are going to examine, room is left for both to be achieved. There are other prime objectives, too. One is that any plan should be flexible. Another is that it should be as practical and realistic as possible. Yet another is that it ought to take

147

some account of likely situations that could change it radically, whilst perhaps the most important consideration of all is that planning should be a continuous process of appraisal, consideration, monitoring and re-appraisal.

8.1 The ideal plan

Planning processes are usually functions of organizations. One single set of finite planning headings would presume very similar business organizations and would, therefore, obviously be wrong. Nevertheless, there are certain things that all plans have in common. In particular, senior managers want firm recommendations – not a set of alternatives which leaves the choice to them. They may not necessarily agree with the recommendation presented to them but it is still helpful to have a set of reasons why one is preferred to another. In addition, they want to know how much profit will result from a plan, over what period and with what degree of certainty (or, alternatively, with what degree of risk).

Differences between planning processes and the eventual document which is the outcome tend to revolve around the factors:

1 The extent to which the past is examined and how far back.
2 How far plans are projected into the future.
3 How much detail is included.
4 What emphasis is placed on strategy, tactics and execution.
5 The number of alternatives to be considered.
6 The degree of flexibility permitted during the plan's life.

The emphasis of this chapter will be on the process of planning – get that right and how you write the plan will not matter too much. Unfortunately, writing the annual plan too often achieves a status all of its own and managers indulge in a sort of ritual self-cleansing process which sustains them through the next 12 months until they write another, and frequently unrelated, plan. Looking at the above list in the light of what this chapter will preach, it will be shown that any plan is all the better for taking as much account of past years as is practical and relevant. Projecting plans some way beyond the year under consideration helps prevent too frequent changes of direction and is a considerable aid to both understanding and involvement by all levels of management. If the emphasis is placed on strategy, detail becomes much less important and, rather than tackle each topic too thinly, it is usually better for full details to be supplied with an individual plan for each tactical exercise. Reference has already been made to one aspect of the consideration of alternatives. Whilst a large number of possible alternatives could be considered, if the emphasis is on a strategic solution, fewer alternatives will suggest themselves. Moreover, it makes life easier for everyone if only two alternatives are presented – the recommended course of action and the action that will achieve predetermined financial objectives if the first does not. Each of these will be treated in greater detail in its appropriate context.

But what about flexibility? A rigid plan is fairly meaningless and is one of the basic reasons for such a high failure rate of business forecasting. A good plan is based on a carefully evolved strategy, one which will last for many years. The outcome of the plan is a profit figure. From strategy to profit consists of a series of carefully planned tactical actions with their timings and costs; many are actions that would have been taken in any case, even without a plan, whilst others are entirely original. If you consider both the strategy and the financial outcome as being thus fixed, flexibility will be necessary if the plan is to be achieved, for it is extremely unlikely that all the events will turn out exactly as planned.

Some years ago, a charter airline decided to carry out an analysis of its timekeeping record. It discovered that on the flight between Luton and Athens it had a remarkable record of being within, plus or minus, two minutes of 'estimated time of arrival' on 94 per cent of occasions. The managing director thought it would be interesting to examine the flight plans and see how often the captain had followed them in full. In 92 per cent of cases where the flight had arrived within the plus or minus two minutes bracket, the pilot had made significant variations from his registered flight plan. Yet he achieved his plan.

All sorts of events had intervened: wind speed changed, wind direction altered, heavy traffic meant diversions and so on. Yet, by trimming his rudder, changing his speed and re-routing in mid-air, he could still achieve his plan. A business is like an aircraft in that respect: adjustments have to be made according to circumstances if the plan is to be achieved. Prices may have to be changed, different product lines may have to be pushed, new service packages may have to replace planned ones and so on. All these should be given first priority rather than, as too often happens, reducing the target or changing the strategy.

Thus, achieving the ideal plan is a matter of:

1 Careful pre-planning
2 The right sequence

3 Producing a plan that has a reasonable chance of success
4 Controlling performance during the plan's life.

8.2 Pre-planning for success

Objectives, strategy and tactics – these three words will be used often enough to justify definition.

Objectives are the numerical targets set by the corporate centre. They should always be set out in quantitative terms, for only then can performance be properly measured and monitored. They can be broken down in various ways for profit centres.

Strategy is the position the enterprise will adopt in striving to achieve the defined objectives. This is the area we were particularly concerned with in Chapters 4 and 7.

Tactics are the means by which the strategy will be achieved.

A simple example will show how the three relate. The objective of Ubique Limited is to achieve profits of £500,000 in year one and increase by 15 per cent per annum thereafter. The strategy will be to appeal to premium markets for hand-produced furniture with traditional designs. Tactics will include direct representation to leading department stores, participation in the Ideal Home exhibition, special shows in local furniture stores dealing in high quality goods and higher than average profit margins for stockists.

SETTING OBJECTIVES

Some kinds of objective are better suited to use at corporate levels, others break down better to profit centre levels. There are three main types of objective, although they may also be used in combination.

Perhaps the most popular is a simple comparative statement of intent. For example, to improve profits by 5 per cent on last year. Its very simplicity hides its virtues. The statement invites the question 'How?'. Answers might include: increase sales volume by 10 per cent; raise brand share to 30 per cent of the market; increase effective sterling distribution by another 15 per cent; increase calling ratio; require each advertisement to generate ten more sales leads; increase the conversion ratio for leads from 30 to 35 per cent – and so on. The deeper you consider the question, the more likely it is to begin to dictate the necessary tactics; and the higher the degree of measurability over a wider area of business planning.

In all planning, it is a good idea to take each aspect one at a time and consider how the plan could be achieved if that were the only avenue open to you. An example from my own experience (a grocery product) went like this:

> Solely by increasing sales: problem, high level of sales per outlet; unlikely without increase in distribution. Increase distribution: sterling-weighted distribution is 78 per cent without Co-ops. The only profitable way to expand distribution is to find a way of getting the Co-ops (who had their own brand) to stock. Rely on advertising – that is, improve effectiveness and increase spending. Same problem as solely by increasing sales.

And so on. It was clear that this brand had gone almost as far as it could without the participation of the Co-operative outlets.

The comparative method is not quite as crude and useless as often assumed. In hard times, even the most sophisticated companies fall back on it. In times of rampant inflation, when standing still means absorbing heavily increased costs, the form of the comparative statement is often amended to something like '5 per cent better than the level necessary to simply absorb higher costs'. The comparative method can be used to define survival limits.

RATIOS

The boom years of the late 60s showed the real deficiencies of simpler methods at corporate levels (even though they may remain an effective way of stating the target share of an overall objective for a smaller profit unit). Many companies who appeared to be doing well were simply not matching up to the performances of other similar companies. In particular it was clear that their money could earn bigger rewards used in other ways. Thus, companies with cash in the business, or under-utilized or under-valued assets, quickly became the prey of those better able to recognize more rewarding uses of cash.

Business ratios were already quite well-known as a method of inter-firm comparison; now they became increasingly used as a means of setting objectives. One in particular was rapidly incorporated into many companies: the concept of return on capital employed (or return on investment – ROI). Simply expressed, the concept is that money invested in any one business ought to earn at least what could be obtained from a reasonably safe investment; otherwise, why take all the risks of business? In any case, if shareholders are to be

151

attracted to the shares of your firm, they must feel that they can earn a reasonable rate of return for their savings.

The formula is simple:

$$\frac{\text{Operating profits}}{\text{Operating assets}} \times 100$$

Although the idea is splendid, in practice the method can easily lead to some dangerous situations. An easy way of improving the ratio when profits are static is to reduce investment. Many sections of British industry (the motor industry was a classic example) are heavily under-invested, a situation which has largely passed unnoticed by the investors who have their eye on a good ratio between profits and assets. There are many other manifestations of this phenomenon, such as sale and lease-back of property (whereby the vendor receives cash for an asset but pays a long-term rental), hiring company vehicles, leasing furniture and so on. They all have one common characteristic: they substitute a cash drain for a paid-for asset. Although profit ratios may look good when the deal is done, the cash receipts can easily evaporate and profits have to increase to pay for the cash drain. The inability to finance high interest rates on cash borrowings was the major characteristic of many financial crashes during 1974/5.

There are two fairly simple defences against these excesses. One is to make sure that the ROI is calculated on *total assets*, including cash. The other, which has additional benefits aside from the safety factor, is to use more than one ratio. Various companies recognize between 18 and 21 business ratios. Three will actually be enough to make sure you aren't simply deceiving yourself. In addition to relating profits to capital employed, use some break-downs that measure some of the fundamentals of your business. Relate operating profits (in the same way as in the formula above) to:

1 Real assets (plant, property, etc.)
2 Stocks (raw materials, finished goods in store and in transit)
3 Net debtors/creditors (the difference between what you owe and what you are owed).

So now you have measures which consider how your investment relates to other uses of money, how the real assets in that sum relate, a measure related to all the raw materials of your trade plus the finished goods that no-one else has yet paid for and, finally, a measure that tells you whether you can expect enough to come in to pay your outgoings. If you have played any of the tricks mentioned earlier, the

152

results will show up somewhere else. For example, a sale and lease-back deal will improve your profit ratio but show up as an adverse factor on cash flow; if something hasn't been done to increase the sums owed to you, the net debtor/creditor figure will become unfavourable. The additional advantage of examining three ratios is that it forces attention on each of the major components of the business: the factory (or office, branch or outlet), the stocks and the cash. (For those engaged in service businesses with little or no stock component, a ratio comparing the number of staff to the profits generated should be used.)

There are many other ways these ratios can be broken down. Some labour-intensive service industries might prefer to put the return on labour employed in the place of real assets, which may be negligible if not actually non-existent.*

CASH SUMS

All objectives have to be converted into cash sums at some time or other; in many cases a cash sum is all that is required. They have the advantage of tangibility and easy monitoring without creating special tools and systems. Managers generally understand money better than ratios and percentages. Something that relates cash to volume has always been the simplest and most effective form of incentive to salesmen and managers alike.

It has been said several times already in this book that no costing system can be entirely fair to all brands and items within it, and we saw from the contribution test how misleading costing figures can be if looked at only in one light. Where a company has many products on the same costing system, and especially when it uses a number of common resources, there are several potential dangers. One is that developing and struggling brands can so easily be 'penalized', whilst others that appear to generate higher-than-target profit rates are actually not worth support (which is often the reason why they appear to do so well – they do not absorb the same costing load that developing brands do). Where it is necessary for the long-term good of a company to 'excuse' some brands from full cost recovery, whilst requiring others to produce more than their allotted target profit rate, there is a great deal to be said for giving the managers of individual profit centres cash sums as their target. On the whole, this is better than giving new brands 'free rides', especially where combined with a

* For a fuller exposition of business ratios and their use and abuse in business, see Chapter 20, 'Profit and Cash Control', of *Directing the Marketing Effort* by Ray L. WIllsmer, Pan Management Series (1975).

steadily increasing cash sum.

A dangerous justification for new lines is that they take no extra resources, therefore they should be excused some elements of cost. The argument holds good only so long as someone else effects full recovery for them.

COMBINATIONS

It is seldom possible to calculate the actual assets employed in the production of one particular product line. In many cases, it cannot even be done for a division. Ratios are usually reserved for the central organization and need to be broken down to profit centres. This is usually done as a cash share of the required central objective and will normally take some account of past performance and reasonable expectations, apart from considerations of fairness. Thus the most frequent combination is a target improvement over the previous year, consistent with the required (costings) rate of profit, which assumes meeting company objectives.

RESOURCE ANALYSIS

Once the objectives are set, the real work of pre-planning begins. The annual marketing plan has as its major (many say only) justification the opportunity to stand back from the trees and look at the wood. This is a question of going through the six questions, examining any changes in life-cycle position, going through your groupings and deciding if you are still on course for your planned strategy or if a change is necessary. Please, please do not get into the habit of change for change's sake. Many young marketing executives believe that they are failing in their duty if they do not change something every 12 months. If they can't change the strategy, they want to change the advertising, which is the vehicle through which the strategy is communicated. It usually requires a major upheaval in a market to justify a change in strategy and one should be careful about changes in component parts, which both reflect and communicate that strategy. If the hardest thing in marketing is discovering the right strategy, the second most difficult is convincing managers to stay with it.

The guiding principle of resource analysis should be the 'SWOT' sequence:

Strengths
Weaknesses
Opportunities
Threats

The order is important. Proceed from strength before eliminating weaknesses; maximize opportunities before tackling threats. The time to tackle weaknesses is when they reduce your strength in the market-place; threats become problems when they limit or reduce your opportunities.

Remember that the basis of all resource planning is identifying profitable opportunities. Remember, too, that real resources only exist outside the business – until you have created customers, all you have is cost.

CO-ORDINATION

One of the principal jobs of marketing is that of internal co-ordinator. Nowhere is this role more vital than in the preliminary stages of planning. A plan which is not fully discussed with all those critically involved and which is not fully communicated to each active participant is not going to work. Clashes must be avoided and priorities assigned where necessary. An agreed strategy can easily be nullified by accepting the basis but not accepting the necessary concomitants. 'We'll have the strategy and we love the plan but we can't afford to increase the sales force' is typical of a common line of argument; then they wonder why such a good-sounding plan failed to achieve their expectations. Yet there has to be some give and take; the best plan for a company almost invariably involves second-best plans for some elements. Planning systems have to allow for this, too.

Pay particular attention to time-lags. Marketing people are always (rightly) concerned with the actual moment of purchase and the time of use. There is a danger of assuming a sort of mystical process whereby the precise item appears suddenly under the roaming hand of a shopper. The time-lag between production and distribution needs a different set of targets from those required for the sales force – which are themselves different from forecast customer sales (using 'customer' in the widest possible sense), whilst the money will come in much later.

Production usually finds it helpful to have warnings of peaks and troughs, the possible range of production requirements, the timing of promotional stock, special packs, deals, and so on. In many cases, labour recruitment is a limiting factor whilst legislation makes it difficult to simply lay employees off for a month at a time. The timing of production requirements affects the amount of raw materials held (and, as we saw earlier, this can have dramatic effects on company profits). Finance need to know the timing of cash flows, what money is fully committed but not yet spent, and so on. A break-down in

155

communications in any one of these areas can seriously damage the effectiveness of any business plan.

8.3 The sequence of planning

I have always assumed it to be a considerable piece of arrogance to suggest to any businessman that my method of writing a plan is better than his; hence my emphasis on the process rather than the plan. One can often suggest the inclusion of items that help understanding and speed communication; one can suggest new forms of measurement and analysis, but these do not basically alter the prime requirement of a plan to fit the organization systems of the company for which it is produced. However, in the system and sequence of planning it is possible to make more positive suggestions, for they achieve one enormously valuable function: they save time and money.

I confess to being somewhat obsessed with the enormous wastage involved in planning. Managers spend long hours, for several weeks, preparing a plan which may then be rejected on the basis of facts that were always known to someone but simply not communicated. The most usual is the inability or unwillingness to provide the cash which creates the resources that give the plan its chances of success. This is particularly true of promotional budgets. The sequence outlined in the following paragraphs is one which appears at first sight to be complicated and time-consuming, but is actually simple and comparatively quick. The essence of it is firing a number of 'warning shots' which require a response and an authority to proceed before moving on to the next stage. This way, managers avoid the ultimate and damaging rebuff, whilst senior management (for whom the final plan is intended) 'grow up' with the plan through these warning shots and ugly surprises are avoided.

The sequence that follows works for any kind of company. It actually describes a fairly complex organization. If yours is less complicated, simply cross out the stages that do not apply. But stick to the principles of firing warning shots across the bows of more senior management, trying out ideas for how they fit with objectives and not moving on until clearance is given. Finally, do not involve other people until you are pretty certain that your plan is going to be acceptable.

PRODUCT STRATEGY
The manager responsible for the marketing of an individual product or line should write this. If he involves other people, he should try to

keep their participation to a minimum. Assumptions can be checked out ('Am I right in assuming we cannot produce any more on the present line and you require a four months' lead time for a new plant?'). In many companies, a brand manager's request has the sanctity of an order and people go away and do lots of work. They must be discouraged at this stage. A manager who has been living with a product line every day of his working life for some time now will usually be able to write a strategy document without any help and in a few hours.

Keep it simple. It is an outline of ideas, hopes and expectations. At the next stage, your manager may have to read large numbers of strategy documents. In the two companies where I operated this system I had, respectively, 46 and 84 such strategies to read over a weekend; it was much better than reading 84 plans with no idea of what I was going to see. The following headings are usually enough, although you may require different ones or even additional ones of your own:

1 *Objectives: short and long-term*   A simple statement such as 'to have 15 per cent of the market and a profit of £50,000 next year but 50 per cent and £350,000 within five years'. This gives an important indication of strategy to the reviewing manager who, otherwise, might regard it as a minor brand with few pretensions.

2 *Consumer proposition*   A piece of jargon meaning 'how we are going to position this brand to our existing and potential customers'. This is a key indicator of the practicality of the chosen strategy and becomes a basic weapon in the armoury of selling and promotion. Thus one might say:

'Eating too much, especially the wrong foods, can lead to a heart attack, so eat less and look after yourself.' (Health Education Council).

3 *Strategy*   The selected strategy should be carefully chosen for its relevance and likely longevity. It should reflect the benefits sought by the customer and the position selected by the company as the best way to present those benefits to the chosen market sector. It is almost as important that a strategy should eliminate unwanted or uneconomic customers as that it should define prime prospects.

4 *Tactics*   Simply an indication of main avenues of attack. As we saw earlier, full details are better left for inclusion with individual tactical plans, but the broad headings here will give an

157

indication of the resources required to put the tactics into effect.

5 *Promotional messages and media* Again, keep it simple. What you are really saying is: 'If this plan goes forward, I shall want to promote our new savings scheme through colour pages in the two Sunday colour magazines and through literature at all our branches. The cost will be around £200,000'.

6 *Promotions and schemes* Very much as for 5 above. 'We plan to have three consumer promotions and four trade deals. Estimated cost – £35,000; timings – periods 3, 5, 9 for consumer and 2, 4, 8, 11 for the trade.'

7 *New resources* New resources created to assist the implementation of the plan for any one product seldom appear in that product's plan. Requests for extra production labour, additional sales force efforts, extra vans, and so on, usually appear in the appropriate expense budgets. This is where brands 'stand up and be recognized' so that a true estimate of worthiness can be made. It is a useful way of identifying clashes, for frequently several brands will require, say, extra sales force effort yet not be able to produce enough extra profit to pay for additional salesmen. If the sales manager is not justified in giving product A some of B's time, the deal is clearly not on.

Really, the final document does not need to be very much longer than the actual examples where they have been given. As time goes on, familiarity will reduce the amount of detail even further.

DIVISIONAL STRATEGY

The essence of the warning shot philosophy is that the next stage of management should be exposed to each phase of planning to secure their endorsement and support. At this next stage, each of the product strategy documents will be considered for their fit into the divisional strategy. (The word 'division' is used to describe whatever next stage may exist. In the very small company this will not only be the next step but also the final one.)

A simple, real example will help illustrate the point. In my days with Lyons, I would meet with my two marketing managers, my two field sales managers and the national accounts manager to consider each of the brand strategies. We would meet somewhere away from the office, having read the documents over the previous week-end. We would consider how the suggestions fitted with our abilities and resources, making notes as we went along about the areas where we doubted the ability of our resources to cope with the demand on them. Of major importance, we would consider how these suggestions lined up with the division's profit objective and where improvements might be obtained if that was going to be necessary. Then, each brand manager in turn would come along to argue for his strategy or hear why his superiors felt that it could not be endorsed or achieved. He or she would then go away either with authority to proceed to the next stage or to produce an amended strategy taking account of the resources that could actually be allocated. Invariably we found that the biggest area of conflict was over demands on sales force time, especially for special sales drives. On average, we needed a sales force twice as big as the one we had, preferably working 104 weeks in a year.

And that highlights the importance of this sort of process. If such a conflict is apparent early on, the manager submitting the strategy can be told to re-examine his strategy and its planned outcome now that he knows that he cannot have as much sales force time as he wants. Otherwise what happens is either that he only discovers this after preparing a fully-detailed plan that has involved most other departments of the company or, worse, only when the plan is running does he discover that the sales force is not giving the time and attention to the product that he believed it was going to get. This, then, is a vital and very useful step which has as its objectives:

1 A check on the ability of resources to meet demands on them.
2 A first rough check of the fit with corporate objectives.
3 A chance to allocate priorities which will be set for the duration of the plan.
4 Authority to proceed to the next stage of planning.

There may be a fifth – the strategies presented may impress the divisional managers sufficiently for them to argue for a change in the divisional objective to accommodate them.

CORPORATE STRATEGY
Depending on the size and complexity of the company, it may be necessary to repeat the divisional strategy procedure at corporate level with exactly the same objectives. The sooner the centre is aware of possible discrepancies from set objectives, the earlier remedial action can be taken. One company of my acquaintance, which did not use such a stage after divisional strategy, had a situation where one part of it took steps to reach its profit target that eventually led to the closure of that particular company. It did not know that two other

companies in the group were planning (and they achieved those plans) to exceed their objectives by handsome amounts. Had there been this extra stage, it might have been possible for the company which eventually failed to have operated its original strategy and built a secure foundation for the future. As was noted earlier, the best plan for a company often involves less-than-best plans for parts of it. The major function of this continual testing for fit with overall objectives is to recognize those parts which need short-term support for long-term benefit and those best able to provide that support.

PLANNED SALES

Let us now assume that clearance has filtered back to whoever produced the original brand strategy. Everything now stems from the sales forecast which is the outcome of the strategy. This stage assumes that there is now a very high probability that the final plan will be approved together with authority for all necessary expenditures. On the assumption that those funds will be forthcoming, the necessary support from other departments is assured and timings agreed, fully detailed sales forecasts can now be prepared in such a way that other departments can make the appropriate adjustments to allow for their timings. All other detailed planning starts from here but it can now begin with the assurance that only some major upheaval will cause the planning to be wasted. Production and distribution planning begins, feasibility studies are mounted, costings are prepared and, possibly, adjustments and reconciliations are recommended.

It is important to refer back to what was said earlier about presenting ranges of probable sales to the production department (which means whatever the 'powerhouse' of the operation is; in service industries it certainly will not be a factory; it could be the credit department or the bookings and reservations section, or service engineers). Close co-operation will encourage a dialogue instead of a subservient response; if factory managers have figures presented to them in such a way that it allows them to make best and worst forecasts, there is more opportunity to recommend changes in timings, for example, that will improve overall profit. There is no point in a plan which produces high profit from sales if this is offset by an increase in factory costs; the figures for the brand may look good but those for the company will not.

The aim of this phase is to end up with 'agreed planned sales' which is, in effect, a considered verdict on feasibility and the most practical means of bringing all the other departments into the act of detailed

160

planning. The outcome is all the figures necessary for the final stage of the plan.

ANNUAL OPERATING PLAN

I prefer to use this name rather than 'the marketing plan'. The latter is rather limiting, whilst the title I suggest infers that it includes all those elements of cost that make up the necessary input to the plan. The format is whatever you wish to make it, although some suggested headings will come later. It is the final request for funds, with the justification for them, the detail of the strategy, the outline of the tactics (it is sufficient only to indicate that this is what will be required if each detailed tactical plan is approved when finally presented in full), and the control figure for the duration of the plan.

For the majority of companies, this stage is the only one, and it has all the dangers outlined earlier, unless there is careful and continual communication from the chief executive down to those producing the plans. The time used in the earlier stages is more than recouped at this phase for, in reality, one is only formalizing and putting in writing a number of steps that have to be taken in any case. Under this system, they are taken with time to amend them and the opportunity to really consider the ramifications of any reductions in resources, enforced increases in targets and so on. When the company in my opening paragraph was told to increase its target profit by £1 million, it was given no extra resources to do it with and, indeed, was able to make no other efforts than those which it had said would produce the lower figure; it was hardly surprising that they did just that.

PLAN AND COMMITMENT SUMMARY

This can either be part of the annual operating plan (preferably as an appendix) or a completely separate document. The reason behind this phase is simply that although the final plan is invariably a confidential document, it cannot be achieved without the willing complicity of a large number of people who will never see it and will not be fully aware of all the inter-relationships involved. It is, in fact, nothing more than a verbal network plan. It is a sheet of paper that really needs only three headings:

Activity   Manager responsible   Completion date

It is no more than a clear indication that involvement in, and commitment to, the plan is both understood and agreed. It can be argued that there is no necessity for this phase, if the marketing people have exercised their responsibility for liaison correctly.

However, on the one hand, it shows clearly to senior management whether they have or not, whilst, on the other, it assures the planner that when other managers have agreed to do things, they, too, have made sure that their co-ordination responsibilities have also been carried out. Some companies find this system such an effective safeguard against error that they insist on a similar procedure for any course of action; for example, they may require that any memorandum setting out required actions must be initialled by the manager responsible for that action. To many managers, this sort of rigidity leaves an unpleasant taste in the mouth. On the other hand, I would have to admit that by far the majority of plans of companies with whom I have been involved, in some way or other, have failed in one or more respects either due to the failure of one function to perform according to plan or (and often the two are associated) because someone has been able to deny categorically any knowledge of being required to do anything or meet a specific timing. A plan and commitment summary, both as an appendix to the annual operating plan and as a document circulated to every named individual, is a simple and not very harsh safeguard. If a plan is to succeed, it must be given every possible chance, both before it is ever written down and during its course.

8.4 Giving the plan a chance

The pre-planning stages already discussed are, of course, the principal ingredients in making sure that any plan has the best chance of succeeding. To that must be added careful control procedures to ensure that new situations are recognized, so that alternative tactics to meet the strategy can be considered and, where necessary and appropriate, put into effect. But there are three other important and often unconsidered areas which can seriously affect the chances of success. They are:

Realistic forecasting
The realism of the plan
Taking account of factors outside the business.

In the last resort, a plan is only as good as the forecast of the outcomes. A realistic forecast is, therefore, a necessary ingredient in a realistic plan. Because forecasts are so important, we shall consider some of the important aspects in the next chapter. At this point it will suffice to say that forecasts must be objective and consistent with reality. 'Hope', if it is used at all in a forecast, should be built on after

162

the objective figures and justified. There is more than just sales forecasting to consider in producing a realistic plan.

THE REALISM OF THE PLAN

Too many plans are merely numerical. Often, the actions required to produce the figures are not even considered. This is especially true of some of the so-called 'Go-Go' companies whose obsession with figures is now proved to have been both excessive and damaging. Nevertheless, skilled managers learn a great deal simply from the figures. One very useful dodge that I used to adopt during my periods of reading large numbers of plans in a very short time was simply to examine the figures for any break in logic. Wherever a break appeared, it had to be questioned. Tables 4 and 5 represent an actual case from a profit centre (a particular, clearly defined operation) of a subsidiary company and, although reassembled to make a particular point, are the actual figures which were presented to me. Table 4 seems to have a logic. The aims of the company are in line with the market as a whole. Market share is going to slip a little but even that is somewhat reassuring in so far as no-one has attempted to fiddle the figures to make them fit.

Table 4   *First plan, Company SK, £000s*

	Year 0	Year +1
Total market	3100	3410
Market growth	—	+10%
SK sales	1147	1250
Sales growth	—	+9%
Share of market	37%	36.7%

Table 5   *Revised plan, Company SK, £000s*

	Year −2	Year −1	Year 0	Year +1
Total market	2562	2818	3100	3410
Market growth	+10%	+10%	+10%	+10%
SK sales	1021	1082	1147	1250
Sales growth		+6%	+6%	+9%
Market share	39.9%	38.4%	37.0%	36.7%

Unfortunately, I did not agree that the figures were logical: there just wasn't enough to justify that statement. I called for past figures (which had never been required in the company before). After some scratching around, they were able to come up with the figures from

163

which Table 5 is produced. Now the situation is very different. There is a clear break in the logic of the figures. Here is a company that has been going along at a 6 per cent increase, suddenly planning to achieve a 9 per cent rise. How? In fact, they weren't planning to do anything in the next year that they hadn't done before. Even worse, looking back at past plans revealed that they had forecast 9 percent increases but achieved 6 per cent. In fact, they were being carried along by the momentum of the market in a section of a very rapidly growing industry, but they were continually losing share by doing nothing to merit increasing at a higher rate. Not a very realistic plan.

There are two lessons to be learned from this. Firstly, the realism of a plan is vastly improved by relating to a lengthy period of time. It is, moreover, a strong defence against the type of plan which changes direction dramatically every year; it affords the opportunity to question the logic of that change. Secondly, if senior management can most rapidly and effectively judge the quality of a plan by querying its logic, then obviously the way to create a realistic plan is to make sure that it is, firstly, logical in relation to the past and current trends and results, and, secondly, that wherever logic is to be challenged a justification must be produced. A realistic plan is the one which demonstrates the greatest internal consistency. But what about external forces?

OUTSIDE FACTORS

In lectures, I usually call this section 'Taking account of the un-expected', which has the merit, at least, of making people sit up and take notice. It sounds impossible and much of it is; nevertheless, it is true that so-called unexpected events have usually happened before, are going to happen again and can be anticipated to greater or lesser extents.

It is always necessary to construct a model (albeit mentally) of the markets in which we operate. Most managers fight shy of the word 'model' as soon as it is mentioned, especially those in smaller businesses obviously unable to afford the people or the computer time necessary to build a vast model of likely influences. However, look at it this way: if you do not build a model, you have just made one! What, in effect, you have just done is to say 'my competitor will not change his price, improve his product, enlarge his sales force, increase his advertising, change his package, increase his interest rate, give more service; the Government will not intervene, produce new laws and regulations affecting our business, increase the rate of interest on hire purchase' and much more. You have postulated that nothing will change and that is almost certainly a very much bigger model than any mathematician would build.

In any plan, only those variables known to be significant can be considered and they should be. Those influences can then be quantified, which will lead to considerations of the probability of success and the degrees of risk. But more can be done. Firstly, it is useful to build into the plan all those assumptions behind the figures. Then you have a readily available list of the significant factors which might account for any variation from plan. Figure 19 shows a form of tabulation that is appropriate to any kind of business. In large companies, it is useful for certain assumptions to be handed down to operating units. For example, in the Thomson Organization, where we had a central economic unit, we would tell operating companies what rate of inflation should be assumed unless they had more positive and certain information relating to their operation. If, for example, we said that wage rates for the printing operations would rise by 15 per cent next year, but Thomson Regional Newspapers had signed an agreement with their unions for 12 per cent, the latter would be the figure they would use. Figure 19 concentrates upon product line factors but could easily start with those assumptions which have been handed down. Secondly, this concept can be taken further. It is useful to build a model of your market, considering all the things that have ever influenced it and those that might do so. The 'Six Day War' and the effects on oil supplies caught many companies out, over a wide range of businesses and materials. Yet it has long been known that supplies of oil will run dangerously low in the not too distant future. A model which included that fact would have invited consideration of alternative sources of supply for materials with high oil content and could have saved many companies from damaging effects. Figure 20 shows a way of doing this. Block one can be your planning assumptions. It might actually contain rather more. Call it something like 'Factors likely to influence the plan'. For example, for a central heating client, items in that list included:

Increase in initial deposit for hire purchase
Reduction in period of payment
Increase in interest rate
Change in ratio of costs between oil, electricity and gas.

The planning assumptions were that most of these would not change; any that did would affect the plan seriously. In fact, all changed simultaneously. This block is the first place to look for the explanation of any deviation from plan. The explanation will be improved if it can be related to the experience last time something like

165

Plan element	Economic environment	Customer behaviour	Competitive behaviour	Own position	Raw materials
Product line					
Prices					
Direct sales					
Delivery					
Advertising					
Packaging					
Credit policy					

Figure 19 *Planning assumptions – the list may be extended to the right and vertically to permit extra elements appropriate to the business*

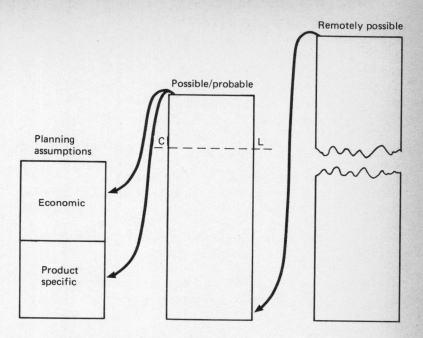

Figure 20 *Expecting the unexpected*

this happened. Keep a diary, or an annotated sales graph. It is surprising how quickly people forget events that were quite significant at the time. The smaller the business, the more significant apparently small happenings can be – like changes of staff, for example. In one classic case in my experience, the explanation for a drop in sales turned out to be related to a change in accounting procedure; sales previously registered at the time of delivery were subsequently recorded only when invoiced. That company ended up with four different sets of figures: orders, deliveries, invoices and payments.

A second block would contain factors that could influence the plan. These may be things that your diary shows have happened before but are fairly unlikely. Most British businesses were affected in some way by the three-day working week of early 1974. It could happen again. It is hardly likely to be in block one but it is indicative of the sort of item for block two. Many businesses have occasionally found themselves affected by a happening at one or two removes from them. Strikes are one example; related item purchases are another. Sales of whisky are shown to be more responsive to changes in their price relative to the cost-of-living, rather than changes in price

167

per se – another example of the sort of item for inclusion.

A third and final block is usually useful. This will contain the remote possibilities. It might include a serious reduction in oil supplies. A general strike might come here. Prohibitive legislation would be another example; the confectionery industry, assailed by dentists for years, might include the possibility of Government legislation on, say, the advertising of sweets to children.

You cannot stop those things happening. You can be prepared for them. Adopting this 'block' theory will give you a sort of ready-reckoner that can be referred to whenever something differs from forecast, good as well as bad. If you can explain good fortune before your competition, you can seize a competitive advantage and that is what it is all about. Any business that has learned to recognize the sort of thing that affects its business for good or ill is better placed to recognize the beginning of trends and, clearly, best placed to handle any sudden acceleration of trend. There are really very few so-called crises that do not contain some predictable elements; many more have fairly regular cycles. If a company starts with a sound strategy, the chances of a crisis seriously affecting anything other than its tactics are substantially reduced; no amount of tactical manoeuvre will correct a basically unsound strategic position. Many marketing men of my generation work to what they call 'the earthquake theory'. Although seismologists cannot predict the exact time of an earthquake, they can plot those areas of the earth's crust where fissures are most likely to occur. With that knowledge, the inhabitants of those places can be better prepared, whilst the experts can look for the tell-tale signs of an impending disaster.

If you are sailing, it is far easier to take evasive action if you can estimate the arrival of a storm. You may not get all the way back to safe harbour but you can reduce the time you are at risk. This is what this system is designed to do. The line 'CL' in Figure 20 is the contingency line. For all the items in block one, and any that rise above CL in block two, prepare a contingency plan. Keep your eye on the events below CL: as soon as one rises above the line (by becoming a more imminent threat), produce a contingency plan for it.

Contingency plans are often called 'What if' plans. This term has been adopted by software producers for micro (or personal) computers. The widespread availability of what are described as 'spreadsheet' programs provides tremendous opportunities for marketing planners. The essence of these programs is the rapid calculation – at the touch of a single key – of the consequences of changing a single variable, or the effects of simultaneous changes, often in conflicting directions, of several. It is the latter that makes planning difficult. Now you can sit at your micro, experiment with different numbers and only commit to tape or disk, and then print, the selected outcomes. By storing those outcomes, they can be recalled again and again and the whole process can be repeated. Only the results you select need be committed to memory. Whilst by no means a computer expert, by using one of the best-known of these spreadsheet programs, I have reduced the calculation aspects of my own business plans from something like two weeks to less than a day, and with the advantage that I can compare many more alternatives in that day. Moreover, incorporating month-end details and changes in assumptions is a matter of minutes or hours, as you choose. Any marketing practitioner is strongly advised to acquire familiarity with the properties of spreadsheets.

8.5 Content of the plan

Here are some suggestions for those who may not have produced an annual operating plan before or who may be considering change. Do bear in mind, however, that the process is more important than the plan itself. The suggestions are presented in the form of notes alone. Where different kinds of business may require something different, that is indicated in brackets after the title of the headings.

1 *Marketing background* Salient features of the market's and product's development since the last plan, showing the way these affect the current situation and the plans.
2 *Current situation* Basically a review of actual against forecast performance. (At this point, the current year usually has to be treated as three quarters actuals and one quarter forecast.) An objective, analytical examination to point up lessons learned and new strengths and/or weaknesses which have emerged.
3 *Marketing objectives and strategy* Major objectives for the coming year, in particular, and the longer term, in general. Quantify objectives and state in precise and measurable terms how achievement is to be determined. Clearly define strategic positioning.
4 *Profit* Bottom line figures compared with past performance and current objectives, noting any significant variances and reasons for them. (Full details of costings etc. are best confined to the appendices.)
5 *Product line* (Appropriate to all; expressed more in industrial

169

terms where greater complexity is likely.) Introductions, withdrawals, phasing out, modifications, lines to be pushed in present markets, and applications; those for new markets and applications.

6   *Pricing*   (As with 5, expressed more in industrial terms where greater flexibility generally exists.) Changes, differential charging, terms of business, credit arrangements (where part of the conditions of business), charged and uncharged or subsidized service aspects. An 'optional extra' in the sense that it need not be included if there are no charges.

7   *Direct sales*   (Normally, not included in consumer plans which, more correctly, deal with income-generating considerations rather than cost terms.) Changes in size and organization of sales force; remuneration, commission, recruitment, training, etc. Conferences, seminars, etc.

8   *Advertising and sales promotion*   Reasons why, not how, at this stage. Funds required and comparison with last year. Creative, media and promotional strategies, prefacing detailed recommendations (possibly from advertising agency). Review of last year's effectiveness and broadbrush picture of type of promotion, anticipating later plans. Promotional objectives.

9   *Technical service*   (Industrial with some service aspects.) Presales: testing, advice, assistance. Applications research. Aftersales: service, advice, training. Spares organization, claims departments, personal counsellors. Size and scope of technical forces. Charging policy.

10   *Physical distribution*   (As for item 7, *Direct sales*.) Delivery time objectives, stock levels, seasonal changes, location of stocks and depots, transportation methods.

11   *Distributors and factors*   (Industrial; similar considerations for some services; e.g. brokers, agents as distributors.) Policy. Discount and/or payment structure. Co-operation, communication, training, motivation, assistance, etc.

12   *Market research*   Desk, *ad hoc*, continuous, product testing, etc. New information required, action planned to obtain it, cost. Use to which it will be put. An optional extra.

13   *Product development*   Optional extra: should relate to recycling and development of existing products rather than completely new ones.

14   *Packaging*   Optional extra. New packaging, materials, costs, reasons why, anticipated effect on sales and profit.

15   *Marketing organization and staff*   A cost item which ideally

should not be on this plan. As a business overhead, it should not be a direct charge on a revenue-generating budget, but should be put with other overhead budgets. Frequently included in industrial budgets where it is often a first charge on promotional budgets.

There may well be others appropriate to your business. In particular, the chief executive or possibly the finance director may want to see key business ratios included or, possibly, capital budgets related to the revenue-generating plans. However, there is one general format that suits any content. It helps digestion by senior management, too. It is, simply, to keep the content as tight and factual as possible with any necessary masses of figures confined to appendices. The whole should be prefaced with a summary, preferably kept to one page, and certain appendices should be common to all plans.

What the common appendices are will be a matter for discussion. The first will certainly be detailed profit figures. If these are not included in both a look forward and a look back, those items should feature in the next appendices. Actually, there is a good case for keeping next year's figures next to the current ones, whilst the longer-term view probably needs fewer details so that volumes and values are more clearly highlighted. Consumer product companies may well find that the next most important appendix is advertising and sales promotion; industrial companies may put the sales force next. The overall idea is that the busy chief executive can extract the essential sense from a plan by reading the summary and three or four key appendices. If the summary doesn't indicate the reasons for any breaks in logic, he will then know which plans he has to examine in most detail, first.

8.6 Controlling the plan

It is not enough to produce a splendidly written plan; it has to be acted upon and monitored continually. Without going into great detail (and some of the areas will receive chapters to themselves), it is worth listing the main headings for continuous examination and making one or two brief comments where applicable.

THE PRODUCT

Many marketing managers use the systems suggested here and then forget to check that the quality of their product is what they believed it would be. The very first place to look for any deviation in sales is to the product or service you are providing. Has it changed in any way?

171

Business history is littered with cases where managers have changed an ingredient or component without testing with the end-user, because they themselves could discern no difference. Regular users know a great deal about the goods and services they buy and can often recognize fine nuances that their suppliers have never recognized or are incapable of recognizing.

Continual testing and quality control is vital, especially with services where devices such as 'test shopping' may be necessary to discover how customers really are treated.

SALES

Everyone checks sales. But are sales records kept purely as historical documents or are they collected in such a way that rapid remedial action can be taken? Few are. The ideal is daily reporting of sales by the lowest possible unit of purchase. If the next stage up in sales management has figures with that frequency, there is every opportunity of a rapid call-back on a previously unsuccessful visit.

The lowest unit of call and frequency will obviously vary by industry but all figures should be kept in a form that allows rapid remedial action to be taken and then, and only then, aggregated into management control figures.

Basic areas to be checked are volume, profit from sales, share of market, repeat sales and sales by area or unit.

PROFIT

Sales figures tend to be under the management microscope all the time and thus get amended frequently. Sometimes too frequently to allow for quirks of timing that will come right a little later. Profit forecasts, on the other hand, tend to be amended only in response to changes in sales forecast, although the size and frequency of changes in raw material prices and wage increases has changed that of late. Even so, amendments to profit forecasts tend to happen more often when they reflect adverse trends than when they seem favourable. Marketing and profit go together: marketing is a profit-generating activity. It is thus absolutely vital that the marketing executive is aware of all the ingredients that go to make up final profit and of any changes in them. It is similarly important that profits are calculated realistically and not by some outdated or irrelevant convention, and that all variances are notified promptly. I spent my first year as a Brand Manager struggling to produce my profit objective in a most inhospitable marketing climate, only to discover at the year end that an item called 'prime cost variances' produced a 'profit' three times greater than the profit on sales had. It may have been possible to have used some of that excess to strengthen the position of the brand but we never had the chance.

For adequate control, and in order to modify plans where necessary to achieve the original objectives, overhead and materials budgets should be subjected to exactly the same disciplines as sales budgets. If marketing management cannot be trusted to use this information properly, that is to improve long-term profits of the business, they have no right to their jobs.

COMPETITIVE REACTIONS

When we looked at the question 'How?', we saw how important a knowledge of competitors' methods and activities is. Adequate and rapid reporting systems must be established if the information is to be actionable.

Competitive advertising and promotional programmes and activities will come under this examination, as will changes in pricing policy, terms, discounts, training and servicing facilities. Indeed, any item that you consider important to your plan is probably important to your competitor, too, and likely to figure in his plans.

BUDGETS

It should go without saying that actual results, in all areas, should be compared to budgets continuously. There are four basic points you should consider about any form of management control information:

1 Does it really help management – or is it just a mass of figures? Ask how often people actually use the figures; that will give a fair indication of their usefulness.
2 Does it show clearly where current performance *does not* match budget?
3 Does it avoid 'information indigestion' when on budget? (If you are on budget, do you really need to know more?)
4 Is the information it presents 'weighted'? Does it take notice of the 80:20 rule; does it take account of the concept of sterling weighted sales and distribution?

Taking all these things together puts a heavy emphasis on 'exception reporting' systems, that is, figures are only reported when they deviate from budget by a predetermined amount.

There are other areas which may need the same degree of continual check. Heavy advertisers, for example, will try to produce crude checks of the effectiveness of their advertising – there is always the ultimate check of whether the sales pay for the expenditure. Similarly,

173

sales force effectiveness will be under continual review by the Sales Director.

8.7 Conclusion

Right at the outset, six factors were described as being those which differ most frequently in different companies' plans. In the light of what has been discussed in this chapter, let us take another look at those factors, adding fresh comment where none has previously been offered.

Reference has been made to the necessity of taking some account of the past and the value of looking ahead. The past helps establish a logic and is an indispensable aid to forecasting. Since the past is thus implicit in planning, there really is no reason why it should not be reviewed more fully and openly. No present plan is ever fully meaningful without some relation to the future. Today's plan has to lead somewhere, and an indication of that direction with some quantification, however inaccurate it may turn out to be, is necessary. It is interesting that complaints about the inaccuracy of long-term forecasts only ever seem to relate to over-optimistic ones; those which are handsomely exceeded generally pass without comment. Again, it is the process rather than the plan which is of greater value. Some quantificaton of a possible future does, at the very least, force the business to consider the consequences of such a future and the steps necessary to get there. How far back and how far forward is a matter that depends enormously on the type of business. The majority of companies find it possible to take five years back and five forward, after quite a short period (although changes in convention can cause havoc). There are few businesses that cannot produce a meaningful profile of three years back and three forward. On the other hand, there are some that need to look very much further forward. The travel business, for example, operates so far forward, on bed deposits, air charters, hotel leases and so on, that the earliest year they can actually do anything about may be three years away. In that respect, the plan they produce for two or three years ahead is the equivalent of the one most companies will produce this September for next January. Such companies frequently adopt a seven-year cycle on the basis that, in effect, year one is two years hence and they want to look five years ahead of that. Others take the simpler view that a large number of leases (of both hotels and aircraft) are based on seven years. It does, however, indicate the sort of parameters that should be considered when setting what are called 'planning horizons'. Look at

174

the critical factors in your business and decide the effective lead time. That will begin to define the horizon for your business.

As for the degree of detail, that is largely up to you and your business. There is a case for the first of a new series of plans, or the first for a product, to be fairly lengthy and provide the basis for a data book. The marketing executive living with the product line may have plenty of knowledge about the market and the buyers, but his seniors know very little. They don't need to be told every year. I know a number of very large companies where the first advice given to new brand managers is 'Never throw old plans away: you can repeat 90 per cent of it next year.' If the sense can be obtained from a summary and about three appendices, and if a consistent logic has been followed, there really is little need for an enormous tome. I can tell you from experience that very few plans get read from cover to cover when they are first received; there is seldom the time to do it.

Moreover, if the emphasis is on strategy, with only the barest indication of tactics and execution in the plan itself, length will automatically be proscribed. An annual operating plan should not attempt to be simultaneously the advertising recommendations, sales force incentive programme, special offer and trade deal recommendations. Indicate what is to come in such a way that senior management can say, in effect: 'Providing the tactical recommendation fits your strategy and looks workable, the money will be forthcoming'. That is the acid test, provided it fits the defined strategy. Every piece of tactics, every scrap of promotional material must have that sole aim – to express the company strategy to its market.

What about alternatives? Although mention was made very early on of two alternatives, the discussion since has really only considered one recommendation. This is because, in the ideal situation, there will only need to be one, because that recommendation will show how the defined objective is to be achieved. Sometimes it cannot. It may even be wrong. Perhaps, as often happens, the only way to produce the profit is to debase the product. In cases like that, achieving the profit in year one is usually at the expense of a very much more rapid decline. Where a manager believes it would be wrong for the longer-term benefit of the company to aim to exactly achieve the target, that manager should propose the one his conscience dictates. But he should also show another which says, in effect: 'If I have to hit the target you have given me, this is how it would have to be done – and this is what I reckon the longer-term consequences will be'. His first recommendation may have to be ignored. But he will have made sure of what was seen in Chapter 1 to be so important – the decision will have to be taken with full knowledge of the possible ramifications and consequences. And, as has been made plain so many times in this chapter, once the plan is set, only two things should be sacrosanct: the objective and the strategy. The tactics will be as flexible as necessary. In the very last resort, if your earthquake maps have failed you, it may even be necessary to change the objective part-way through the year. When so much time and trouble has gone into choosing a strategy, just as much thought should be given before changing it.

8.8 Summary

General (later President) Eisenhower had a sign behind his desk when he commanded the Allied Forces in Europe. It read:

Plans are nothing.
Planning is everything.

The emphasis of this chapter is that if the process is right, the plan will come right too. Careful pre-planning, 'giving the plan a chance', with consideration of alternatives, possible competitive reactions, your own reactions to any such moves, and the preparation of contingency plans will produce the best set of outcomes.

Although difficult, the aim should be to produce the best fit between resources and results so that any change in one will result, at least, in the need to reconsider the other. Using a sequence like the one outlined gives the best chance of an acceptable reconciliation between the results expected and the resources applied.

8.9 Checklist

1 Any plan *must* produce firm recommendations after considering all reasonable alternatives. Except in exceptional circumstances, the recommended plan will be that which produces the best long-term result.

2 Occasionally it may be necessary to produce two alternatives: the plan which achieves the pre-determined objectives and the one the planner believes to be the best in the long-term interests of the company.

3 The best plan for the company is seldom the total of all the best plans for individual products, units or companies within it. Compromise is normally the case and the inability to resource all the individual plans will mean changing some of the outcomes.

176

4   All marketing plans should aim to achieve company objectives. These should be carefully arrived at, realistic, and fully communicated to all those responsible for achieving them.

5   Objectives may be simply comparative, based on cash sums or the use of business ratios. Some combination is usually the case, mainly because the shared use of assets and human resources normally makes it difficult to apply relevant ratios to any individual part of the business.

6   Before the plan is written down, the techniques described in earlier chapters (the six questions, portfolio analysis, etc.) are combined in the resource analysis stage. If this has already been done, the findings are reviewed and form the basis for the SWOT analysis.

7   All resulting aspects of the possible plan must then be communicated and co-ordinated to ensure that everybody will pull in the agreed direction. Care should be taken not to commit departments to undue or unnecessary action before the plan has been agreed, at least in outline.

8   A sequence that begins with a series of 'warning shots' is recommended as the best and safest way to reconcile resources and results.

9   'Product strategies' are reviewed and combined to form 'Divisional' and/or 'Corporate' strategies, as necessary.

10 The aim of these strategy documents is to check the fit of individual plans within corporate objectives and receive authority to proceed to detailed planning. Once detailed planning begins, money is often irrevocably committed, as are the early stages of the plan.

11 Since the people responsible for achieving the plan do not always see the documents, a 'Plan and commitment summary' is a good idea and forms a verbal network plan of the sequence necessary to make the plan happen and, like a formal network plan, of the dependencies of departments upon each other.

12 Plans must obviously be realistic. 'Hope' should be kept only to an unavoidable minimum. 'Realistic' usually means that they are the outcome of an inherent logic, or that the plans and tactics recommended are capable of changing that logic.

13   Few things are totally unexpected, although their timing is often unpredictable. The three-block system suggested enables one to consider contingency plans for those events most likely to occur or change. The discipline encourages all managers to look for events with either opportunities or threats well before they become problems or missed opportunities.

14   The plan is controlled by continual examination of the product or service, sales, costs and profits. All elements within the plan or which could affect its outcomes and achievements *must* be subject to the same disciplines, reviews and timing.

15   The complex relationships and interactions within a plan, and especially the response to competitive reactions (which may trigger off a further reaction from competition) are most easily assessed by the use of a spreadsheet ('What if?') program on a microcomputer.

16   Once set, the objectives and strategy are sacrosanct. Tactics should always be regarded as flexible. Moreover, since they are likely to spark off competitive reaction (from their own flexible tactics), an alternative should be prepared at the same time as the first-choice tactic.

9

What the Future Foretells

Long foretold, long last;
Short notice, soon past.

17th century proverb

With this chapter, we reach a turning point and turning points are one of the things we shall consider. Until now, each chapter has been concerned with what has been defined as the philosophy of marketing and practical applications of that way of thinking. Several times, it has been necessary to make passing reference to some technique or other; forecasting is, perhaps, the most appropriate bridge between philosophy and techniques. Moreover it is the one technique that every kind of business has to employ over a wide area of business situations and especially in planning.

Forecasts shape plans and plans shape forecasts. In one direction, the plan is derived from consideration of possible alternatives involving forecasts of the results of possible action; in the other direction, a plan is evolved that requires accurate forecasts of its outcomes. Like so much in marketing, forecasting is part art, part science. The sensible manager uses science wherever possible, but no forecast is likely to be the best possible unless it contains an input from those people in the business most closely connected with, and who understand the market. Indeed, we shall see that it is more likely that circumstances will arise where total reliance has to be placed on personal opinions than it is that a completely mathematical method will suffice.

In the majority of companies, far too little forecasting is used. Sales forecasts are often the only ones attempted, for it is universally recognized that the sales forecast is the bedrock from which all others stem. However, there are many more business areas than simply sales which are amenable to forecasting. Profits, for example, need not necessarily arise only from sales, and the possible outcomes of these

179

alternatives can and should be predicted. Forecasts of investment and labour requirements may relate directly to own-company sales, to possible alternative plans and to demands for labour from neighbouring companies, demands for machinery from other manufacturers and countries and so on. Consideration of such forecasts often prompts actions which could not even be considered unless the inter-relationships between variables had been noted. Since the sales forecast is the bedrock, since marketing personnel are most often involved in that area – perhaps to the exclusion of others – and because the techniques and methods apply to most types of forecast, the primary concern of this chapter will be with the forecasts most directly affecting the sales of the company.

9.1   Selecting the method

There is no single or simple method of forecasting which is applicable to all circumstances and companies. Unfortunately, many managers appear to believe there is and usually rely on something like the moving average projected forward, when that is no more than an ingredient in a technique and needs careful handling. Different objectives help determine the method to be used. Different factors affecting markets and differing time periods are other highly significant variables. Factors which may be very important to a forecast for three months ahead could well be totally insignificant to one for twelve months and yet others would be required for a five-year plan. Even then, no one method may suffice. The same forecaster working with the same products and facts may well try several different approaches and compare the results, making reconciliations wherever they seem to work.

The type of business will help determine the method used. Consumer products and the majority of services usually have far more of the significant factors under their own control. Even though they may not own the actual means of distribution, many of the key factors involve decisions which they themselves can take: price, promotion, deals, distribution channels, delivery times, and so on. Truly industrial companies, that is those meeting a derived demand, tend to have far fewer areas of direct influence. Moreover, it may be impossible to obtain information about what is happening further along the total system of which the product is only a part. Obviously, this kind of forecast is going to be more difficult and involve totally different techniques from one concerning a product where there are fewer factors outside the influence of the company. On the other hand, derived demand occurs because the product is necessary to the manufacture of another and often, to ensure necessary supplies, the customer goes to the supplier with forecasts of likely needs.

The position on the demand life-cycle is one of the determinants of the amount of information and the need for a particular type of forecast. Of especial importance is the amount of assistance that forecasting needs in different stages; in the very early stages, one needs to know if it is the same buyers repeating or different ones, for example. The total sales curve can look exactly the same but the forecast will be completely different. The further along the cycle one is, the more important it is to use a technique that gives the best possible indication of likely turning points, Half-way up the curve, one may be more in need of accurate estimates of final steady demand so that production, raw material and labour resources can be planned accordingly. Without going any further, it should be apparent that not only the type of forecasting method used may differ but the requirement for accuracy changes. As we shall see later, there is normally a trade-off between cost and accuracy, so another matter of concern will be the likely benefit of the results of the forecast. For example, if a forecast costs £10,000 to prepare but the profit on the resulting sales is only £8,000 it doesn't appear worth doing – unless the longer-term ramifications can provide a 'pay-back' in terms of the ultimate benefit related to the immediate cost.

The purpose of the forecast will also determine the method. If you are considering entering a business for the first time, it may be sufficient to have a fairly rough estimate of market size. (It comes as a surprise to many managers to realize that a rough and ready size of market estimate *ought* to be enough; a decision that has to be taken on finite results accurate to the last £100 is obviously a very risky decision, whilst one that still works to plus or minus £100,000 in the market size estimate is far less so.) If the purpose is a budget or a target for performance (always assuming the latter is not based on stretching performance when it is in fact possible to achieve profit budget with a sales performance of 10 per cent less), then much greater accuracy is needed. When the purpose is to set standards, you can afford to ignore the measures designed to lead to changes. If you are looking for forecasts of the effects of changes in strategy or tactics on growth, you will need highly sophisticated techniques most able to take account of the effects of planned events. This is an area where the spreadsheet computer programs can put quite sophisticated, and otherwise time-consuming, techniques in the hands of non-mathematical forecasters.

181

There are many other factors that help determine the method, including:

The context in which the forecast has to be made
How much historical data is available
How relevant that data is
How many changes from past events are planned
How much time is available for making the forecasts
The margins of error that are permissible before disaster strikes the firm.

Finally, when one forecast (almost certainly the sales forecast) is used as the basis for others, there are four questions to be asked which may help decide whether the same method is correct and if the method used in the first instance is trustworthy for the new purpose; in many cases, additional factors may have to be taken into account and the base forecast amended before other factors can be considered.

1   What methods and techniques were used to achieve the base forecast?
2   What economic assumptions were included?
3   What assumptions have been made about competitive behaviour and possible reactions?
4   Were standard costs used or have any price or cost changes been incorporated?

Without further elaboration, the importance of these questions in the production of additional forecasts should be obvious.

9.2   The stages of forecasting

Good forecasting procedure employs this sequence, or as much of it as is necessary to the forecast required:

1   Set background assumptions, for example will Britain stay in the Common Market, will laws be harmonized?
2   Define planning assumptions (as set out in Chapter 8).
3   Identify trends ('trend fitting').
4   Project into a defined future (remembering the relationship between method used and the time-span of the forecast).
5   Convert projections into predictions of market behaviour (to be explained in the following sections).
6   Add 'circumstantial evidence', that is the evidence of your own eyes, such as closure of customers, changes in ownership, changes in attitudes to services, etc.

7   Apply business judgement, relevant experience and the intuition of the proven 'best guessers'.
8   Integrate the human elements.
9   Forecast.

This same method will work, as will most techniques of forecasting, for total markets, industry sectors or individual customers. The weighting you give to the different elements may change quite markedly.

9.3   Projections

Most forecasting methods attempt to discern a pattern in past behaviour which can be carried forward into the future. At one extreme is the computer-based, highly sophisticated technique, whilst, at the other, is the laying of a plastic ruler across a set of figures or the drawing of a freehand curve as a continuation of an existing shape. Actually, the two extremes are not so far apart as they may seem. If you have a good eye for putting an equal number of plottings on either side of an imaginary line, the plastic ruler (which, of course, allows you to see what otherwise would be covered) may be satisfactory; if you have both a good eye and a steady hand, the freehand curve will work for you. After all, what the computer does is really the same as these two alternatives – it simply uses complex equations to ensure the greatest possible accuracy. It really scores in those cases where sales figures jump up and down all over the place and no human eye can discern a relevant pattern. In between the more obviously 'do-it-yourself' methods and the use of the computer come simple moving averages and totals, trend analysis and fitting and exponential smoothing, with the latter not infrequently using the computer for greater speed.

The problem with a projection is that is assumes a future just like the past. In the very short term, this may be accurate enough; when longer time-spans have to be forecast, the assumption usually proves false. Things like new products, changes in use and usage patterns, price alterations, new competitive strategies, and so on, all reduce any similarity between the past and the future. Nevertheless, there is often considerable value in projections based on the past and this will be seen more clearly when we consider how trends are fitted to data. There is a not inconsiderable number of cases where simple statistical projection has actually been more accurate than managers' predictions of future events. For this reason, as much as any other, a simple projection is normally the first mathematical stage of any eventual forecast and is often, and usefully, known as the 'What if?' forecast: what if the future is exactly like the past, what actions would we need to take, is that future good enough, what should we do to make it better? Most good marketing planners make such a projection before starting detailed planning, to prompt those very questions.

9.4 Predictions

Now we need far more information. To make a prediction, it is necessary to try to discover what events seem to go with others ('correlation') and what factors account for what changes ('causal relationships'). Obviously, the more we can learn about such events the greater the accuracy of both our forecasts and our plans. The accuracy with which the sales of the company (for example) can be predicted will itself depend heavily on the accuracy with which movements in the relevant factors can be predicted. Long-term trend fitting and projection can be of great assistance in determining such relationships, especially where they are lagged in time. For example, a long sequence of events correlates at a distance with the birth of a child – baby clothes, starting school, school uniform, changing schools, opening savings accounts, bank accounts, houses, baby clothes again (as they have their own families) and so on. The age of a population is often a significant lagged indicator. Purchase of plant presages entry into an industry and may generate a lagged demand for packaging material, banking services, insurance, advertising and many others. Those are fairly simple causal indicators and enough to convince most managers that this is not an area they can afford to ignore completely. The search for other indicators may be far more complex. It is often very useful indeed to simulate not only known causal events ('what would happen if . . . ?') but also less likely ones. The three-day week which resulted from the miners' strike in 1974 might have been less damaging if more businesses had simulated the effect of a dramatic reduction in fuel and power supplies. Different levels of unemployment, changes in interest rates, raising the school-leaving age are all examples of the sort of event which may have a causal relationship in the future, even if the absence of the event now obviously means there is no such correlation.

Any business should search for its own significant 'leading indicator' – the event that sets off a chain of purchasing events. Not every business will find one. Some may find several, not always pulling in the same direction. In addition to those already mentioned, significant leading indicators for many businesses include: new housing starts; levels of employment; volume of advertising (like new investment, an indicator of confidence in the future).

9.5 Forecasts

The process began with projections, looked at causal relationships and predicted likely outcomes of these additional factors. For it to become a forecast, it is now necessary to add the best possible opinions about planned and/or expected events. This is where the possible outcomes of your actions begin to shape the figures. Obviously, the opinions used should be based on the best possible evidence and experience of similar events and their effects. Beware of expecting an exact replication under circumstances where that cannot possibly happen. Unfortunately, in marketing few things repeat themselves with the same order of magnitude. For example, any drive to open new distribution channels must take account of the fact that those which featured in the success of the last effort cannot be opened again; similar considerations apply to new buyers and users. Science, and particularly statistical and mathematical methods, leads in both projections and prediction; art is to the forefront in converting the earlier stages into a forecast.

The significant difference between the projection and prediction stages and the forecast itself is that the first two provide logical and mathematical outcomes; the forecast is a quantified statement about what you intend to make happen. Thus it includes plans and hopes. Obviously, these must be realistic, objective and, preferably, based upon market tests or customer trials.

9.6 Statistical methods

Statistical techniques can be used where several years' data exists in continuous form. Their use does depend also on clear trends and stable relationships between relevant factors: they cannot predict the effect of new and changing relationships. Since an understanding of time series and trend fittings is essential to the appreciation of statistical methods, these two topics will be considered briefly.

TIME SERIES ANALYSIS

A time series is a set of raw numbers in date order. Submitting them to analysis helps to identify, and hopefully explain, several important factors, especially:

185

1 Any regular or seasonal variations from a norm. (The word 'seasonal' is normally used in statistics to describe any regular variation, not simply a summer/winter difference. Thus, the fact that certain customers' factories close down for two weeks every August would be classed as a seasonal factor.)
2 Any kind of cyclical feature that repeats itself every two years or more. (Recurring seasonals in shorter periods are usually obvious enough not to require complex identification methods.)
3 The direction of trends.
4 The rate of growth or decline of those trends.

The techniques work best for short-term forecasting, but they can be used for longer periods where an industry has very stable relationships between factors and stability in its data. Their inability to predict means that they are bad indicators of turning points in sales and profit curves.

EXTRAPOLATION
This is a word used frequently in time series analysis. It simply means that some method has been used to project a relationship beyond the range of the supporting data. It means 'to take out'. Thus, one takes out the pattern of the past and uses that to produce a pattern for the future. You are, in effect, saying 'There is no evidence for what I am doing other than it is the sort of relationship that has worked in the past'. You project by extrapolation.

TREND FITTING
Sales trends are much more clearly apparent from a long series of data than from a few plottings, and often no great amount of work is necessary to enable one to discern them. This is especially true where one of the three basic shapes is apparent without the use of any smoothing techniques. Trend fitting is of greatest help where such shapes are not obvious. Look at Figure 21. There is a fairly simple upward trend visible, but consider what would happen if one looked only at the most recent data: the projection would be very different.

An objection to trend fitting and projection is that the future is unlikely to be like the past. All experience shows that the vast majority of well-formed patterns hold their shape for at least half a year. Things like changes in economic conditions (other than short-lived emotive reactions to the actions of the Chancellor of the Exchequer) hardly ever lead to dramatic short-term market changes. Most projections last long enough to justify the course of action

186

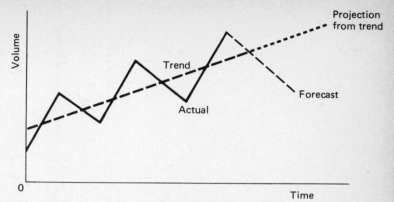

Figure 21 *Projections from trend and short-term data*

proposed and can stand changing half-way through the year, since the difference between the first plan and the amended one should not be big enough to have affected the first decision. (Simulation of the possible alternatives could have helped decide whether it was or not.)

Before moving on to look at some of the major ways trends are actually fitted, let us take a look at the three basic shapes of curve:

1   Linear trends are straight lines which means they increase by the same, or nearly the same, amounts each year. Thus, in Table 6, the increase each year is 20 units. A graph on normal paper would show a perfectly straight line. Equations for various slopes are easy to derive and thus projection can be made very accurate indeed,

Table 6

Year	Linear trend	Exponential trend
1	50	50.00
2	70	60.00
3	90	72.00
4	110	86.40
5	130	103.68
6	150	124.42
7	170	149.30
8	190	179.16
9	210	214.99
10	230	257.99

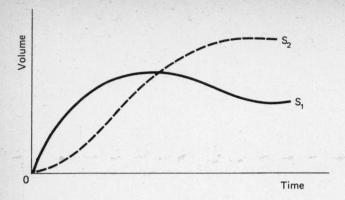

Figure 22 *Typical S-shaped curves*

  although such techniques are hardly necessary when a ruler will
  do much the same job.
2 Exponential trends, on the other hand, would normally appear as
  a curve (unless plotted on semi-log paper where they appear as
  straight lines). The key this time is that they increase by the same
  percentage each year. In Table 6 the increase is 20 per cent *per
  annum.*
3 The third shape is the sigma or S-shaped curve. This is a very
  familiar pattern in marketing and readers will recognize that the
  growth stages of the life-cycle conform to this general shape.
  There are several descriptions and corresponding equations of
  various complexity to both describe the shape and provide the
  projection means. Figure 22 shows just two of the more common
  shapes. The dotted line is fairly typical of new launches – a slow
  build-up, rapid growth as the product takes on and then maturity.
  The solid line illustrates the 'penetration' launch in which
  everything possible is done to obtain rapid results: high levels of
  promotion, low prices, trade deals, etc. (We refer to penetration
  pricing policies in Chapter 11.)

SMOOTHING THE TREND

If you are ever faced with a sales history like that in Figure 23, you will
have problems. It does, however, exemplify several important aspects
of smoothing techniques. Obviously, unless the shape is smoothed,
the eye cannot discern any overall pattern. Although each year seems
to have two peaks and two troughs, corresponding peaks and troughs
have varied widely. In such a case, one single act of smoothing may

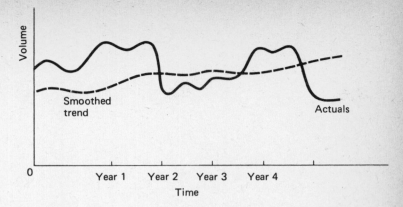

Figure 23 *Problems of projecting from seasonal data*

not be enough and it might need repeating several times before a shape begins to appear. Obviously, the more times this is done, the greater the distance from reality. If the final smoothing were to come out like the dotted line in Figure 23, one might well have serious doubts about any projection from that line which varies so much from the most recent points on the sales curve.

The simplest, and most used, method of smoothing is the moving average. Decide on a period, say 12 months. Aggregate sales for the chosen period and divide by 12. When the next monthly sales return comes in, add that to the previous total but deduct that for the first period of the original 12. Divide the new total by 12. The simple formula is:

Period 1 to 12;	Period 2 to 13;	Period 3 to 14
12	12	12

Calculated moving average plus or minus difference between periods 1 and 13 divided by 12

Unfortunately, there is a serious practical difficulty with the moving average: it produces figures people have difficulty in recognizing at periods when they clearly didn't happen. If, for example, you take a 12-monthly average, the first figure will fall not against either period 1 or 12 but mid-way between periods 6 and 7; it will also represent one-twelfth of what any salesman knows he has sold. In an effort to correct this, the moving average is 'centred'. You do this by adding each pair of moving average figures and dividing by 2: now you can

189

put the first figure against period 6.

There is a much easier and far more practically effective way. Do not divide the answers: this way you are dealing with a moving total. Each figure represents the period ending; thus, a 12-monthly moving total will be the total for the 12 months ending at each month-end. This is a real figure that every manager can identify with. I have actually worked in a company where a factory manager was fed with moving averages and actually produced one-twelfth of the requirement in the first month using the averages as evidence of what he was asked for.

Either method will give a fairly smooth curve although, as we have noted, it may be necessary to adjust periods or carry out successive smoothing to get the shape clear. There are problems. Firstly, there is no attempt to understand the underlying forces at work; they are simply taken for granted. That is one major reason why trend fitting is only a first step. How close is the trend to the raw figure? The more variable they are, the less certain will be any projection. Figure 23 is an example of a variance that throws considerable doubt on the projection. If there are any plateaux, consider carefully whether you can ignore the lower steps as irrelevant influences on the future. Do you know what caused those steps? Keeping a diary of events would have been useful. Be careful to distinguish between demand and sales when interpreting the trend. If demand has not been fully satisfied in the past, the trend will not be a true indicator of the future possibilities when supplies are increased. Finally, do make sure that no conventions have been changed to affect the trend. Figures for the United States tea and coffee markets have been totally confused by differing interpretations of the ratio of leaf tea and bean coffee in instant products. The tea market in that country shows one trend by sales of packages but another by leaf tea equivalent – hardly surprising when instant tea mixes (lemon tea) contain as little as 3 per cent tea by volume and are substituted for packets of pure tea.

Not all of those questions can be overcome by different smoothing techniques. It is, however, possible to give greater weight to recent events (so that, for example, more account could be taken of that steep fall in recent months shown in Figure 23). There are even methods which would allow one to weight different periods in very markedly different ways. In Figure 23, you might want to ignore year 3 on the grounds that it was quite exceptional and unlikely to occur again. It can be done but now you are into computer programs. If this is your problem, talk to leading software houses about the packages they have, which will produce the results of many years of manual labour in almost the same amount of minutes. The basis, however, will be exponentially weighted moving averages.

Even here, the technique is quite simple, especially once the right factor has been found. The method is to start with the latest period for which figures are available *and* the forecast for that period. Calculate the error (actual – forecast *or* forecast – actual). Now you adjust the former forecast by adding or subtracting – as appropriate – a proportion of the error and this gives the new forecast. Notice that you do not add the whole error, only a proportion of it.

The proportion of error that you add has to be established by trial and error. If may be helpful to be aware that the most common figures seem to be 0.2 and 0.3; the largest I have found to be meaningful is 0.8 but this seems to be an unusually high figure. Once the proportion has been found, it can be handled by any manager; many companies rely on personal secretaries to keep the forecast up-to-date on this basis. Where there is a very large number of calculations, a computer may be useful.

9.7 Putting back the kinks

Nearly all projections from smoothed figures suffer the considerable disadvantage that they are too flat to be meaningful as forecasts. Figure 23 clearly needs some seasonal kinks added back. We take them out by the de-seasonalizing data (the technique is well described in standard statistical texts) and we can add them back almost as easily in most cases. What would have been better for Figure 23 would have been to have produced our trend by de-seasonalization and then we could have added back a series of plusses or minuses to our smoothed line, so that we ended up with a line of the right shape to take account of the way business is clearly done in that company. Most methods project from a smoothing basis not at all unlike the moving average. If it is then necessary in your business to separate out trends and seasonal variations with greater forecasting precision, more time and more money will be necessary. In summary, the method involves:

1 Plotting the rate of change in underlying trends.
2 Projecting the rate forward over the chosen period.
3 Adding or subtracting that growth rate to the raw de-seasonalized data showing present sales rate.
4 Projecting the seasonals for the period covered by the forecast.
5 Multiplying de-seasonalized forecast rate by the seasonals.
6 Forecasting total sales rate from results.

191

9.8 Qualitative techniques

Sometimes, it just isn't possible to use numerical techniques. This is where qualitative methods come in. Any situation where data is scarce presents an opportunity for considering one of these non-statistical means. However, there are often new situations to consider where adequate data exists for statistical techniques but where, perhaps, the relevance of the past to the future is in doubt. They can be valuable, too, when adding the human element to a projection such as when considering the possible outcome of a course of action. Thus, qualitative methods can be used alone or in combination.

These methods basically attempt to make use of human judgement and employ various rating schemes to put numerical values on expert opinions. That means bringing together not only all the possible factors in a system under investigation but also the judgements about them, and doing so in the most systematic and logical way that can be devised. The great danger, obviously, is bias and the possibility of 'management ego' clearly stares one in the face unless adequate safeguards exist. The best way to avoid these problems is to seek as many views as possible and provide adequate feedback to other views and any new and different opinions that may be expressed in different parts of the company.

SUBJECTIVE PROBABILITIES

At the heart of the qualitative techniques is forcing people to put numbers on their opinions. For example, a group of managers is divided equally between those who rate a new product as a likely success and those who rate it as a probable failure. With a 50:50 split, the final decision is usually taken by the most senior manager. However, when asked to assign probabilities to their views, those arguing for success say they are 65 per cent certain; those who think the product will fail are only 55 per cent certain of their view. If we add the two favourable probabilities $(65 + 45)$ and the two unfavourable ones $(35 + 55)$ and divide by 2 (because we have two sets of opinions), we get:

$$\frac{(65 + 45):(55 + 35)}{2}$$

$$= \frac{110:90}{2}$$

$$= 55:45$$

Because one group of managers is more positive in its opinions about success than the other is about failure, the balance of probabilities comes down firmly on the side of success.

Clearly, the outcome is obvious in this example; if a dozen managers have very different probabilities of success and failure, the balance of opinion may not be so clear. Do not confuse a 50:50 split in numbers expressing an opinion with a 50:50 probability.

DELPHI TECHNIQUE

The best known, and probably most universally applicable, of the qualitative methods is known as 'the Delphi technique' – another way of saying 'consulting the oracle'. That is precisely what happens. A questionnaire, possibly about the likelihood of success with a new product, is submitted to a wide cross-section of management likely to have valid views to express based on solid experience. The various opinions on each sub-section are collated and passed back, anonymously, for comment. Each original participant is asked to review the feedback and comment, giving the reasons for their views and why they reject any views. This goes on until either a clear consensus is emerging or until it becomes clear that there is going to be no more 'bending' of views. The reporting stage summarizes what might be termed the 'average' opinion and indicates the spread of viewpoints.

There are variations around the basic method. Many practitioners prefer to conduct personal interviews at the feedback stage, especially when it is the first use of the method in a company. Personal contact does allow one to feed opinions back in a way that guarantees comment: 'Some people have expressed a view that the market will be at least double the size you suggested for these reasons . . . what do you say now?'

Figure 24 shows how outcomes are typically expressed and is an actual example of the method in use. A company manufacturing expensive heavy plant had a problem in that it had to rely on sales force forecasts of sales. In fact, they were 95 per cent correct in their forecasts of *who* would buy – and 80 per cent wrong in their forecasts of *when* they would purchase. This meant that the production process could not begin until a firm order had been placed, producing long lead times and uneconomic production runs.

The solution was to encourage the sales force not only to assign probabilities to the actual order (they were already good at that) but to give probabilities to the earliest time an order might be placed, the latest it could be expected, and the most probable time of ordering.

193

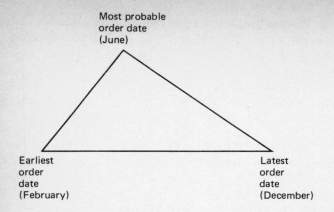

Figure 24 *Delphi expression of order dates*

Within three months of adopting this method, production costs were reduced by 40 per cent, lead times from 12 months to 4 and profits were dramatically improved. The combination of 'earliest' and 'latest' dates allowed the company to commence manufacture in high anticipation of firm orders. Within six months, the company reported that the 'most probable' date had reached a 70 per cent level of accuracy and was still improving.

9.9   Econometric methods

These are the models that strike such terror into the hearts of so many managers. They are conscious attempts to improve the accuracy of forecasts by including economic factors in the considerations. They are based on the existence in many industries of 'leading' economic factors. For example, changes in hire purchase terms and interest rates frequently lead to changes in sales of a large range of commodities. Such changes are themselves often preceded by other changes in economic activity, such as the balance of payments, the general state of trade and so on. The search is for causal factors in the economy, that is those which change before related events in specified industries.

The basic necessity is for adequate data. The systematic search for relationships will involve complex statistical methods and probably require the use of computer programs if the work is to be completed in sufficient time to be of use. Many industries have found such models valuable; others have found that they themselves may lead the very events they are examining. In the Thomson Organization, we found that significant indicators of the future of advertisement revenue, that is the income from the sale of advertising space, were the rate of sale of second-hand cars and the number of job vacancies advertised. After a good deal of work with Government statisticians, we ended up feeding them with our indicators, for we had discovered variables that seemed to presage changes in the level of the economy.

9.10 Testing as a means of forecasting

If you need to know what the effect of change might be on your forecast, it will often make sense to try that change out in a sector of a market. Such tests can include the trial of a new product in an area of the country chosen for its similarity with overall market characteristics and the possibility that results can be scaled up in some way to national equivalents on a realistic basis. Area tests may be used for changes in price, packaging, service levels, distribution, advertising weight or effectiveness, new promotional messages and schemes and many more. In every case, an attempt is being made to provide more accurate – and numerate – opinions about the effect of future activities upon forecasts.

However, there are many slips possible in the choice of an area and results can easily be invalidated by destroying the objectivity of the test, albeit in a minor way. Many companies find it almost impossible not to try to force the test to succeed – without measuring whether the efforts they are able to put into a small part of the country (or into one customer) can possibly be replicated on a larger scale. Nevertheless, they can be extremely useful to give indications of the effectiveness of alternatives and as exercises in viability. It is when they are used to predict that great care has to be exercised.

Think of a test operation as an attempt to contain an otherwise expensive operation to affordable risk limits and you won't go far wrong. Pilot instead of full-scale plant, low marketing investment instead of heavy expenditure, a small trial sales team instead of total upheaval of the whole sales force – these are typical examples of the sort of event where total and final viability will depend on the accuracy of the forecast. Even where the absolute numbers are open to some doubt, the exercise of trying schemes out will often reveal 'bugs' which will have a far more beneficial effect on the accuracy of the final forecast. Consider such testing as an insurance policy taken out against the risk of heavy loss.

Tests of this kind tend to be thought of primarily as part of the process of new product development and secondarily as a way of

195

testing changes in the marketing mix as a whole or in elements of that mix (for example, price, advertising, sales force deployment). Nevertheless, there are general guidelines that apply to all tests:

1 Try to contain the test to only one variable and don't change your mind about what to test half-way through.
2 Stick rigidly to what the test was designed to do, for example, if you are testing the effects of heavier advertising, don't try to evaluate sales force effectiveness from those results.
3 Allow sufficient time; few tests reveal anything in much less than a year. Time will show which results might have happened in any case, even without your activity.
4 Do nothing to upset the integrity and objectivity of the test.
5 Design appropriate measuring tools and understand the margins of error of the measures. (For example, most market research is conducted to a margin of error of plus or minus 5 per cent: if a 2 per cent movement will decide you to go ahead, you need more accurate – and more expensive – measuring devices.
6 Make sure the chosen area contains a representative proportion of the population (however you may define that for your business) that you will eventually market to.
7 Remember that the population you should be interested in is that which uses your type of product or service – not the national population profile, unless you happen to conform to that.

Finally, it should be noted that a vast amount of market research which seeks opinions about existing and possible future users is in the nature of a test designed to improve the input into the forecasting sequence.

9.11 Uses of forecasts

Space precludes the examination of every possible use to which a forecast might be put. In this section, a few of the more usual types and some of the associated problems will be considered. Together with what has gone before, it will be possible to decide on what type of forecast to investigate for most kinds of use.

SIZE OF A MARKET

When thinking of a possible new market, or an entry into an existing one, one of the first questions asked is how big is the market. From that, the obvious question is where the market is going.

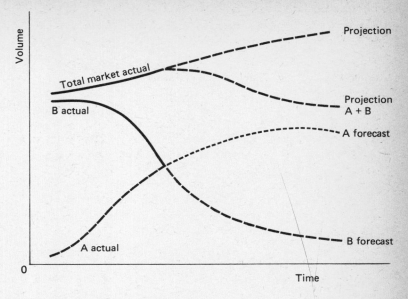

Figure 25 *Projecting market size*

There are many ways in which market size can be forecast and one should be well aware of some of the pitfalls that can trap the unwary. Firstly, consider carefully whether you need to make forecasts: for many markets there are published estimates of size and forecasts of future growth and you can make your own judgements upon the worth and validity of these. Certainly, for what is often called 'first order scanning', that sort of analysis can be enough to decide on questions of basic interest, delaying more precise measurements until it is possible to make them in the context of a finished and tested new product or service as an entrant to that market.

Markets are made up of different and competing products or brands. Care is needed to ensure that a forecast of a total market is consistent with the likely progress of brands within it. Look at Figure 25, for instance. The total market line has been growing steadily and any of the mathematical techniques or the freehand methods of projection would have that line going upwards forever. Now look at the progress of the two brands in the market. In the period under review, B has fallen right away; A, on the other hand, grew healthily but now seems to have passed maturity and is heading for a plateau if not actual decline. Add the two together and for a time the growth of

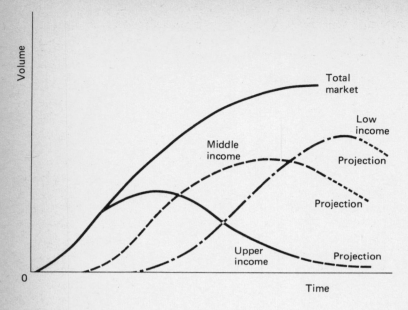

Figure 26 *Segmentation of a market*

A offsets the decline in B. Within the period of the projection, the most likely estimates for A + B produce a totally different curve for the market from that based on a straightforward 'What if' projection of the total.

Another phenomenon which must be noted is the different rates of progress of segments within a market. Markets are not only made up of different brands but of very different kinds of buyer. Figure 26 represents a segmentation analysis of a market. It could well be, for example, the growth rate of hi-fi equipment for domestic use. Initially, price was very high and the appeal would be more likely to be greater to the upper-income groups. The spread of knowledge about hi-fi, the growth in distribution of models and the gradual reductions in price would bring in those groups with lower disposable income, so that, by the time the market is well-developed, saturation of the first buyers means that only a small amount of replacement buying is taking place. In the example shown, all three groups have passed their peak and the market forecast has now to be derived from estimates of replacement buying, trading-up and adding extra items

198

to a system. There are close parallels in all types of business. Instead of socio-economic groups, they may be types of firm, size of business, adventurous and cautious investors and many others. To sum up, the forecast of a market may be either or all of the following:

1 The growth rate of the total market
2 The total of the individual products
3 The addition of the growth rates of different segments of buyers
4 The amalgamation of different reasons for buying.

Some particular markets run into another problem: the situation where the total market is more than the sum of new production. Any market where trade-ins feature largely (from private cars to office typewriters; commercial aircraft to bicycles) will have this problem. If you were to count the total number of sales of aircraft in any one year and add them to the figures for previous years, the result would be very false. Some aircraft would be counted several times because they have been sold several times during their flying life. In other words, the forecast for the market for new aircraft must allow for trade-ins and write-offs. Presenting the calculation as a conventional sum, the demand for new aircraft would be:

Opening stock of aircraft *minus* write-offs *plus* growth factor *equals* demand for new aircraft

But even that assumes that the total stock has been carefully calculated not to include all the second-hand sales during the preceding year.

What has been said so far indicates clearly that simple application of even the most sophisticated statistical techniques is likely to be highly misleading as a forecast of market size and growth unless combined with sound common sense, market research, segmentation analysis and a thorough knowledge of the way the market behaves. Some businesses will require more of these steps than others whilst others may need to get involved in test situations before they can really estimate a market including themselves, as distinct from the one in which they have not been involved.

Consumer businesses (including durables) and services will generally find that the analysis of market segments and their different buying rates and behaviour will be crucial. As we saw when discussing the identification of the position on the product life-cycle, prediction of market turning points is much easier from analysis of buyer behaviour than it is from pure projection techniques. For some industrial companies, the use of input-output analysis could be valuable. This technique, pioneered in the USA by Liontieff, analyses how each part of industry draws raw materials and components from others and to what extent its products are, in turn, taken up by others. In theory, inputs and outputs in the total must be equal. If there is complete information about a total system, then it is possible to trace changes in any one sector back to the original suppliers thus easing the task of prediction about the resultant changes in demand for the intermediary products of other sectors. Unfortunately, the UK does not collect figures in this form (the United States does) so that methods other than Government statistics have to be used. Nevertheless, even incomplete analysis can be better than none at all, and using the theoretical concept – that every input has an output – can enable the industrial company to build a total system picture which must improve its knowledge of the background to its forecasts and, consequently, the market predictions it makes. Obviously, too, the value of predictions about its own products will be improved.

COMPANY SALES

To a very considerable degree, forecasting total company sales is like predicting total market sales. Total company sales will only reach forecast levels if each of the component parts behaved as predicted. A similar plotting to that used in Figure 25 will at least show what gaps have to be met by either new products or re-cycled old ones. Apart from that use, which many believe to be of more value to long-term forecasts of where the company will go with present products, it is generally far better to produce a forecast of total company sales from the sum of the forecasts of individual products or services. You then become concerned with predicting the movements of brands within markets.

On the whole, markets tend to move much more slowly than individual products or services within them. This will obviously be more noticeable within large markets with several competitors where even a marked change in the sales of one company will not upset the momentum of the market. Growth will either be at the expense of other brands, and therefore leave the total unchanged, or the effect will be dissipated by the movements of the many other products in the market. Predicting the sales of an individual company in those circumstances means forecasting share of market. Although many models have been built, and although some have been quite successful as predictors of behaviour in individual markets, it has to be said categorically that no universal tool exists which is capable of

200

predicting brand share under any circumstances in any market.

Having said that much, most of what has been said under the headings of market size (especially regarding segmentation analysis) and statistical techniques will apply to company sales forecasts when confined to individual brands. Classically, such forecasts rely heavily on smoothing and extrapolation techniques and these have been fully discussed.

NEW PRODUCT FORECASTS

Again, techniques which have already been considered can apply. However, there are many occasions where a new product really does enter totally into the unknown and it is difficult to know where to start when attempting a forecast. In such cases, the first thing to ask yourself is how necessary a forecast really is. Often, all the company needs to know is the minimum level of sale necessary to equate with company forecasts. If this is so, simple break-even analysis may suffice; historical market trends may provide sufficient information; input-output analysis could give the answer. That sort of information combined with expert market opinion about the possibility of reaching those levels of viable sale may be all that is necessary; it will depend on the sophistication of the market and the complexity of the decisions to be taken within the company regarding the degree of risk inherent in a mistake.

It is generally the case, where the risk is high, that the questions requiring accurate forecasts are of a longer-term nature and are of the type that ask:

Should we enter the market at all?
With what involvement?
In which sector(s)?
With what investment?
What strategy?
Which tactics?
What alternatives should be considered?

Naturally, the longer the period covered by the forecast, the higher the likelihood of error. Nevertheless, as was heavily emphasized in Chapter 8, making these forecasts does at least indicate the risks inherent in different courses of action and what kinds of measures would have to be taken if those risks are to be contained to what the business can afford.

In general, the main tools of this type of forecasting are elements that many do not consider to be forecasting methods at all. They are areas like market research, market tests, measures of buying intention, likely penetration and the differential rates of that penetration among different types and groups of buyers, usage rates of old products likely to be replaced by the new one, and so on. Predictions are then made on the basis of the most relevant of those factors and the best estimates of the likely effects of the launch strategy and follow-up tactics.

There is, however, a difference between forecasting sales of a new product into a known market and into one in which the company has no valid experience at all.

In a market you know, the planned product can be compared with competitive products and any known development in the market. The relevance and effectiveness of market research is increased and so is any comparative market testing. One additional method that might be applied (to all kinds of business) is 'Product Difference Analysis'. Known qualities of importance to buyers are compared on a semantic scale, that is, a range of opinions from markedly superior to markedly inferior with, perhaps, five points in between, to give a comparative numerical score. The opinions expressed must be completely objective and totally unbiased or the method has no value. Be warned, however, that all this will give you is a likelihood of success, provided that you can communicate those qualities successfully to the potential market: they can't be expected to know what you know unless there is some means of telling them.

A more formalized method, much favoured in the United States for industrial and consumer durable products, is disaggregated market analysis. It simply means breaking a market down into its component parts and segments (by use, buyers, income groups, etc.) and from these attempt to identify the factors most likely to influence growth. Thus, a company may be able to say that no successful markets for its product will exist unless certain key areas of business buy first. A simple and very obvious example would be synthetic fibres: they have to be made up into garments before people can buy suits made of synthetic fibres. Other examples are much more complex.

Quite often, that method is combined with a much more universally applicable one: a comparison with a similar product in a market with a well-chronicled history. Obviously, it should be as similar as possible. The first television manufacturers looked hard at the early history of radio and how sales grew and spread through communities, reasoning, realistically, that there would be very close parallels. For colour television, they looked at the growth of black and white: who bought first and so on. They also looked at the disaggregated data

202

since a supply of valves and tubes was a prime necessity to the growth of the market. A very useful forecasting tool is the question 'Which existing market are we most likely to resemble?'.

There are several markets where the best judge of a potential new entrant may be an experienced and closely involved individual. Two very different examples of this can be found in perfumery and hair cosmetics, at one extreme, and crockery and pottery, at another. The knowledge and experience of individuals has to be built into all new products; if that is combined with careful pre-testing of product performance to check that the individual is still in tune with the market, one probably has the best of all possible worlds in business.

However, and especially in industrial markets, often nothing is known about the market to be entered and there is no readily available (or sufficiently well-chronicled) product or market to learn from. History may not help either where new technology is involved. Input-output analysis can be extremely helpful in this context (it can also help define possible new areas for services by revealing gaps and areas where interchange can be eased) although the paucity of information about industry as a whole is a present limitation. Constructing a diagrammatic model of all the flows within the total system that is an industry, from raw material to end use, can be of great value nevertheless.

In many of these cases, there is no real option to using the Delphi method, perhaps with some measure of probability analysis to assist quantification and indicate margins of error and, more importantly, the confidence of management. Once again, it is careful marketing analysis, backed up by independent research, where applicable, that provides the input from which forecasts can be constructed, rather than precise and universally applicable statistical techniques which just do not exist.

9.12 Accuracy and cost

Enough has been said to have made it abundantly clear that different methods have very different uses and values. The position on the life-cycle will help decide the applicability of some techniques and assist in the definition of both problem and opportunity areas for forecasting and prediction methods. It is always necessary to have some concept of cost/benefit analysis in mind. Is the cost of the method and the time involved going to prove worthwhile? There are many computer-based techniques which could improve the accuracy

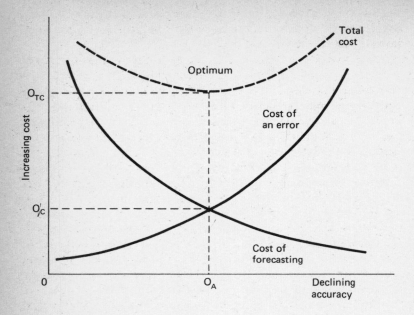

Figure 27 *Cost and accuracy*

of a forecast enormously but that would be of little value if the cost exceeded the returns from the sales, or if it took so long that the company lost its sales opportunities whilst waiting for the results.

In Figure 27, a model of the decisions involved is shown in simplified form. The highest accuracy goes, not surprisingly, with the greatest cost, whilst the reverse is also true. The cost of an error rises from left to right: declining accuracy is associated with increasing cost of mistakes. If the two cost elements are now added together, they produce a gentle curve which reaches its optimum low cost point immediately above the intersection of the individual curves. In other words, every manager should strive for the ideal reconciliation between cost and accuracy in forecasting.

Do remember the steps necessary to turn a projection into a forecast. It cannot be done without human input. The human and the mathematical must be put into balance. Over-emphasis on human values can so easily lead to dangerous signs of omnipotence; it is in such circumstances that mathematical methods often perform better than humans. Human judgement and common sense, applied to statistical projections and backed up by market research and market tests where they can be both used and economically justified, will always produce the best results.

'And common sense' – I have seen highly complex mathematical models applied to situations where common sense could have told them the same answer in minutes and at no cost. If you are a house builder and you know that a roof has 3,000 tiles and you are going to build 300 new houses, you don't need a lot of back data or a mathematical model to forecast your need for roofing tiles. If you are a tile manufacturer, knowledge of how many new houses are likely to be started and the average number of tiles used per house not only provides the parameters for any easy forecast but tells you the leading economic indicators (all those that affect housing-starts), the disaggregated demand factors (builders and architects will be prime among the areas to be examined) and will indicate pretty clearly how an upsurge in new house-starts one year might affect future building programmes – and consequently the long-term demand for roofing tiles. People close to the business will make rapid mental adjustments to their forecasts with every new piece of relevant information that comes their way. That is the final point: forecasts should not merely be amended – they must be updated. Recording a variance from a forecast is one thing; taking account of that variance and predicting how that will be carried through into various periods is quite another. Waiting another 12 months for a formal planning and forecasting period might be fatal.

9.13 Summary

Forecasting is a marriage of knowledge, science and art. Science can do little more than throw past events forward in time and assume that whatever influenced them in the past will do so again, and in the same proportions, in the future. Even the more sophisticated methods of weighting different periods to change the level of importance will not improve that situation dramatically. Thus human judgement and evaluation are essential to convert a projection to a prediction and a prediction to a forecast.

The precise method used will vary with need but every manager should aim for the best possible reconciliation, which will almost certainly entail the greatest accuracy with the lowest risk of loss through a bad decision – at the lowest absolute cost in money and the shortest time-span in preparing the forecasts.

9.14 Checklist

1. 'Forecasts shape plans and plans shape forecasts.' Consideration of sales trends helps to identify the limits on future plans. The outcome of recommended plans produces sales forecasts which set-off departmental budgets and profit projections.

2. The method selected will depend upon:
   - a The type of business and the degree of control it has over key factors.
   - b The position on both the demand and product life-cycles.
   - c The purpose of the forecast.
   - d Its context.
   - e The amount of relevant past data.
   - f How much time is available.
   - g The acceptable margins of error.

3. The full sequence of forecasting begins with setting background and planning assumptions, identifies trends, projects them forward in time, amends them by reference to leading indicators and all known facts about the market and, finally, adds the human element.

4. The final stage is to add the outcomes of plans, preferably pre-tested.

5. Projections assume that the future will be like the past although it is possible to select which bits of the past will be allowed to influence that future.

6. Predictions rely on the use of indicators, correlations, facts and opinions to condition projections.

7. The forecast is what it is intended to do about the possibilities revealed by the earlier stages.

8. Statistical methods relate to projections and extrapolations. Mathematically accurate (in that they project by formula), they are often wrong (because markets do not conform to formulae). They work best up to three to six periods ahead.

9. Qualitative techniques rely on quantified opinions. They provide a safeguard against undue influence by seniority or 'best guessers'. Probabilities can be assigned to events, times or opinions to measure outcomes.

10 Econometric methods are more accessible via the mini or microcomputer but still remain mainly in the province of the mainframe computer. There is no evidence that any model has universal applicability and few are accurate for long periods, even for individual products. Their main use is in simulation of the possible outcomes of changes in interrelated variables.

11 Market tests may also be used for forecasting purposes, but especial care is necessary in the selection of the factors from which predictions will be made.

12 Such tests must never involve anything that could not be replicated on a wider scale. They should, preferably, run for 12 months, test only one thing at a time and be very carefully monitored and measured.

13 When forecasting market size, the possible influences may be:
   a The growth rate of the market.
   b The sum of the individual products within the market.
   c The growth rate of market segments.
   d All the different reasons for buying added together.

14 Where replacements, trade-ins, etc. are important, demand will be opening stocks, less write-offs, plus a growth factor. 'Opening stock' must not include second-hand sales.

15 Company sales forecasts are very similar to market forecasts except that markets generally move less rapidly than products (because products compete for shares of that market).

16 New products in new markets may require more specialized techniques of input-output analysis, disaggregated demand analysis, the use of analogy or the Delphi technique.

17 It may not be necessary to forecast the total market accurately if all that is necessary is to decide if company sales can break-even or if a market of sufficient size exists to absorb total or profitable capacity.

18 Cost and accuracy must go together. If the cost (which may be time as well as money) exceeds the profit, it will not be worth doing. However, the less time and money spent on forecasting, the greater the risk of error.

19 Forecasts should not simply be amended (as when variance to

207

data is simply added or subtracted from the original forecast).
Every change should signal the need for a complete review.

10

The Vital Difference

It is a socialist idea that making profits is a vice; I
consider the real vice is making losses.
Winston Churchill

The vital difference is, of course, profit. Without profits, no company
can survive beyond a very short-term. Implicit in all that has gone
before is the concept of earning a profit as the reward for taking
commercial risk. In the vast majority of cases, the practical alternatives
are along a spectrum with low profit rates but high turnover, at one
end, and high profit rates but low turnover, at the other. There are
remarkably few cases where the opportunity to make very high
profits at enormous turnover levels exists. That would be a situation
that would encourage competition at lower prices and profits.
However, this is one of those areas where a knowledge of marketing
realities can be somewhat uncomfortable, as was pointed out at the
end of Chapter 1. The marketing realist has to acknowledge that there
are situations where the consumer does not value the product or
service except at a price that affords an 'abnormal' level of profit.
Those cases exist far more often than is generally accepted by most
businessmen. It is always easy to see when you are charging too much;
people stop buying. Unless you actually try it out in some way, it is
impossible to foretell how much more they might buy if the price was
higher. There are literally thousands of examples of products and
services where this has been proved beyond any reasonable doubt –
from precision engineerng to cake mixes; hotels to holidays; houses to
furnishings; cars to coffins.

This is a book about marketing, not finance. Therefore, in this
rather short chapter, just a few of the more pertinent aspects of profit
as it affects the activities of the marketing executive will be
considered.

10.1 What is profit?

Next time you feel like throwing a spanner into a management meeting, ask each of the people there for their definition of profit. You are likely to get answers like this:

1 'The value added in production' (*from the factory manager*).
2 'What is left after company expenses have been deducted from sales revenue' (*from the sales manager*).
3 'The brand contribution after deduction of all fixed and variable costs and divisional overheads from sales revenue' (*from an experienced brand manager*).
4 'The final operating profit after the deduction of all costs, expenses, charges and taxes and which represents the sum available for distribution to shareholders and retention as reserves in the company' (*from the finance director*).

Each is likely to believe his or her definition yet (other than by pure accident) no two will produce the same result.

Profit means different things to different people for two fundamental reasons. Firstly, because they have been allowed to adopt unrealistic attitudes to the part their job plays in total company welfare. Secondly, the concept of company profit is essentially a set of conventions which vary considerably from company to company. If each of those four definitions is looked at briefly, it will be seen how both the attitudes and the conventions cause this dilemma.

What I have ascribed to the factory manager is very much what the classical economist would have liked profit to have been. It is undoubtedly true that many of the dramatic business collapses of the mid-1970s may well have been avoided if both the companies themselves and those who invested in them (individuals and institutions) had remembered that there is a world of difference between real value added, in either production or marketing, and purely numerical changes in valuation, which can only reflect attitudes at points of time. To be fair, it is often quite difficult to distinguish between additions to value affecting intangible items. If a travel company puts together a package of ticket booking, hotel reservation, transport from door-to-door (or nearly so) and an adequate supply of food and entertainment at the resort, it is adding value in the buyer's mind and this addition is comparable with the act of, say, harvesting peas, grading them, processing, packaging and supplying them refrigerated to retail outlets. On the other hand, most people find it very difficult indeed to appreciate how any value can possibly be added to an unoccupied building that is deliberately kept empty for a long period. Whilst added value is not profit as such, it is a vital ingredient in both profit and consumer satisfaction. And since the marketing philosophy tells us that no business can have profits until it has customers (for, until then, it can only have costs) then it behoves any company to carefully monitor the degree of value that it is adding in whatever might be termed its 'production process' and to ensure that the customer still has the same idea of value.

It all too often comes as an enormous shock to salesmen to discover the concept of 'working capital'. Not only has no-one taken the trouble to disabuse the sales force but the whole emphasis on selling and sales policy (often including remuneration) usually mitigates against any clearer understanding of how sales need to be financed. At the back of most salesmen's minds is the thought that company profit is basically affected by how much the company takes away from the cash the sales produce. In times when sales volume and revenue go up but profits go down – a common feature of inflation – it is easy to blame the unseen hands in head office for the company's ills.

In fact, as anyone who has ever started their own business knows only too well, a business starts with costs: that is why capital is needed to fund the setting-up costs until revenue begins to flow in. Most businesses find, too, that there are significant operating plateaux which have to be financed. A piece of machinery does not become efficient and economic until it is producing at 80 per cent capacity; one salesman can handle 20 customers but the 21st needs a new salesman, and that customer alone will not be economic – even worse, the extra cost of the additional salesman will now reduce the profitability of the other 20; a van that goes full to Glasgow has to come back empty and so on. Thus any company is continually having to find cash to cover not only existing business but planned future expansion. For this is usually needs three things:

1 Satisfactory profit levels from existing business.
2 Access to cash due to it as rapidly as possible.
3 Sources of new finance for those needs it cannot immediately finance itself.

A proper appreciation of the concept of financing sales is necessary among sales forces if they are to complete their task – which means collecting the cash for orders obtained.

Marketing specialists tend to work within a narrow and special concept of profit. This is the idea of profit contribution. It is usually applied where there is a holding group of some kind distinct from the

211

operating divisions or companies. However, it may be applied in very much smaller operations, where it may be impossible to allocate fixed investment correctly to individual products or services and where there may be a large number of shared services and overhead expenses. Simply expressed, profit contribution arises after all the specifically allocated costs, charges and expenses have been deducted from sales revenue. Final company net profit is not produced until non-specific charges have been deducted.

This not only means that very few marketing executives actually work with true net profit, but it also accounts for the degree of effort which is often necessary to maintain some level of contribution from product lines which, under other circumstances, would be prime candidates for withdrawal. Where this happens, the senior management should look very seriously indeed at the level of central costs to see whether the company might not be all the better for a pruning there and product rationalization elsewhere (along the lines of the analyses in Chapter 6).

And, finally, there is the finance director's definition which, fairly obviously, is going to be closest to a commonly accepted definition of corporate net profit. Unfortunately, although a high proportion of corporate accountants might be able to agree with most of the definition, they might find it possible to disagree violently about the figures such a definition actually produces. Neither company law nor accountancy practice lays down any common standard. Thus it is possible for companies in exactly the same kind of business to do the same amount of turnover with the same costs and expenses, with the same sort of charges from banks and yet produce different profit levels. They may value their stocks differently, for example. They may take different attitudes towards writing-off development expenditure on new products launched during the year. They could have different depreciation policies. Just read the different views on the same set of published results from different financial commentators and you will see clearly not only how conventions can vary but how very differently the same convention can be interpreted under varying conditions and by different people. Another interesting thing to do is to examine the first set of accounts to incorporate a new acquisition. It is often found that using the new owners' conventions reduces the profits of the acquired company for earlier years; when the General Electricity Company acquired Associated Electrical Industries in late 1967, they took over a company with forecast profits of £10 million. When the accounts were amalgamated, GEC showed that AEI had produced a loss of £4.5 million for 1967. In the swing of £14.5 million only £5 million could be attributed to facts; the remaining £9.5 million was due to differences in the way the AEI figures had been certified in audit, and the conventions required for the new amalgamated accounts to be certified in line with procedures agreed in the past.

Where does all this leave us? Obviously, profit is a largely individual concept based upon a few generally accepted conventions, some rather stronger ones laid down by the Inland Revenue, and a very large area of discretion where you will find professional advisors to agree with you. There is only one inescapable fact – cash. Companies fail when they can no longer finance their sales or when they are no longer able to convince their backers of their ability to service their debts, that is, pay interest charges on borrowed money and be capable of repayment in full on a due date. Thus, marketing activities should be concerned with the generation of cash resources. This is a basic truth whatever the circumstances but is never more vital than in times of inflation. It may, for example, lead to a policy of deliberately concentrating on good payers and ensuring that neither you nor they are subsidizing bad customers. It will certainly encourage a realistic look at customers and the realization that the customer who never pays until the final demand is hardly a customer at all. It also encourages very careful consideration of the ways in which profits arise and the methods by which they can be increased.

10.2   Increasing profits

By now, the thought may well be crossing your mind that if you were to do all the things I have suggested in this book, there would be little, if any, time left to do what you do now. On the one hand, it could be that some of your priorities are wrong and they certainly will be if you have not been giving sufficient attention to your customers. On the other hand, it could be that your business needs the services of an employee or possibly a consultant to help you cover the ground more quickly. Nevertheless, I would readily accept, as the owner of a business myself, that time is one of the enemies of the modern businessman and never more so than when we are diverted to attend to bureaucratic demands. There is some comfort I can offer and it is that so many of the basic arts of business can be reduced to fairly simple lists. We have seen how there are really only six questions you can ask and how they can be used to prompt a whole series of other relevant pointers. Similarly, the three kinds of competitive advantage show that the way you compete with others in your line of business can be pulled back to a very few headings. So it is with increasing profits: there are four ways you can do it and most companies go about it the wrong way.

However, having made that sweeping condemnation, let me be absolutely fair and admit that, for many businesses in this day and age, full freedom of action does not exist and that it is not always possible to raise prices or easily reduce costs. With that proviso, here are the four ways:

Raise prices
Reduce costs
Sell more
Improve the profit mix.

Three of these can easily be illustrated in the same table; the last of the four is more complicated.

In the second column of Table 7, prices have been raised by 5 per cent. If we were all in the happy state where that was both possible and permitted, and if the price rise could be imposed without any increase in costs, the whole of the increase would fall through to the bottom line as extra profit. Because nothing else has changed, a 5 per cent increase in price becomes a 45 per cent increase in profit. In the third column, costs have been reduced by 5 per cent. Each of the three cost lines has been reduced by the same amount. Clearly, it would be

Table 7   *Improving profit by single steps, £s*

	Current figures	After 5% price increase	After 5% cost decrease	After 5% sales increase	After 15% sales increase
Sales turnover	720	756	720	756	828
Material costs	300	300	285	315	345
Wages & salaries	180	180	171	189	207
General overheads	160	160	152	160	160
Net contribution	80	116	112	92	116
Increase in net contribution		+45%	+40%	+15%	+45%

unrealistic to believe that many companies could reduce all three simultaneously; however, the overall effect might well be achieved by concentrating on just one area. Even labour costs can be reduced in times of inflation by redundancy, natural wastage and improved productivity. This time, sales revenue does not increase and the fall in costs is not quite enough to produce a profit increase equal to that given by a 5 per cent rise. Nevertheless, the overall effect is a 40 per cent increase in profit.

Now look what happens when price remains unchanged but sales revenue goes up by 5 per cent. This time, the increase does not fall through to the bottom line. Some of it becomes dissipated in increased costs of financing the sales. (For those who want to check, figures have been rounded up, but equate with, roughly, material costs at 42 per cent of revenue and wages and salaries at 25 per cent.) The net effect is only a 15 per cent increase in profit. In fact, if we want to produce the sort of increase in sales that will come through as a 45 per cent increase in profit, we will have to sell 15 per cent more.

How realistic is that? If it can be done now, why wasn't it done before? Yet isn't that just what most managers ask for when profits must be raised? The natural tendency is to push the sales force to sell more, yet it is by far the most difficult way of increasing profits, simply because of the need to finance sales. Different sets of figures will produce different results but you will find that the order is always

Table 8   *Improving profit by combined steps, £s*

	Current figures	After 5% cost decrease	Plus 5% price increase	Plus 5% sales increase	Plus 15% sales increase*
Sales turnover	720	720	756	794	869
Material costs	300	285	285	299	330
Wages & salaries	180	171	171	179	200
General overheads	160	152	152	152	152
Net contribution	80	112	148	164	187
Increase in net contribution		+40%	+85%	+105%	+134%

*15% increase on 5% price increase column

the same: sales increases are the hardest way of increasing profits.

Table 8 shows what happens when the three things are combined. It makes sense to start by cutting costs, then raising price and then selling more. Now the sequence looks really exciting. It is this second table that gives us the ideal discipline for profit planning. First make sure that products or services are provided at the most economic levels, without undue wastage of people or materials, without unnecessary frills and with continuing value-analysis, to make sure that things stay tight. Then be sure that the price is right; that is, what the customer rates it at. Then it makes sense to exhort the sales force for greater effort.

However, many companies will actually find that it is the item not in the tables that will produce the greatest benefit. Getting the business priorities right means selling more of the higher profit lines, wherever feasible at the expense, if need be, of lower value ones. Whereas, even with hypothetical figures, there is an easily discerned logic in any example of the other three means of raising profits, it is not possible to demonstrate the effect of improving a profit mix with the same degree of conviction. However, Table 9 uses figures relevant to the company on which Tables 7 and 8 are based. From the summary of contributions per case, it is clear that – other things being equal – it will require about two cases of products A and C and six of D to equal the contribution of B. If this was all that had to be taken into account, then B is the line to push at the expense of the others and especially of the unrewarding product E.

If, however, the situation is that all the products use the same resources and a position of scarcity of machine or labour capacity is likely to arise, then it is necessary to look at contribution per unit of machine time before arriving at a conclusion about the ideal product mix to yield maximum profits. Now the picture changes. A is the best line to promote. The contribution from A is worth two of C and more than double the contribution of B.

Table 9   *Contributions summary, £s*

	Contributions per case	Contributions per unit of machine time
Product A	6	6.00
Product B	11	2.75
Product C	6	3.00
Product D	2	0.70
Product E	–3	Negative

10.3 Profit and sales

Picking up from what has already been said about salesmen's attitudes to how profit arises, it should be obvious that there is a great deal to be done if the sales force is to enter into a true profit partnership in the company. In particular, there are two areas of prime importance. The first is that the snobbery that puts cash collection and invoice-chasing as menial tasts not befitting a sales executive must be dismissed from sales forces, if necessary by dismissing the salesmen. It cannot be too strongly emphasized, particularly in times of rampant inflation or recession, that a salesman's task is not complete until the cash has been received. Some companies even believe it is worth the effort of identifying prompt payers before allocating bonus payments against sales.

A good deal of what I regard as an unsatisfactory situation has arisen from the refusal of company managements to allow sales forces even a glimpse of profitability calculations. Sales forces are traditionally given volume targets and all forms of bonus calculations and other incentives are geared to the pursuit of volume. Yet, as we saw in the very first chapter, this can be very dangerous. It isn't necessary to expose all your secrets to the sales force. All that is required is some simple indicator of the company's profit priorities. Such a device is to measure all sales in some form of standard units. For example, instead of measuring all sales in cases, give each a weight according to its profit contribution. We might take the first column of Table 9, and allocate the following standard units:

Product A   3 standard units
Product B   6 standard units
Product C   3 standard units
Product D   1 standard unit

In this example, D is taken as the base product and the others are geared accordingly. If bonus payments are based on the standard units, the sales force will quickly see where both their own and the company's interests lie.

Suppose the company runs into some production problems and now has to take account of machine-time contributions. If it believed that this was only a short-term position, it might not wish to go to the trouble of changing all the standard units, but simply make a few temporary adjustments. It might say, for example, that for the next three months A and B will change places; that is A will be worth 6 standard units and B worth only 3. Obviously, this can be used to give

217

appropriate incentives during periods of promotion, slack sales, and so on. The only caution that is necessary is not to change the values too often or they will become debased.

Standard units present a very practical way of relating sales efforts to profitability without divulging confidential information that may become insecure. However, they can be used to give any kind of emphasis or change of weight in sales efforts.

There are many other ways in which profitability and sales effort may be more closely related, such as break-even charts to decide on any new cost elements (new salesmen, new vehicles, opening area offices, etc.), but these belong more properly in books on sales management. It is enough to say here that, because other methods usually produce more profit than increasing sales alone, some guidance is needed by sales forces on where their efforts will most benefit their company; until that information is provided, no company will ever know the true contribution that a good sales team can provide.

10.4 Profit and the marketing executive

There are still many, many companies who do not allow their marketing people to have full profit information. It is rather like sending a boxer into the heavyweight championship of the world with both hands tied behind his back and blindfolded. Marketing is indelibly linked with profit and all the ways in which it might arise. As a co-ordinator between departments, the marketing executive should be ideally placed to identify opportunities for profitable action. If he knows that the factory has a problem re-engaging any labour that has to be laid off during the summer months, he may be able to devise schemes that will prevent the lay-off. At least, it will be possible to calculate whether it is better to try to promote at that time or to allow the labour force to be reduced. Where the marketing executive is reduced to seeing only the results of sales effort (and I know of large British companies where they do not even have access to that information, at least not directly), then not only are possible opportunities ignored in other areas, but there is a danger of over-emphasis on one area of the business, with the remainder regarded as nothing more than a series of expense budgets.

Not only should whoever is in charge of the marketing analysis have access to profit information, but he or she should also have rapid access to any information about changes that may affect profitability. It is a strange fact of business that sales budgets are

218

amended frequently (often too frequently to allow random movements to show themselves for what they are), whilst other changes which are known to be longer-term are not. Most companies report such differences as 'prime cost variances' or even 'unexplained differences'. I know of a tea and coffee company that reported prime cost variances against a standard set in 1938 until 1968; a printing company which normally enters its financial year with agreed wage rates (trade-union negotiated) but nevertheless calls these 'unexplained differences' at the year-end. It is possible – I put it no higher than that – that schemes could be devised that might help to offset such differences. With a team of brand managers, I once sweated through a year trying to make a profit target. We got within £30,000 of the target and thought we had done pretty well in a tough year but we wished that we hadn't had to do so much surgery to get there. When the final figures were published, they were £1.2 million higher than we thought we had achieved. The company had been sitting on favourable prime cost differences which produced that final result. The thinking was that if these young marketing men got to hear about the money that wasn't being spent, they would want to use it for advertising or some wild sales promotion scheme. Had we known, we might have avoided some of the drastic measures we had to take, measures that eventually led to the demise of three of the largest brands in the company and the very ones that had provided 80 per cent of the favourable differences.

My plea is a simple one. The enterprise is presumably in business to make a profit. The more people there are who know what their part in that objective is, the better the chance of achieving it. They do not all need to know every shred of information; coded and weighted information (such as standard units) can be enough. But they do need to know, and know quickly, when things change. And they should be positively invited to suggest how adverse changes might be overcome.

10.5   Inflation

We have lived through a long period of inflation. It must be seriously doubted whether modern attitudes to wealth and employment together with aspects of social welfare will ever permit a return to times of really high unemployment and rabid deflation. Many businessmen seem to have become numb in the face of constantly rising costs and, faced with practical limitations on price increases, feel unable to influence their own destiny beyond minor efforts.

If you have done all the things suggested in this chapter, you will, ironically, be closer to the point of being able to do little to influence your own destiny; if you haven't done those things, there is a great deal that can be done to improve your lot. However, there are two particular opportunities during times of rapidly increasing costs and prices. The first is to concentrate on getting the right profit mix. Obviously, this may change more rapidly than you would like but attitudes tend to move in your favour. Because of inflation, customers may gradually become somewhat disenchanted with the product or service, whilst you are becoming distressed at the reducing profitability. They may actually welcome a switch in emphasis themselves and may be looking for a lead of some sort. You may find it pays to hasten the decline period of the life-cycle, unless you can find a profitable way of re-cycling.

Re-cycling presents an attractive alternative to falling profits. If you can revamp products or services to give additional customer benefits, those additional benefits can reflect current costs. The more the new aspect is seen to present new and additional benefits, the more acceptable the new price will be. Where controls exist, it may present a legitimate way to avoid restraint orders on existing products.

A re-cycled product is a form of new product and new products are the meat of inflation survival policies. New products have two great advantages: they lack historic cost and they are launched into updated price expectation patterns. Historic cost is the enemy of profit in times of inflation. If new methods of production and new ingredients (or their service equivalents) cannot be found, then new products with new cost and price structures will be the answer.

10.6   Marketing in hard times

There are three fundamental things to understand about hard times if you are to make the best of them:

1   Accept the fact that there will be a period of, at best, only slow growth.
2   Growth will only be possible at the expense of others.
3   Because times are hard, it doesn't mean that technology will stand still; changes and new developments still happen.

They may seem simple yet the root cause of so many financial disasters in hard times is the refusal to accept things for what they are and the tendency to respond far too late to lower levels of growth, turnover and profit. When volume is short, competition gets tougher.

Failure to control costs will be fatal. Nevertheless, there are things you can do.

It is rare that the whole of a market is in decline. In fact, there is usually some growth sector to be found. This may require some segmentation and even producing differentiated products to meet the needs of the growth sector. If your planning process has involved careful market analysis, these sectors should come as no great surprise to you. Assessment of the vulnerability of different segments of a market should be second nature and may lead to decisions about maintaining contact with sectors that offer better long-term security than others.

Your customers are probably having hard times too, and this is the time to search for better cost-benefits. It is often the case that higher prices will be paid for items producing better cost-benefits than can be reflected in costs of production. Now, more than ever, is the time to emphasize product quality, not to drop it (which seems to be the reaction of many companies to hard times, often as a justification for lower prices).

We saw that improvements in technology still happen, so this is a good time to produce innovative improvements, especially if they can be combined with customer cost-benefits.

Particular attention should be paid to the efficiency of your marketing mix. All your marketing activities will need to be sharper and more clearly cost-effective. Wherever possible, concentrate on the more measurable activities and think twice about those that are uncertain or immeasurable. It usually pays to look hard at stock-holding and at distribution methods and efficiency. If volume falls, inescapably, are the old delivery and stockholding standards still applicable? Are the sales force call frequencies still appropriate; are the sales tasks relevant or should they be doing something different?

In short, hard times call for creative analysis of sales opportunities and for frequent questioning of why things are done that way and whether the old standards are still relevant. Above all else, one needs to be poised and ready to take advantage of any upswing as soon as it happens, not to have become so lean that the company has no energy to attack new opportunities.

10.7 Profit and price

All profit is at a price. It may seem strange that so little attention has been given in this chapter to price, other than to emphasize that, of all the ways of increasing profits, raising prices gives the greatest multiplier effect. So much so that few companies are likely to lose such a volume of sales as to wipe out the beneficial effects. Simple break-even analysis (of the type discussed in Chapter 11, Figure 30) will show how much sales would have to fall to produce a nil-effect.

Price is such an important aspect of profit, and profit such a vital factor of marketing, that it is the one item of the marketing mix we shall examine (in the next chapter) in a book which otherwise avoids considering those elements in detail.

10.8   Summary

Profit is capable of many definitions yet the only one that has real meaning, in the marketing context, is that of a cash surplus. There are four major methods by which profits can be increased:

Raising prices
Cutting costs
Selling more
Improving the profit mix.

Consideration of these four methods suggests a priority in operations that gets costs right, prices correctly in line with customers' ideas of acceptable range and risk, puts due emphasis on the most profitable items in the range, and then gives incentives to sales forces to sell more according to the new priority. The more profit information is disseminated, in appropriate forms, the more chance there is of changes in cost areas being offset by positive marketing action. Not only should this information be provided to responsible executives but it should be updated and amended at least as frequently as sales budgets are.

10.8   Checklist

1   Wrong prices are quickly discovered when they are too high. It is far more difficult to establish when sales and profits might be higher if prices were raised.

2   In most companies, the marketing function works with the concept of profit contribution. True, final net profit does not arise until all shared costs, general overheads and company charges have been deducted.

3   In the search for higher profit, those central costs should be subjected to the same searching examination as in the effort to increase product contributions.

4 The necessity of covering central costs can easily lead to the maintenance of products which make some gross contribution, even though they fail to make a net – or target – contribution.

5 Raising prices produces such a significant multiplier effect on profits that it ought always to be the first option to be explored.

6 The effect of cost reductions will depend upon the cost structure of the product. For most manufacturing companies, this will be the next most effective method of increasing profits. However, the more efficient the company, the less room it will have for further cost reduction.

7 Improving profits by increasing sales is much the most difficult method. Because sales have to be financed, the sales volume increase needed to secure quite a modest profit improvement will be high and often unreasonable.

8 The ideal priority for improving profits is:
   a Get the cost structure right (that is, as low as is consistent with the necessary customer standards of quality).
   b Decide on the most profitable assortment of products and direct sales efforts to the more profitable products, if necessary, at the expense of the least profitable.
   c Set prices as high as is consistent with the required volume/ profit aims.
   d Sell more.
   Extra sales effort without the three preceding stages will be far less rewarding than it could be.

9 Sales effort can be better directed towards more profitable sales by the use of a profit-weighted incentive system (for example, 'standard units' instead of profitable sales, by the use of a profit-weighted simple, unadjusted volume).

10 Those responsible for product marketing must be aware of all the ingredients that produce or influence final profit. It is especially important that other profit centres do not exist (for example, buying better than standard costs) which might lead to unwise short-term decisions which prove to have been unnecessary.

11 In times of inflation, the key to profitability lies in getting the optimum profit mix, re-cycling existing products to present added values, justifying higher prices and launching new products with today's prices covering today's cost levels.

12 The prime requirement in hard times is to recognize that they are hard and take action accordingly.

13 The only place to gain volume when markets stand still is from competitors . . . and you are the only place for them to get *their* gains. *the question: if I were the competitor, what would I do?*

14 Customers will be searching for cost-benefits and hard times are good times to emphasize product quality and to make innovative improvements.

15 Particular attention should be paid to the cost and efficiency of marketing activities. Measurable methods of sales and promotion should take precedence over immeasurable or less certain methods at such times.

11
Pricing

Cheat me in the price not in the goods.
    T. Fuller: *Gnomologia: Adages and Proverbs*, 1732

Pricing is only one of the 'direct' elements in the marketing mix. Arguably, after the product itself, it is the most important. For over a decade now, price has been the single most important variable in the marketing activity of most companies. Through the years of rampant cost inflation, it was necessary to set prices that recovered rising costs yet did not reduce volume by unacceptable amounts. As recession hit virtually all the developed nations of the world, buyers insisted on lower prices, and price competition between nations as well as between domestic competitors became rife. This became especially difficult for companies selling to other businesses. Falls in total demand led to heavy over-capacity in many industries and this, in turn, led to lower prices, in desperate efforts to keep factories working. Additionally, companies selling 'derived demand' products are not well-placed to resist demands for lower prices when the companies they supply feel themselves forced (or elect) to offer lower prices. Hence the reason for looking at price, when this book deliberately ignores other marketing mix elements and other technique areas. However, it can justifiably be claimed that although there are several pricing techniques, their application is, to a large degree, an art.

11.1 What price is

To most people, price is a measure of value added. Two things must immediately be said about that statement:

1 'Value' can be highly emotive and vary considerably between individuals.
2 Something that has no use, has no value for that individual.

The economist distinguishes three kinds of value that may be expressed by price:

1 Cost
2 Use
3 Esteem.

Cost, wrongly, is still the basis of most companies' pricing methods. Selling at cost merely avoids a loss. Companies sell at cost for promotional reasons or to keep facilities (including labour) working, and thus avoid write-off and redundancy expenses. 'Use' value is what it is worth to the buyer to have the goods or services. If the value in use is not greater than the cost value, no-one will buy. For example, a very high proportion of householders do their own decorating. They place no value on their own time and conclude that it is cheaper to do it themselves than employ a decorator who will charge for his time. However, nuisance value also enters the calculation. It may cost more to use the services of a travel agent but you feel more secure employing an expert. Suppose you elect to fly first-class to your holiday destination. Why? You won't get there any faster. The sun won't shine more brightly. You may travel more comfortably and receive more attention in-flight. In fact, your decision will contain a heavy element of 'esteem value'. 'Esteem value' presents a great deal of confusion in price theory. There are many fields in which scarcity creates high prices (from gold to Ming china). To the buyer of a designer dress, the price is a guarantee that there will not be another like it. The amateur buyer of a Hasselblad camera will be buying a good deal of esteem when he or she pays highly for many mechanical qualities that may never be put to the test.

How can these three values be put to use in business? Cost clearly sets the lower limits. The high failure rate of many small retail businesses is often due to not attracting sufficient customers to pay the basic costs of the business. I was once asked to advise the owners of a prestigious hairdressing salon in a prime location in London. The salon, financed by the bank, was lavish, the prices were high. So too were the rent and rates. So high, in fact, that even if the salon was full all day, every day, it could not take enough money to pay the rent and rates!

'Use value' is the important one. Unless your customer has a use for your product and values it at a level that affords a satisfactory margin of profit, you simply aren't in business. But 'esteem value' begins to tell us what every experienced marketer knows – that there is a 'right' price, and sales volume and profit will be maximized at that level.

Moreover, that price may well be higher than a simple cost plus percentage mark-up would produce. Marketing history is replete with examples of products that have only really taken off when the price was raised. People not only have 'esteem values', they also possess notions of what might be termed 'negative esteem'. It occurs when they are put off buying a product or using a service because the price was out of line with its perceived qualities. It provokes reactions like 'If it is that good, why is it so cheap?'. We all react to the idea that something can be too dear; it can also be too cheap. The psychology of price, as we shall see later, is vitally important.

11.2 Cost-based pricing

Repeated research has shown that the great bulk of British industry totally ignores the customer in setting their prices. If the customer buys, they assume they have got the price right; if they don't, it must be wrong, which is usually assumed to mean it is too dear.

We can distinguish seven main methods of cost-based pricing, although some of the differences are subtle.

ABSORPTION COSTING

Take all the costs, calculate a required overhead contribution, add an agreed profit margin, and the result is ex-factory selling price (that is, a price before calculation of any margins, discounts, etc.). Thus:

        Direct material costs
    +   Direct labour costs
    +   Overhead contribution
    =   Total product costs
    +   Agreed percentage mark-up
    =   Ex-factory selling price

DIRECT COST PRICING

Also known as 'contribution costing', price is the result of the summation of all direct costs *plus* a contribution to cover all other costs (for example, overheads, promotion, etc.) *plus* profit.

Figure 28 shows how this method works. At an output of X_1 direct costs (D_1) are £15.00. Total unit costs (F_1) are £30.00. The price for output X_1 of £35.00 allows a profit of £5.00. The line F_2, D_2, X_2 shows the volume at which the price of £35.00 will exactly cover total unit costs. Suppose that sales fall back from F_1, D_1, X_1 to F_2, D_2, X_2, then the profit margin will fall unless a new price is set. The mark-up used to set the price of £35.00 was 16.66 per cent. Total unit costs at the lower volume are £33.00 (at F_3) so that using the same mark-up will produce a new price (rounded-up) of £38.50.

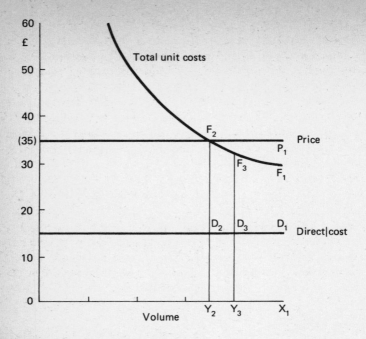

Figure 28 *Direct cost pricing*

How practical is this? How many companies would have the courage to raise prices against a decline? If volume falls further, prices will have to rise yet again. Nevertheless, despite this obvious problem, the method is a useful way of considering entry into a new market and deciding if it will be profitable to enter at ruling prices, or as a means of assessing the probabilities of satisfactory profits at different levels.

INCREMENTAL COSTS

This method takes account of the actual extra costs involved in moving from one level of output to another (always remembering that it is possible to suffer incremental costs of *reduced* output too). As a costing/pricing method it makes sure that changes in cost levels are adequately reflected in price. It is particularly suitable for jobbing firms, jobbing printers being a good example. The cost calculations generally show the cost advantages of long, continuous, smoothly programmed orders. Thus, the 'run-on' cost of printing an extra 1000 catalogues is mainly paper, and makes the cost per catalogue cheaper on a 5000 run than on a 2000 run.

228

MARGINAL COSTING

Strictly speaking, a form of incremental costing but a method with positive dangers. The 'marginal' cost is the actual production plus selling cost of one extra unit (or batch). Its dangers are seen most clearly when marginal costing is applied to a standard costing system. The temptation is to remove all the standard costs you can to justify a price that will secure an order. There's nothing wrong with this, provided you can be 100 per cent sure the cost can be wholly removed and the order genuinely represents extra business. Nine times out of ten, it is not wholly justifiable to remove all of a standard cost. You assume no delivery cost because a van is calling in any case. On the day you need to deliver, there is no van calling and there has to be a special delivery. And so it goes on. And what if the marginal deal you do is with Tesco and it draws volume away from nearby Fine Fare outlets? Part of the fully costed sales to Fine Fare, which supported your deal with Tesco, have now gone. Only use marginal costing with extreme care.

OPPORTUNITY COSTS

If the same plant can be used to make two products, manufacturing one could mean foregoing the profit that could be earned from the other. A notional value – or opportunity cost – is put on the cost of producing A rather than B, or B instead of A. 'A notional value' – the *real* opportunity cost is not always so obvious. There may be a discrepancy between short-term profit and long-term opportunity, for example. As a pricing method, it works best with one-to-one situations, and tends, therefore, to be widely used in the professions. If a fully-employed barrister earns £100 per hour, the 'opportunity cost' of his round of gold may be £200-300. On the other hand, the chance of a brief at £150 per hour might justify him paying someone else £120 per hour to take over the £100 per hour brief.

MARK-UP PRICING

The simplest form of cost-plus pricing – the term 'mark-up' is used because of its wider implications. The mark-up is usually a traditional, habitual or generally accepted percentage. Mark-up pricing is the convention of wholesaling and retailing and traditional patterns exist in many industries. Such mark-ups tend to continue unchallenged until it is clear that the level of service or effort is not given to, or by, everyone in receipt of that margin. The demise of retail price maintenance was largely due to companies able to buy in bulk at high (traditional) discounts and preferring to increase their volume sales

229

by passing on part of that margin in the form of lower prices. Self-service retailing lowered labour costs and effectively meant that part of the traditional margin was no longer necessary.

TARGET PRICING

This method is also often described as 'profitable pricing'. The company sets the price that will give the required rate of return at various levels of volume. Figure 29 shows the kind of break-even analysis used to determine price. At a volume of 50,000 units, total costs are £400,000. If the required rate of return is 20 per cent, £80,000 profit must be earned. Price per unit will be:

$$\frac{£400,000 + £80,000}{50,000} = £9.60 \text{ per unit}$$

It is, again, a cost-based method because demand is ignored: price is determined by hypothetical levels of volume. No attempt is made to determine what price is *necessary* to sell those volumes.

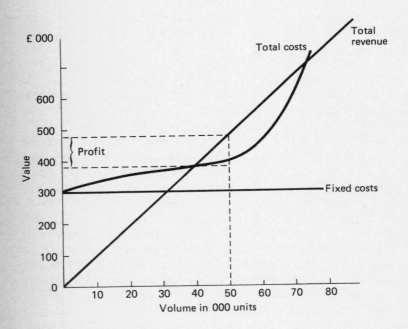

Figure 29 *Target pricing break-even chart*

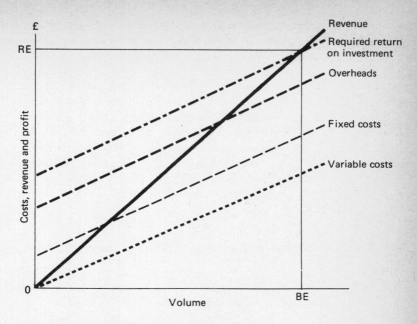

Figure 30 *Sophisticated break-even analysis*

11.3 Break-even analysis

We have already noted two uses of break-even analysis in Figures 28 and 29. Reference was also made in Chapter 10 to the value of simple break-even analysis in checking by how much volume might have to fall to wipe out the profit created by higher prices. Figure 30 shows a relatively sophisticated break-even analysis: sophisticated only in the sense that it is possible to identify recovery of different types of cost, as well as achievement of required rates of return on investment. Break-even volume is shown at BE, where revenue exactly earns the required return on investment after meeting all costs and contributions. However, the definition of 'required return' varies enormously between competing companies. The company looking for 30 per cent return on total assets will have to set a higher price than the one looking for 15 per cent. And if one company can get a price that meets a 30 per cent return objective, why should its competitor necessarily accept a lower one?

The big danger with the slavish use of break-even analysis is that when times are bad, and revenues reduced, prices will have to rise. Conversely, when times are good, revenues rise, as the result of higher volume, and prices can be reduced. Both reactions might be the opposite of what is required in such situations. Additionally, there is nothing in break-even analysis itself that allows competitive reaction to be taken into account. In theory, if your competitor lowers his price and steals some of your volume, you will have to increase prices!

Break-even analysis has its uses but should only be used with great care. It can become a useful discipline if probabilities are assigned to the chances of achieving the necessary volumes at various price levels (see Chapter 9). Break-even charts are especially useful in calculating by how much sales will have to rise to offset lower prices, or by how much they would need to fall to outweigh the advantages of higher prices.

11.4 Demand-based pricing

Although clearly the best way to price is according to what the market will bear, it is not always easy to discover the correct level, and some painful experiences may be gathered along the way. The ones you never know about are the sales you don't make because your price is not high enough. 'Charging what the market will bear' usually comes down to segmenting the market and producing different prices for each segment. In other words, price discrimination. The very term invokes fierce reactions, yet we commonly accept many forms of discrimination. We do not expect all seats in a theatre to cost the same; even though a child occupies a seat on a train, we expect to pay less than for an adult. In fact, discrimination, by customer, by time, by place and by volume or value, are so common as to pass almost unrecognized in many instances.

DISCRIMINATION BY CUSTOMER

There are six justifications for charging different customers different prices:

1   They have different degrees of price responsiveness.
2   They have different intensities of demand.
3   There are different levels of knowledge.
4   There are different levels of awareness of levels of market prices.
5   There are differences in the urgency or timing of demand.
6   The belief that different prices indicate different levels of service, quality and expertise.

DISCRIMINATION BY TIME

Where there are peaks and troughs of demand – and especially where costs remain level through the sales variations – price discrimination may be possible. Thus, hotels charge more at peak holiday times but may be prepared at off-peak times to accept low prices that merely make a contribution to the necessary costs of keeping a hotel ready for business. Public utilities have off-peak, reduced rate tariffs. Hairdressers have special days (ones which would otherwise be slack) for senior citizens.

Discrimination by time is often a way of maintaining necessary services. For example, 'Awayday' fares of British Rail make a contribution to getting the trains in position ready for the peak (full cost) travel hours. British Rail combine discrimination by time and by customer when they heavily discriminate against the commuter who is forced to travel at certain times. A problem with discrimination by time is that it could lead to customers adopting new patterns. Those who can delay their departure until cheap fares come into operation will do so.

DISCRIMINATION BY PLACE

Seats in the dress circle, first-class berths on ships, hotel rooms with bath and a balcony overlooking the sea, are all examples of discrimination by place. So, too, are products sold ex-works, delivered, FOB (free on board). The price is higher, and the profit greatest, for the customers who involve the supplier in the most cost or effort or whose estimates of scarcity or esteem value are greatest.

DISCRIMINATION BY VERSION

The characteristic of this type is a disparity (up or down) between the differences in price and the differences in marginal or direct attributable cost between the versions. For example, a 35mm camera with a standard 50mm lens is cheaper than buying the body and the lens separately. It ensures that a maker's lens is sold with the body rather than losing a lens sales to an independent manufacturer. Most cars are available in a range of options. It could also be argued that the hotel room with bath is a different version from the one without.

DISCRIMINATION BY VOLUME

This is the most common, especially in relationships between manufacturer and intermediary, or between suppliers and direct customers (as when one business sells direct to another). Here we are concerned with volume and quantity discounts or, where end-users

233

are concerned, lower prices for higher volumes (for example, the giant pack at less than half the price of the two packs that make up the same volume).

The effect of this type of discrimination is to create different final net prices for customers buying different quantities (although customers buying the same quantities receive the same terms).

Normally, the prices charged reflect the advantages of manufacturing or delivering higher volumes, or the effects of various cost plateaux. Delivery is probably the most-used cost factor, world-wide; for example, a container load, a truck load or a ship load. For the same reasons, a form of reverse discrimination is also practised, as when a minimum order quantity is fixed or there is a small order charge.

DISCRIMINATION BY VALUE

It is possible to use values instead of volumes. This method is not widely used because the value steps tend to need constant revision. Each revision makes the recipient feel less well rewarded than previously. There is a problem of whether to continue to offer, say, 10 per cent on a higher price, or maintain the value by a combination of higher price and lower percentage margin. History shows that it is very difficult to remove a percentage allowance even when the lower figure represents the same net benefit.

DISCRIMINATION IN INTERNATIONAL TRADE

Selling in another country normally involves additional costs which must be recovered through higher prices, if profits are to be maintained. However, different countries place different values on products and the harmony of product/price may be better satisfied at higher levels than in the domestic market. This is an argument that now falls on deaf ears within the EEC. In December 1977, the Distillers Company Limited (DCL) were ordered to cease dual pricing of whisky (that is, a home price and an export price). At the time, the Prices Commission in the UK would not allow DCL to raise UK prices to overseas ones. To avoid the EEC ruling, DCL withdrew Johnny Walker and Haig Dimple whiskies from the UK market.

11.5 Competition-based pricing

THE GOING RATE

You may find this method referred to elsewhere as 'pleasant pricing' or 'follow the leader'. In well-established markets with traditional prices, it is usually wisest to enter at, or very close to, the ruling rate unless you present significant added benefits. It does mean that you need similar cost structures and that you must keep very careful control of those costs. It also tends to mean that you cannot alter your price until the price leader in the market does so.

PLATEAU PRICING

An extreme form of the going rate, it is still found in international trade, particularly with commodities and raw materials. Price is often maintained at the plateau by government subsidy and/or control by buffer stocks. Although price cartels are officially banned in most parts of the world, 'gentlemen's agreements' exert the same influence on prices in many industries.

SEALED BIDS

Many companies operate in businesses where there is no option but to tender against competitors (known and unknown). Companies in such businesses would be well-advised to study the expanding literature on bidding, much of which makes extensive use of probability analysis in order to estimate possible success rates against different competitors and the outcomes of various bids.

11.6 Pricing new products

There are five major methods to be considered under this heading, but the first two involve the most critical decisions and have the greatest ramifications as far as the total marketing mix is concerned. In short, are you going to try to build up the market as fast as possible at a low price or will you aim for slower growth but at a higher rate of profit? Either decision involves the whole of the company's marketing mix.

PENETRATION PRICING

A low price is set which, together with heavy promotion, will ensure a rapid take-off and, thus, early recovery of the initial investment. We are all familiar with the FMCG new products which are launched with massive television advertising, door-to-door couponing or sampling, and further cut-price activity at the stores. This is a typical example both of the pricing technique and the way the marketing mix is involved in supporting the price strategy. The root reason for the strategy is that the price which has been set to achieve volume aims requires heavy volume to justify it. Further, substantial economies of scale will be achieved at those volumes. It is assumed that the market is going to be price elastic; that is, more will be bought at a lower price. It is also hoped that the low price and the supporting marketing activity will discourage competitors. Indeed, any competitor is likely to be forced to enter at the established going rate.

MARKET SKIMMING

Since the full title of this method is 'skimming the cream', it will hardly surprise you to learn that it is also known as 'creaming'. If the previous method assumes that the market is capable of rapid growth, this second method assumes the opposite. Moreover, it requires a considerable lead-time over competition. The prime exponents of skimming are the ethical pharmaceutical companies who, under the provisions of the Sainsbury Committee rules, are allowed seven years to exploit a new market before competition can enter. Price is set very high to recoup the heavy investment in developing the product. The aim is that high profits will be earned whilst the period of protection lasts, so that when competition enters, the first company has the option of switching to a penetration policy to deter them, staying where they are and relying on the reputation they have built up, moving down but preserving a margin, or simply waiting to see what competition charges and meeting it. Clearly, the company that can use a skimming policy is presented with a range of options. Perhaps the best is that it has a period in which it can establish a price/quality relationship that may prove to be detrimental to new entrants at lower prices. It is possible to compromise between penetration and skimming, and this is often done by industrial companies who have high investment to recover but do not wish to limit the development of the market by setting too high a price. Thus they set a sort of 'mid-way' price.

EARLY CASH RECOVERY

Obviously, both the methods described have, as part of their aim, early recovery of investment. This third method is rather more than that; it is aimed at quick cash. Often, such an aim is indicative of a lack of real confidence in the product or the market. It is vital to use a method that guarantees rapid cash recovery and profit if you work in a market characterized by short life-cycles (like certain parts of the confectionery market). You need to be sure of getting your money back before the market declines.

PRODUCT LINE PROMOTIONAL PRICING

This is a whole topic in itself and space precludes all but an indication of the possibilities. The method is seen at its zenith where the use of one item is dependent upon the use of another. For example, you could price your copying machine very low but the paper needed to operate it, very high. If your copier uses plain paper, you can't do that. Instead, you only rent out machines and charge a rental based upon metered paper usage. 'Conditional pricing' is often used to describe these very close relationships. King Gillette was an early pioneer when he gave away razors that only his blades would fit. Retailers use 'loss leaders' in a similar way; a low price offer brings people into the store who then buy higher-margin items.

RATE OF RETURN

It is possible to employ one of the cost-based methods of pricing. The most widely used of them is the one that we referred to earlier as target pricing. Clearly, a company that has developed a new product or service will have invested in it and will require a return on it. By the use of break-even analysis it is possible to arrive at prices at various volumes that, if the volume is achieved, will satisfy the rate of return objective.

It should be obvious that there are three key factors to be taken into account when setting new prices. The first is the degree of competition that is likely and the extent to which you are protected from it. The second is your calculation of which will produce the better net result: high price times low volume or low price times high volume. Thirdly, how responsive are customers likely to be to price levels and changes in price?

11.7 Elasticity of price

Elasticity is a measure of the degree of responsiveness of demand to price. Proportionate changes are the important ones. Elasticity is said to be at unity when a change in one element leads to an exactly equal change *in the opposite direction* in the other; for example, a 5 per cent drop in price leads to a 5 per cent rise in demand. Products are said to be 'price inelastic' if a change in price does not lead to any significant change in demand, and 'highly elastic' when, say, a rise in price causes a steep drop in demand. The measurement is simple to state but complex to achieve and experience proves the better guide. It is obviously important that you have a feel for the degree of elasticity in

237

your market. There is little point in price promotion in an inelastic market.

One point to beware of is the fact that elasticity often occurs at one remove; it is well established that the price of whisky *per se* is not a cause of elasticity in demand; however, the relationship of the price of whisky to other items in the price index is. Only when the price of whisky increases faster than the cost of living does demand fall. Many products are related to others in the same market. The demand for certain types of car is clearly related to the cost of petrol and oil; the demand for others to the cost of servicing and insurance.

Elasticity is an important concept and vital to the consideration of the place of price in the marketing mix. For example, a price reduction will be of no benefit unless it produces enough extra volume to offset the lower revenue per unit.

11.8   The psychology of price

There are many more aspects of pricing that could be considered but they are outside the scope of this book. We have considered the general principles that are adaptable to most types of business. One important area which we have only touched upon so far is that of the psychology of price. Enough has been said to indicate that it is very, very important. In areas of uncertainty, price is an indication of quality. The lady who goes to a new hairdresser and is uncertain of the standards (or searching for esteem value) asks for the leading stylist. Faced with two alternatives and no apparent differences, most people will opt for the slightly higher priced of the two.

It is rare for some psychological factors not to enter into a buying situation. Obviously, some buying situations are more objective than others, but it is well established that even in the apparently emotion-free industrial buying situation, many more things than just product quality and price are important. Since many companies are capable of offering the same product, the final decision has to have more components than quality and price. The psychology of price is associated with the degree of risk involved. The higher the risk, the greater the care that has to be taken. High-priced products tend to be seen as more risk-free than low-priced ones. At very low prices, people tend to say 'I can't lose much at that price' and accept the risk. At very high prices, they feel they could justifiably complain and expect recompense if things go wrong. Cost-based methods of pricing could well be dangerous in that they take no account at all of the psychology of the buyer when considering prices.

11.9   Changing prices

Whether or not you can determine the prices in your market or even initiate changes, will depend on a number of circumstances. These are:

1   The extent of competition
2   How close that competition is
3   What effective and acceptable substitutes are available
4   The strength of demand for your product
5   The elasticity of demand for the product or service
6   The price/volume relationship
7   Volume and cost relationships
8   Psychological factors in your market
9   Whether you are by tradition a price-leader or a price-follower.

It should be possible to use this list to determine what circumstances favour price changes and which ones make it difficult. But the list assumes that you are the one initiating the price change. What happens when your competitor moves first? If he raises price, your first reaction should be 'If he can get away with it, why can't I?'. Then start thinking whether you can seize a real marketing advantage by either not going up with him or not going all the way up. It is the price reduction by a competitor that usually causes most problems. The two key questions for you to answer are:

1   Do we have to reduce our prices too? Are there any valid non-price moves we could make?
2   If we cut price, what will it do to our image?

If the answer appears to be non-price competition, it pays to simulate the effects carefully, probably using the subjective probability method described in Chapter 9. Remember, if your competitor hasn't exhausted his resources in making the price cut, most non-price methods are easy to respond to and it can be done quickly. Simulation has to take the form of: 'If we do this and he does that, what do we do next?'.

If you feel your image is not going to be a problem, you can consider meeting or beating the competition, on price. But first consider whether that competitive price cut is a permanent one or a promotional one; a once and for all, or the first in a series. Above all else, *do not panic*. Stop and think; a few days won't make all that much difference. A large number of customers will interpret a price cut as a sign of a company in trouble; perhaps that is why your competitor has done it. If so, don't let him take you down too.

11.10 Summary

Setting the right price is a critical decision for any business. Like all aspects of marketing, the right price is the one acceptable to the customer. It is easy to discover when a product or service is over-priced; it is extremely difficult to discover when a product is under-priced. The psychology of price is important in determining a person's price/value relationship. Attitudes to price also relate very closely to the amount of risk the prospect feels is involved in the purchasing decision. For all these reasons, cost-based methods of setting prices can be very dangerous. Their real value is in determining the lower limits of price.

11.11 Checklist

1 Next to the product itself, the price is the most important element in the marketing mix. Indeed, customers rate the product at a price; without price, there is no real indication of value.

2 Something that has no use, has no value for the individual. The value placed on a product or service is individual and often highly emotive.

3 Value in a product or service can be expressed in terms of cost, use and esteem.

4 Cost-based pricing methods:
   a Absorption costing: takes account of all costs plus a profit margin.
   b Direct costing: price is calculated from a break-even chart. Theoretically, every time volume declines, price must rise, and *vice versa*.
   c Incremental costs: the costs of moving from one level of output to another.
   d Marginal costing: the cost of one extra unit or batch. Can be dangerous unless the extra costs are realistically assessed and the business is genuinely extra business.
   e Opportunity costs are the costs of foregone profits when taking one course of action rather than another. Very difficult to calculate in most businesses except where scarcity of resources makes the choice obvious.

f Mark-up pricing: widely used in wholesale and retail trades.

g Target pricing: setting the price that gives the required rate of return.

5 Break-even analysis is not a good way of setting prices but a useful way of determining minimum price levels and of calculating the effects of price changes.

6 Demand-based pricing is based upon charging what the market will bear and involves discrimination by:

a Customer

b Time

c Place or position

d Version

e Value

f Nation: frowned upon by the EEC.

7 Competition-based pricing

a What the going rate in the market is. In many markets, one is forced to accept that rate or something very close to it.

b Plateau pricing is most commonly government (or international agency) supported. That support may take the form of subsidy or buffer stocks. It is most used in commodity trading and raw materials.

c Sealed bids are common in certain types of industry. Contrary to popular belief, they are not all based upon the lowest tender.

8 Pricing new products: the first decision is whether to penetrate the market fast or go for a skimming policy. Not all companies will have an option; the conditions for skimming are arduous and essentially require a certainty of a lengthy period without effective competition.

   Early cash recovery is a necessary strategy in some markets but can be seen as a sign of lack of confidence in the product or the market, in others. Of the cost-based methods, target returns is the most appropriate.

   The pricing of new products must always be seen as part of the total marketing mix and there are appropriate mix strategies for each pricing technique.

9 Promotional pricing can be used for the launch of items in a product line. Forms of conditional pricing are especially suitable for product lines where the use of one item is dependent upon the

241

purchase and use of another.

10 Price elasticity describes the proportionate effects of a change in price in one direction and changes in volume in another. Difficult to calculate precisely, a feel for the elasticity of demand in any market is important, for it describes the ability to make profit out of price changes.

11 Price is an important indication of quality to most people, and the psychology of price in any market or purchasing decision must always be considered most carefully.

12 The ability of any company to initiate price changes depends upon the extent and closeness of competition; what acceptable substitutes are available to the market; the strength and elasticity of demand for the product; how price, volume and costs relate; what the psychological factors are; and the tradition of the company as a price-leader or price-follower.

13 Reactions to competitive price changes may depend upon the ability to respond by non-price means and the best estimate of the effect on the image of the product (and its quality), if prices are changed.

14 Non-price reactions can often be quickly copied by competition, leaving you no better off than before. Successful non-price actions invite response from a competitor anxious to defend his position.

15 If a change is unlikely to damage the product image, you can match the competitor, beat him or go part-way towards his prices.

16 Try to calculate why your competitor has changed.

12
Chiefs and Indians

Not everything that goes by the name 'Marketing'
deserves it. It has become too fashionable. A gravedigger remains a gravedigger even when called a
'mortician' – only the cost of the burial goes up.
Peter Drucker, *Managing for Results*

Marketing is primarily a state of mind. Although there are numerous
techniques that can be used to improve our marketing ability, they
can do nothing if the environment is wrong. That was what Chapter 1
was about and right at the very beginning the emphasis was placed on
understanding and action. Without the right sort of understanding,
the right action is unlikely. Thus it is that the ultimate marketing
authority in any company is the chief executive. The question is: does
he need any other marketing assistance?

12.1 Why have a marketing department?

You can adopt the marketing philosophy without a marketing
department. Often, the chief executive's particular skill will be in the
marketing area and the other calls on his time may not preclude him
from exercising an executive function in the marketing area. There
are occasions when the size of the business will simply not stand
another specialist. Nevertheless, it is somewhat strange that any
business can 'afford' not to have someone to look after the customer-
creating process, when it has someone to look after the product-
manufacturing side.

In reality, the considerations that lead to the appointment of a
separate marketing specialist (with or without a department) are
exactly the same as those that lead to the appointment of any other
specialist function. If there is any difference, it is in the less tangible
nature of the marketing output and the high level of necessary
subjectivity involved. Since nearly everyone claims to know all about

advertising and selling, it is rather easier to justify not employing a dog when you fully intend to bark yourself.

The very existence of specialist management roles, from chief executive down, is part of the managerial revolution – a phenomenon so well-established that most modern managers take it for granted and will not know of the excitement generated by those words a couple of decades ago. As ownership and management of businesses divided, the old beliefs in the omnipotence of the owner gave way to the opinion that skilled managers should be responsible for operational units within enterprises. The spread of this development was associated with the growth of businesses and their increasing complexity. Whilst the earlier functions tended to be production, accounting and sales, later developments led to such posts as personnel, distribution and other more specialized positions, according to the particular needs of the business. Because the concept of total marketing (in the sense that it has been described in this book) did not exist until late into the 20th century, marketing did not take its place in these other developments. Thus, it has had to fight for recognition and carry the burdens of subjectivity and intangibility. yet it makes at least as much sense to say that the chief executive should not have to be his own marketing specialist, as it does to say that he should not have to be his own accountant or factory manager; after all, it is still true that more British chief executives know more about those disciplines than understand marketing techniques.

In short, if yours is a business that needs continual and close analysis of the customers for your goods or services, or needs to apply some of the more specialized techniques of market research, advertising, sales promotion, public relations, selling and so on, then there is almost certainly a very strong case for some kind of marketing department – even if it is only one person. And there are half a dozen good reasons why.

TIME

Even growth and complexity could be handled, given enough time. Unfortunately, people are not like machines; most of us break down more easily after prolonged running and we need more frequent and regular breaks. It is true that a fair proportion of the marketing task could be done by the majority of intelligent managers, but they would need some training and a good deal of time in which to apply both the philosophy and the techniques. Although every effort has been made in this book to simplify and to reduce alternatives, it is perfectly obvious that considerable periods of solid, unbroken time do need to be given to simply thinking through the ramifications of possible alternative courses of action. Trained and experienced marketing executives are more likely to be able to reduce the time factor, quite apart from freeing busy chief executives for other productive work.

ATTITUDE

No amount of training or experience can change some people's attitudes. Some people think more creatively, more laterally than others. In today's fast-moving times, it isn't good enough to get there eventually, you have to get there fast and first. The kind of mind that can define the potential for ¼-inch electric drills as the market for ¼-inch holes is both rare and valuable. When they are that valuable, you want them working for you, not sharing their talent as is the case when you hire their services through some outside service agency.

SKILLS

Apart from a peculiar kind of mind, marketing people have other special skills. Good marketing people are 'generalists' – a sort of Jack-of-all-trades and master of one. That one can be any of the techniques and preferably the one most appropriate to your business. If you spend heavily on promotion, someone with experience and skills in advertising may be advantageous; if industrial market research is the key activity, that sort of specialization may make sense; in either case, a prime prerequisite will be the knowledge of where to buy the best services.

VOCABULARY

Most kinds of marketing training provide a person with an extensive vocabulary; the better ones also teach the understanding of the use of the techniques under a wide range of conditions. Experience can provide much of the same information. That knowledge is an enormous time and waste saver. Knowing what to do, where to go, what services can be hired and who is best at them is part of the function of any specialist manager. With marketing training and experience still relatively limited (compared with other specialist skills), the marketing vocabulary may be currently more important to more companies than some of the more conventional and accepted specializations.

MANAGEMENT

In many companies, the marketing department will be quite sizable, especially if it includes the sales force under the overall wing. Like any other well-staffed unit, it needs detailed management and guidance. A marketing director or manager has to perform all the personnel and training functions that any departmental head does and nothing disturbs any specialized skill or talent more than reporting to an uncomprehending and unsympathetic management. Obviously, the position of a one-person or very small unit is different, but where the scope exists, the marketing department is no different in management and budgetary terms from any other in the company.

RESPONSIBILITIES

For all the reasons outlined above, chief executives frequently choose, and should at least consider, delegating detailed consideration of certain functions to specialized marketing deparments. In the vast majority of cases they do no more than recommend. They consider alternatives, question the possible effects, outline all the ramifications and then recommend. If the recommendation is accepted, they then may be given executive authority for certain sections of the plan, working under targets and budgetary constraints similar to those of other departmental managers. And the areas over which they are likely to exercise this delegated responsibility are those we saw in Chapter 1:

Assessing markets
Specifying products and services
Pricing policy
Sales and distribution policy
Advertising and promotion
Co-ordination.

12.2 What kind of person?

Anyone who has got this far will already have a very good idea of the kind of qualities that would be desirable in a marketing executive. Obviously, he or she should be a good generalist. Good marketing people have lively and active minds; in interview they usually reveal a wide range of interests and seem to know rather more about a bigger range of often unrelated topics than the average manager. Most of the best marketing people I have worked with have interests that range from the esoteric to the extremely commonplace. What used to be called 'the common touch' is usually a sound recommendation, especially in high frequency, mass markets – it is a sign that they can easily identify with customers.

246

They should have sound analytical abilities combined with pronounced flair. Marketing involves sitting in darkened rooms with metaphoric towels around one's head, reaching conclusions, raising objections, and, when one is convinced that the right answer has been found, rushing out into the world at large and selling the ideas enthusiastically. Part of the time, one behaves as an introvert; the rest as an extravert.

It is the middle part of that sequence that causes trouble and sorts the men from the boys and the women from the girls. Too much flair and creativity and the possibility is that there will be too many wild schemes; too much analysis and opportunities may be lost through delays. Courage and commercialism are essential ingredients. Marketing people are usually more prone to risk-taking than managers with a more scientific background. Although the marketing philosophy (and some of the techniques) can be applied to non-commercial undertakings, in business the idea of a non-commercial marketing executive is a *non-sequitur*.

Where there is a fairly large marketing department, it is possible to be rather more flexible in the choice of skills, for it is then possible to engage complementary skills and abilities. Nevertheless, it has to be said that too much specialization and too narrow a range of personal skill and ability can lead to problems. By and large marketing departments work best when individuals have the delegated responsibility for all that concerns a particular product or group of products or services. Problems easily arise when, say, one person sets the strategy and has responsibility for budgets but another produces the advertising that is the basic means of achieving the targets. Specialized skills can be bought from companies who devote all their energies to those areas, and it is generally best to do just that and make sure that only well-rounded marketing people are employed in-company.

12.3 The product manager concept

In those last remarks, I have begun to talk about the product management function. The system is simply that whereby a single executive has full delegated responsibility for the overall performance and conduct of a product or a group of products.

Many of the problems of understanding of the role of marketing executives within companies are due to the product management system. Nowhere else in most companies has so much apparent power been yielded so quickly to people at such junior levels. The concept of power without authority was not always easy to understand

247

either by the product managers themselves or by those who had to work with them. In many cases the confusion was multiplied by the use of a definition once much favoured in the USA of the product manager as the 'managing director of his brand'. This was nonsense. Any power the product manager has is delegated. At the best, it covers only the co-ordinating role. Although, for example, he has delegated responsibility for ensuring that sufficient product is available to achieve the agreed plans, he does not run the factory. He has no responsibility or authority over personnel. He cannot authorize capital expenditure. And so on. Rather than elevate the role to a grandiose title, it is better to reduce it. In reality, the product manager is almost certain to be the lowest person in the organization who knows all about the affairs of a particular product area. There are others above him who also know, but they don't attend to detail. There are others who attend to such fine detail that they often have little knowledge of where their part of the exercise fits into the whole. As long as someone co-ordinates those efforts, it will not matter. That someone is the product manager.

How necessary is the product manager? That depends very much on the complexity of your operations. Generally speaking, the role is seldom necessary in companies with very few products or services, unless they either use entirely different resources or involve different methods of reaching the final customer. It is better to think of a company as needing one good senior marketing person. Then the need for product managers will arise where it is necessary to prevent the management overload from simply transferring itself from the chief executive to that senior marketing manager and where that manager will otherwise be unable to give enough attention to all the product areas that need it.

A major problem with the introduction of this system is that the early needs are likely to be far greater than the later ones. If a company were to staff-up to carry out just the analysis suggested in this book on a large range of products, it would almost certainly require at least twice as many people initially than it would require in two years' time. This makes a very good case for using consultancy help as a task force in the early stages, under the close direction of the person who is going to run the final department. That will take care of most of the necessry once-only work and help ensure that the right-sized department is established when the time is ripe. It may also help other managers to understand the role of brand managers when they arrive, for the concept represents an organizational anomaly in all sorts of ways. Above all, for the majority, the title 'manager' is a pure courtesy one.

12.4 Some problems of the co-ordinated marketing department

Essentially, there are two kinds of marketing department: one includes the sales force under the wing of the marketing director or manager, whilst the other does not. The only really good reason for not combining them is a management one and they should be put together as soon as the management problem is solved. To keep them separate is rather like asking the accountant to produce the annual results without giving him the figures. It is not a question of marketing taking the ascendancy over sales or *vice versa*; sales people generally have more man-management experience and, other things being equal, ought to make better departmental managers than the people with the best marketing abilities. But the separation is merely artificial; marketing is a sort of federal government in which specialized functions like selling, advertising, public relations and market research are merely states. Some states are more important than others at different times. Some are meaningless to certain types of company. It is difficult to co-ordinate the efforts of truly separate functions when inter-related ones are themselves artificially divided.

There are other types: some companies keep public relations, for example, outside the marketing department, either as a separate entity or possibly reporting to another function. There is probably more case for this in many companies than for most other kinds of separation of essentially related components. In many companies, the public relations function is essentially non-commercial in the selling sense although it may well have important commercial aspects in terms of personnel, welfare, relations with institutions and local and central government. Where the role is that of product promotion and general customer satisfaction (enquiries, complaints, trade relations, etc.) there is, again, no valid case for a public relations function outside the marketing department.

Advertising is sometimes outside, too, especially in large technical companies which need a good deal of technical literature. Here, the very same considerations apply as for the sales force, although it would be far less likely that the best man-manager of an enlarged department would be found in the advertising department. Personally, I find it absolutely inconceivable that any chief executive could even think of asking one manager to make plans, another to promote the product and a third to sell them, without ensuring that there was adequate overall direction and co-ordination. Possibly even worse, is the case where the advertising function is within the marketing department but there is a separate role (usually concerned with

249

advertising content). This effectively means that strategy and execution are separated. If the separation is rigidly enforced, as it frequently is, it usually results in advertising agencies receiving inadequate and incomplete briefs with the inevitable results. It always compounds the anomaly of the product manager: the advertising manager now has power without responsibility over part of the product manager's power without responsibility. The case where the separate function is merited within a company marketing department is where there is a strong corporate image and need which transcends individual product identities. The case for an in-house advertising production department is harder to argue in the abstract. Although I have owned an advertising agency, I left a position where I felt it absolutely right to have an in-house operation. The justification is usually to be found in the special needs of the company. If you can justify employing specialists, it may pay you to have them under your own roof. Generally, the overhead costs ensure that it costs you more in the long run than putting work out. Generally, too, the difference in cost would permit you to buy the services of really top-flight creative talents on a one-off basis for individual jobs. The half-way house of employing an experienced buyer of creative services with possibly a small in-house studio for small day-to-day jobs is much more desirable, less costly, more efficient, but seldom used. Market research can be a problem although the attitude of market researchers is so much closer to that of product managers that actual difficulties arise far less often than they do with selling and advertising. Problems can arise because market research involves so many very narrow specializations that most brand managers find this the area where the gap between vocabulary and practice is greatest. That justifies a market research manager. The problem is: does that manager simply act as a buyer, advising on techniques for problems and recommending suppliers, or does he or she decide on the need and feed the result to the product manager? You will find companies that work both ways. By and large, opinion favours the market research adviser/buyer role, whilst practice has the market research manager and the product manager working together in that relationship without friction and actually achieving the better points of both alternatives.

There is a great deal to be learned from that example. People who accept the fundamental role of the marketing philosophy and who have no fears for the future of their own function or activity, manage to slot into the total company organizational structure without any problem at all and simply confirm that marketing is really no different from any other justified specialist department.

12.5 Summary

A marketing department isn't absolutely necessary, but in the majority of cases it will be justified by ensuring adequate attention to customer creation and satisfaction, and the attention to detail involved in those activities. People trained and experienced in the application of the marketing philosophy will reduce the lead-time in creating customer-satisfying strategies, and will have the knowledge and experience to apply the appropriate techniques in the best way for the company. Ideally, all those techniques will be under unified control and any apparent exception to that rule will be seriously questioned and fully justified. It may make very good sense to use outside task forces to deal with the initial heavy work load of a new marketing department, and delay the full staffing until continuing needs can be assessed. This will also assist decisions regarding the appointment of managers to individual products or product groups, and related questions about whether they should be responsible for each of the technique areas on that product, or whether parts should be the responsibility of specialist managers. Care has to be taken in the latter case that you do not simply compound what is already an organizational anomaly – the manager with delegated power without ultimate responsibility.

12.6 Checklist

1   A marketing department isn't necessary to the adoption of the marketing philosophy. It may be essential to the use of the relevant marketing techniques or, alternatively, those services could be bought-in.

2   The decision to employ marketing specialists involves essentially the same factors as those used to justify employing any other specialist.

3   For marketing specialists, the key justifications are:
    a   Time: the ability to both reduce the time taken to make decisions and implement them, plus the release of time to other busy executives.
    b   Attitude: training in a discipline that always puts customers first in satisfying profit objectives.
    c   Skills: breadth of knowledge, plus one or more areas of deeper knowledge.
    d   Vocabulary: what can be done, how to do it, where it can be obtained, etc.

251

    e   Management: reducing spans of control and providing 'sympathetic' man-management and control.

    f   Responsibility: assuming delegated responsiblities for defined aspects of operation.

4   Where there are many products requiring special attention, the product manager system may be appropriate. The product manager is, ideally, profit-responsible for the product or products assigned, and exercises that authority by knowing about all that may affect that product and co-ordinating the separate departmental efforts involved.

5   Product management is most necessary where there are many products and/or they use different resources or involve different methods of reaching customers.

6   In the early stages, the work load may far exceed that required later. It may make sense to buy-in a task force to handle work which may not need to be repeated.

7   Ideally, all functions aiming at the same end objective or customer should be under common control. Under no circumstances should responsibility for tactical planning be divorced from the responsibility for strategy.

13

The Technique Sequence

> True science teaches, above all, to doubt and to be ignorant.
>
> Miguel de Unamuno, *The Tragic Sense of Life*

13.1 Scientific marketing

Marketing is not a science. Mostly, it is an art. Very, very occasionally marketing makes use of true scientific principles. Even when they are used, they are usually employed under circumstances that are so far from the ideal that the original purity is lost. Science relies on the principle of falsification: an activity is repeated under different conditions until it would seem that no trial alters the performance. It is impossible to submit the event to every conceivable situation but, under the most common circumstances it is usually possible to forecast that the same result will occur. Then, we call it a law. Even then, things sometimes go tragically wrong and we are reminded that the number of possible variables is so vast that, perhaps, nothing truly has scientific sanctity. A relaxant drug was submitted to all the likely test situations that might be encountered in use; it proved to be the drug the world was waiting for – until doctors prescribed it to expectant mothers, when it was discovered that thalidomide reacted unfavourably upon a small proportion of unborn children. A small proportion, but a tragic result.

In marketing, we hardly ever get that far. There are few cases where we can get anywhere near scientific purity. They occur most often in the field of market research where the laws of probability and significance can be applied. Then, pure commercial factors force us to move away from the ideal random sample conditions where those laws apply, to more contrived and affordable samples where, strictly speaking, they do not. Moreover, the mathematical rules of significance and probability tell us that even then there is a measurable possibility that the result we have achieved could have happened by pure chance. And, as everyone who has ever prepared a forecast knows full well, a result that has occurred in the past is far less likely to happen again, with the same effect, in the future. A new buyer gained last time cannot be gained a second time.

For these reasons, cost-benefit analysis – the prediction and determination of the result that will attend any expenditure – cannot apply in marketing. It is sometimes possible to find reasonable predictive models of certain markets over a limited period of time, but it is absolutely impossible to find any kind of universally applicable predictive indicator. Thus it is that the results of advertising campaigns or sales efforts cannot be accurately forecast in relation to the precise amount of effort involved.

So what are techniques? – Techniques take the guesswork out of hunch, as one of our cliché definitions said. They help reduce the risk which is inherent in any commercial decision. Although this book has shied away from techniques in favour of the arts of marketing, the fundamental principles which have been enunciated form the basis of a progression which gives a semblance of scientific authority to an otherwise subjective area. In many parts of the marketing mix, we gain strength of information and precision from trends, when none of the individual figures is capable of any high degree of trust-worthiness. It is the same with the techniques; alone, no one carries a great deal of conviction. When they are used in steps, and especially when they follow a carefully ordered sequence, they add a great deal of strength and contribute significantly to the reduction of business risk.

This is what people mean when they use the phrase 'scientific marketing'. There is a certain sequence that successively eliminates uncertainty and progressively ensures that customers' needs are both understood and catered for. What follows is no more than a set of notes which outline that sequence. There are certain individual components that not every business will require. If you don't advertise, you won't need to test any advertising copy; not every business is able to test its goods or services in a representative area in one part of the country, but is forced to expose its services to the world at large, or possibly is unable to reduce the nature of its risk but has to provide the product on a large scale. You must discard where necessary. Some of the items have been touched upon in this book; others have not and will be only thinly described here. Hopefully, the description will form a bridge between the arts and the techniques that will encourage the reader to go on and learn more about the specific areas of technique which would appear to relate most closely to his or her business needs. So we start with the idea of going into business and we follow these stages:

1. Reconcile objectives with customer needs.
2. Define possible customer consumer needs.
3. Research needs.
4. Identify new customer needs.
5. Test the concept or the product.
6. Make any necessary alterations to concept/formulation/performance/price/pack/blend/flavour/service, etc.
7. Test again.
8. If necessary, refine the product (and repeat the testing procedure until satisfied that a market does or does not exist).
9. Refine forecasts.
10. Test advertising/packaging/promotional concepts.
11. Test communication effectiveness of copy, visuals, packs.
12. Decide next step:
    national launch;
    test market, that is, restricted entry into a representative section of the country to contain costs and provide indicators of likely extent of success;
    launch on a rolling basis, that is, area by area.
13. Launch.
14. Measure: monitor chosen significant variables, for example, sales in, sales out, customer off-take, usage, frequency of purchase, etc.
15. Evaluate success against pre-determined factors.
16. Forecast future events:
    decide on controllable/predictable variables; make simple correlations, that is, what goes with what; make complex correlations (using multi-variate analysis to examine the inter-relationship of several apparently related variables);
17. 'What went wrong?' Examine all variations from forecast against 'controllable/predictable' variables for causal relationships. Question validity of planning assumptions.
18. Look for possible and plausible new planning assumptions and causal relationships.
19. Revise forecast.
20. Repeat the appropriate stage for any variation, for example, product reformulated – test new version with customers; advertising copy change – test communication effectiveness of new version; increased promotional activity – review sales forecast, etc., etc., etc.

And now you are firmly entrenched in the planning sequence described in Chapter 7.

13.2 The forecasting sequence

It is helpful to look at another sequence that employs many of the techniques available to us to evaluate performance and guide the accuracy of our forecasting. This is shown in Figure 31. It reviews the three routes that can be taken. In every case, the stage furthest away from the forecasting 'box' represents one of the simpler (if not the simplest) methods; that nearest the 'box' indicates a level of sophistication not every situation will demand. However, if the methods you are using are not providing satisfactory answers, the probability is that you should be moving nearer to the box. The more stages you use in conjunction, the fewer risks in forecasting and the greater your ability to evaluate what is happening.

The three streams examined are sales, demographics and attitudinal/sociological factors. Sales are obvious even if the method used is not: above the 'box' indicates what you should be examining; below the 'box' shows the means of doing it. In every case, the final stage above the 'box' shows a degree of sensitivity analysis where attempts are made to predict alternative courses of action. Thus, the sales stream begins by looking at your own performance, by examining your sales figures. To look at competitors' sales, some method of measuring total market performance and identifying named competitors within that market must be found: these are the retail and/or consumer audit stages. The closer one gets to an actual forecast, the more likely it is that one will need to use the more advanced techniques described in Chapter 9.

Demographics are concerned with the description of buyers – by location, importance as buyers, age, sex, class, size, and so on. The stages above the 'box' are the same as for sales, simply substituting the closest parallel. The simplest form of research to discover such facts will be inclusion in an overall piece of research looking at other goods and services, in order to share the overhead costs of contact and fieldwork. Consumer audit is the final stage in this stream, although it could be less sophisticated than a specially structured *ad hoc* study. It is in this position because it has appeared already in the first stream and in a very much lower position. In some cases, demographic information can be regarded as a by-product of the consumer sales audit, whilst in others it is the basic reason for its use. A consumer audit especially set up to examine changes in the

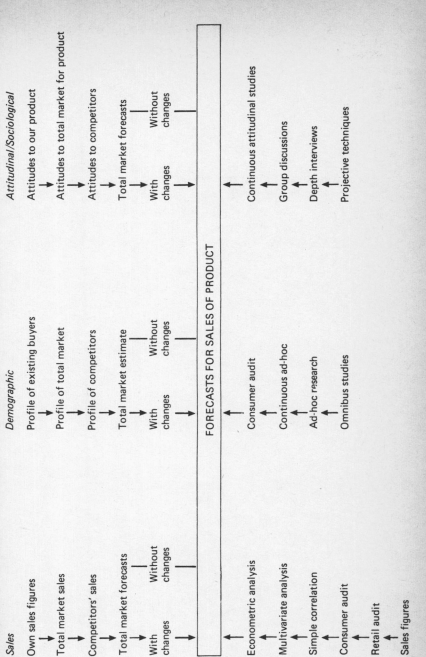

Figure 31 *Three routes to market forecasting and evaluation* (Distance from 'Forecasting' box indicates simplicity; nearest, especially if followed in sequence, indicates sophistication.)

structure of buyers would be a very sophisticated and quite costly piece of research. (The Tea Council in the UK has subscribed to such research over a very long period, being especially concerned with the problem of the rate of usage by different age groups.)

Attitudes are much more difficult to discern and consequently more expensive to measure. Thus we have not only a measure of distance from the middle of each stream but actually a different sense of 'distance' moving from left to right. We normally collect sales information before demographics, whilst many companies never concern themselves with studies of customer attitudes. Simple answers to uncomplicated questions will not suffice in this stream. In projective tests, people are literally asked to put themselves (or other people) into new situations. Such methods as showing pictures of domestic situations are employed, with the respondent asked to describe what sort of people would live there and what brands they might buy. From such methods, attitudes to brands and companies can be elicited. Depth interviews are those detailed, probing, one-to-one situations where reasons for answers are sought. Group discussions attempt to replicate the psychiatrist's couch, but reduce the time factor by taking groups of people at a time. The continuous studies often go hand-in-hand with consumer audit, in an attempt to discover which attitudes lead to what kind of purchasing behaviour. Thus, the UK Tea Council has looked at the attitudes of the different age groups and discerned behaviour patterns which have shown themselves capable of being influenced by advertising, and thus amenable to change.

And that is precisely what the marketing sequence is all about.

13.3 Summary

Marketing is neither an art nor a science but an art and a science. The art is used all the time; the science rarely. But, by adding the arts together and using techniques in a carefully ordered sequence, risk can be reduced and business improved.

13.4 Checklist

1 The number of variables likely to influence any marketing situation is too great to permit pure scientific accuracy or the status of laws of behaviour.

2 To overcome this, managers should use whatever aids science can provide.

3   Many of the deficiencies inherent in marketing can be minimized by using a sequence of activities.

4   This sequence begins with reconciling corporate objectives with customer requirements, then tests products and/or concepts, submits products to customer trials or market tests, evaluates results and provides feedback loops to enable corrective action to be taken and more accurate forecasts of future performance to be made.

5   Three routes to better market forecasting and evaluation are:
    a Sales
    b Demographic
    c Attitudinal/sociological.

6   Each route begins with examining our own product or service, expands to the total market, then looks at competitive products in order to provide total market forecasts for each aspect examined.

7   These final forecasts are made with *and* without changes from present conditions (that is, 'What if?' forecasts).

8   The main techniques associated with each of the three aspects are described in Figure 31 and, in each case, begins with the simplest (and normally cheapest) and then moves in steps to the most complex.

9   Very few companies will need to employ each technique along any particular route. Only the most complex market situations will require even a preponderance of them.

14

Reading

14.1   General reading

It is assumed that readers of this book will not wish to follow
immediately with any heavy theory. Three fairly general text books are
therefore suggested, any one of which will take the reader a little
further, but not out of his or her depth, into the techniques (and their
associated theories) of marketing:

Fundamentals and Practice of Marketing, John Wilmshurst, Heinemann
(1978).

Marketing: an introductory text, Third Edition, Micheal Baker,
Macmillan (1979).

Directing the Marketing Effort, Ray Willsmer, Pan Management
Series.

Marketing Today, Gordon Oliver, Gower Press (1981).

Marketing Management: a planning approach, David Hughes, Addison
Wesley (1978).

14.2   Buyer behaviour

Several works were referred to in Chapter 3. The models mentioned
in the text (except the final simplified version which is my own) can be
found in the following books:

The theory of buyer behaviour, J. A. Howard and J. N. Sheth, John
Wiley & Sons, Inc. (1969).

Consumer behaviour, Third Edition, J. F. Engel, R. D. Blackwell and
D. T. Kollat, Dryden Press (Hinsdale, III).

Consumer decision processes: marketing and advertising implications,
F. M. Micosia, Prentice Hall (1966).

Attitude and prediction of behaviour in attitude theory and measurement,
Ed. M. Fishbein, John Wiley & Sons, Inc. (1967).

'Attitude, attitude change and behaviour', M. Fishbein, in *Attitude*

research bridges the Atlantic, Ed. by P. Levine, American Marketing Association (1975).
A theory of cognitive dissonance, L. Festinger, Harper & Row (1957).

An excellent, more extended, summary of these and other models is to be found in:
Behavioural aspects of marketing, Keith C. Williams, Heinemann (1981).

Two other, very readable, works are:
Testing to destruction, Alan Hedges, Institute of Practitioners in Advertising (1974).
How do we choose?, Mary Tuck, Methuen (1976).

14.3 Pricing

The literature on price is extensive. The books suggested are either general or specific to topics not dealt with fully in the text. In my opinion, the best general text is:
Pricing: Principles and Practices, Andre Gabor, Heinemann (1979).

Also good in a general sense is:
More Profitable Pricing, Arthur Marshall, McGraw-Hill (1979).

Those interested in tendering and bidding will find the next two books useful:
The Pricing and Bidding of Capital Goods, D. Cooper-Jones, Business Books (1976).
Bargaining for Results, John Winkler, Heinemann (1981).

Finally, one excellent article:
'Pricing Policies for New Products', Joel Dean, *Harvard Business Review* (November/December 1976) (reprint of an article which first appeared in November 1950).

Index

skimming, 236, 241
skin-care products, 64–5
sleepers, 133
smaller businesses, 30–2, 37
Smith, A., 8
smoothing trend in forecasting, 188–91
social
  inputs, 50
  marketing, 10, 21
socio-economic conditions, 43
sociology and forecasting, 256–9
specials, profitable, 131–2, 144
specifiers, 92
specifying products and services, 14
spreadsheet programs, 168–9, 181
stages/sequences
  forecasting, 182–3, 206
  planning, 156–62
  scientific marketing, 255–6
standard units, 218, 223
standards, maintenance of, 31, 37
'stars', 141–2
stationery, 23, 45, 81, 107
statistical methods in forecasting, 185–91, 207
sterling-weighted sales, 92
stimuli, 48–50
stock, buying for, 35, 42–3, 59
straightforward products, 130–4, 145–6
strategy in planning, 148, 150, 157, 169, 174
strengths, customer, 83
strikes, 167–8, 184
subjective probabilities, 192–3
subjectivity in buying decisions, 20–1, 33
substitutes, 239, 242
Sun, The, 11–12
suntan cream, 5
supermarkets, 82, 133
switching gear, 24
SWOT analysis, 154–5, 177
Symbol Biscuits, 76–7, 106
synthetic fibres, 24

tactics in planning, 150, 157–8
tangible service products, 24, 36
target pricing, 230, 241
tea
  changes, 90
  costs, sales, 13
  Council, 258
  decisions about buying, 41
  encouraging established markets, 45
  life-cycle, 96, 104, 111–12
  profitable specials, 131–2
  quality, 11, 77
  regional differences, 83
  seasons and, 86
technical service, 170
technique sequence, 253–8
  forecasting, 250–8
  scientific marketing, 253–8
techniques of marketing, 6–10
technology, 22, 36, 221
television, 20
  advertising, 43, 65–6
  tendering, 48
  Terylene, 24
  Tesco, 82, 133
testing and market research, 170, 195–6 202, 207, 255
Tetley, 13
textiles, 24
Thalidomide, 253
Thomson Organisation, 69, 165, 194–5
tiles, ceiling, 12, 96
time
  changes over, 86–91
  discrimination by, 233, 246
  lags, 155
  marketing deparment and, 244–5, 251
  series analysis, 185–6
  span, and industrial goods, 22–3, 36
  under–costing, 27, 36
  value of, 26–7, 36, 137

271

Times, 76
timing, questions about, 85–9, 92
total product concept, 78–9
trade unions, 72–3
traditionalist buyers, 97, 101
trend
  in forecasting, 184, 186–91
  –setters, 97, 99
trials *see* testing
turnover, high, 20

Unamuno, M. de, 253
unconscious decisions *see* habit
under–costing of time, 27, 36
under–investment, 152
understanding marketing, 5–6
unidentified industrial products, 23
Unilever, 30
United Biscuits, 77
United States, 9, 111–12, 200, 202, 248
unnecessary and unprofitable products, 138–40, 144
use and value, 226

value
  added, 210–11
  analysis, 105–6
  cost and, 226
  curves, 96–8, 106
  price and, 225–6, 234, 240–1

variances
  input and output, 48–50, 56, 60
  prime cost, 219
variation in marketing mix, 122, 125 128–9
version and price, 233, 241
vocabulary and marketing department, 245
volume
  cost and, 299
  price and, 233–4, 239, 241
  profit and, 13
  value curves, 96–8, 106

warning shots, 156–8
washing machines, 20
wastage in planning, 156
Weetabix, 45
welfare benefits to staff, 26, 36
Willsmer, R.L., 153n, 260
window cleaning, 21
women
  magazine for, 5, 140
  as purchasers, 71–2, 74, 92
wool, 24
working capital, 211

Xerox, 90

Yellow Pages, 70